SHERWOOD ANDERSON

A Study of the Short Fiction

W0006617

Also available in Twayne's Studies in Short Fiction Series

Twayne's Studies in Short Fiction

Gordon Weaver, General Editor
Oklahoma State University

SHERWOOD ANDERSON
Courtesy of Virginia Greear and Greear Studio

SHERWOOD ANDERSON

A *Study of the Short Fiction*

Robert Allen Papinchak

TWAYNE PUBLISHERS • *NEW YORK*
Maxwell Macmillan Canada • *Toronto*
Maxwell Macmillan International • *New York Oxford Singapore Sydney*

Twayne's Studies in Short Fiction Series, No. 33

Twayne Publishers
Macmillan Publishing Company
866 Third Avenue
New York, NY 10022

Maxwell Macmillan Canada, Inc.
1200 Eglinton Avenue East
Suite 200
Don Mills, Ontario M3C 3N1

Macmillan Publishing Company is part of the Maxwell Communication Group of Companies.

Library of Congress Cataloging-in-Publication Data

Papinchak, Robert Allen.
    Sherwood Anderson: a study of the short fiction / Robert Allen Papinchak.
        p.   cm. — (Twayne's studies in short fiction series; no. 33)
    Includes bibliographical references (p.) and index.
    ISBN 0-8057-8339-3
    1. Anderson, Sherwood, 1876–1941 — Criticism and interpretation. 2. Short story. I. Title. II. Series.
    PS3501.N4Z76   1992
    813'.52 — dc20   91-32990
                                                                          CIP

10 9 8 7 6 5 4 3 2 1

Contents

Contents

APPENDIX

Preface

Sherwood Anderson has an assured place in the history of the American short story. Washington Irving, Nathaniel Hawthorne, and Edgar Allan Poe, whose stories, like Anderson's, contain reclusive figures, isolated characters, and monomaniacal obsessives, created the native genre. The later writers Henry James, Stephen Crane, and Theodore Dreiser, among others, led the way for Sherwood Anderson's revolt. And revolt he did, in large measure.

Unwilling to accept the direction of the American short story, Anderson developed what we now recognize as its modern incarnation by making revolutionary contributions to its form and content. He re-shaped the American short story, making it his own, and at the same time prepared the groundwork for the revolutionary writers who would follow him, chief among them Ernest Hemingway, F. Scott Fitzgerald, and William Faulkner. Stories by writers as various as Katherine Anne Porter, Flannery O'Connor, Eudora Welty, J. D. Salinger, Philip Roth, John Updike, Shirley Jackson, Bernard Malamud, John Barth, and Donald Barthelme owe an enormous debt to Anderson's pioneering contributions to the genre. The same can be said of contemporary short-story writers; whether traditional, experimental, or minimalist, Raymond Carver, Richard Ford, Tobias Wolff, Alice Adams, Robert Coover, and Joyce Carol Oates have all written stories that are direct descendants of "The Egg," "Death in the Woods," "I Want to Know Why," "The Man Who Became a Woman," and *Winesburg, Ohio.*

This study of Anderson's short fiction examines the aims, the directions, the final products, and the legacy of his assault on the genre. Opposed to what he called the all-too-familiar "poison plot," Anderson sought out his own themes and broke new ground with his tales about sex, loneliness, repression, thwarted potential, and unlived lives. He used ordinary characters in ordinary situations to reveal the life that is lived beneath the surface.

Part 1 of this book looks at Anderson from the beginning, starting with his rejection of the poison plot and his search for his own form. He found that form through the creation of what he called "the gro-

tesque," an isolated figure resembling the recluses of Irving, Hawthorne, and Poe, but nevertheless a modern figure growing out of a
new social context.

Anderson's short fiction falls quite naturally into three groups: the
early pre–*Winesburg, Ohio* stories, the stories in *Winesburg, Ohio*, and the
stories after *Winesburg, Ohio*. His first stories—only half a dozen, published from 1914 to 1918—provided the foundation for his later fiction
and established his perennial themes and subjects: loneliness, isolated
writers, the crass business atmosphere of the art world, the turmoils of
unhappy marriages. *Winesburg, Ohio*, published in 1919, derives its thematic and structural unity from its recurrent imagery. The short fiction
after *Winesburg, Ohio*, much of it discursive narratives and convoluted
visions, coalesces into stories of childhood and adolescence.

Part 2 contains representative selections from Anderson's self-reve-
latory writings in his letters, diaries, memoirs, notebooks, autobiographies, and essays. Part 3 presents a group of critical essays that provide
an overview of Anderson's work as well as responses to particular short
stories. And, a unique catalogue of the sites in Clyde, Ohio, as reference points to episodes and locations in *Winesburg, Ohio*, has been
added as an appendix.

I wish first of all to thank Prof. Kichinosuke Ohashi of Japan for his
kindness and generosity in supplying me with the necessary volumes
of *The Complete Works of Sherwood Anderson*, which he edited for the
Rinsen Book Company. I also wish to acknowledge here a long-stand-
ing debt to Walter B. Rideout for his support and encouragement over
a number of years. Thanks, too, to Gordon Weaver and Liz Fowler for
their editorial guidance, to Welford Taylor, to Diana Haskell of the
Newberry Library, and to the late Thaddeus B. Hurd, who gave me
and my wife a private tour of Clyde, Ohio, during a hot summer day,
pointing out Andersonian landmarks. Marion Anderson Spear provided
the contact to Virginia Greear, who supplied the frontispiece photo.
Finally, I wish to acknowledge the enduring love, support, and encouragement of Lynne and Martina.

Part 1

THE SHORT FICTION

Anderson's Contribution to the American Short Story

Sherwood Anderson's American models for short-story writing were the realists (William Dean Howells, Henry James, Mark Twain) and the naturalists (Hamlin Garland, Stephen Crane, Theodore Dreiser). But he was satisfied neither with the surface of things the realists explored, nor with the deterministic treatises the naturalists followed. Anderson sought a new short-story form. He believed the "true history of life is but a history of moments. It is only at rare moments that we live."[1] To represent those moments, a writer had to break "with the rules of structure literally to embody moments, to suggest endless halts and starts, the dreamlike passiveness and groping of life" (Kazin, 214). In his search for a new form for the American short story, Anderson also developed a new style and a new concept of character and theme.

Character and Incident—The Foundation of a New Prose Form

Anderson distinguished what he called "form" from the previously established notions of plot. In *A Story Teller's Story* (1924), he laments the usual approaches to the American short story:

> There was a notion that ran through all story telling in America, that stories must be built about a plot and that absurd Anglo-Saxon notion that they must point a moral, uplift the people, make better citizens, etc., etc. The magazines were filled with these plot stories and most of the plays on our stage were plot plays. "The Poison Plot," I called it in conversation with my friends as the plot notion did seem to me to poison all story telling. What was wanted I thought was form, not plot, an altogether more elusive and difficult thing to come at.[2]

And come at it he did. Anderson's form and style infused new life into the American short story.

Although some literary critics have classified Anderson as either a

3

new realist[3] or an old naturalist (Kazin, 205), he in fact moved away from the strictures of both those movements, synthesizing a new approach to the short-story form and adopting a prose style that has been described as "mellow, lyrical, controlled, and glowing with sonorous warmth" (Walcutt, 224). A less effervescent critical assessment of Anderson's form notes its dependency on an essentially "organic element which follows the contours of an image, or a symbolic cluster of sensory impressions aimed toward delivering an objective immediate presentation of a character's inner struggle, the specific quality of inwardness that constitutes the 'roundness' of his personality."[4]

Anderson's description of the role of character and incident in the conception of a story is close to the ideas of both Henry James and Virginia Woolf on the subject.[5] In *A Story Teller's Story* he discusses an incident that could have been developed into a short story. Sitting with a friend on a bench in front of the cathedral of Chartres, Anderson observed "a little drama played . . . out in the open space before the cathedral door. An American came with two women, one French, the other American, his wife or his sweetheart. He was flirting with the French woman and the American woman was pretending she did not see." Anderson admits to having watched the situation for several hours because he was sure there "was a woman losing her man, and she did not want to admit it to herself" (*CW*, 12:400). The three people went into the cathedral, but soon the American woman came out, stood for a moment outside the door, cried softly, then returned inside. Soon thereafter, the man and both women came out of the cathedral and walked away. As Anderson says, "That was all," and yet it is enough of an incident to suggest characters and a story.

> There was just the material for a tale, a novel, perhaps. One might fancy the man a young American who had come to Paris to study painting and before he came had engaged himself to an American girl at home. He had learned French, had made progress with his work. Then the American girl had set sail for Paris to join him and, at just that moment, while she was at sea, he had fallen desperately in love with a French woman. The deuce, the French woman was skillful with men and she imagined the young American to be rich. With what uncertain thoughts was the breast of the young American torn at that moment. (*CW*, 12:402)[6]

This is just the sort of material Henry James made into stories and novels that explored the contrasts between Americans and Europeans.

Just such characters and incidents were the genesis of Virginia Woolf's stories. Anderson claimed that "all tales presented themselves to the fancy in just that way. There was a suggestion, a hint given. In a crowd of faces in a crowded street one face suddenly jumped out. It had a tale to tell, was crying its tale to the streets, but at best one got only a fragment of it" (*CW*, 12:402).

Out of such fragments Anderson told his best stories and formed his best characters. The fundamental dilemma of every Anderson character "involves chiefly a search for order—primarily, an order between intention and act, thought and deed, dream and reality" (San Juan, 153). These are people faced with the most important issues of their lives, which are full of contingency and frustration. Wanting to "see beneath the surface" of such lives, Anderson found new meaning in one kind of American character.[7]

The "Grotesque" Character in Industrialized Society

The person Anderson called a "grotesque" is someone who has interpolated the truths of the world into an individual credo. This character is a direct descendant of Washington Irving's recluse, Nathaniel Hawthorne's isolate, and Edgar Allan Poe's monomaniac. The grotesque is "anyone who identifies himself absolutely with fixed schematic ways of doing, feeling, and thinking." Inevitably, such a figure "distort[s] the inner self and its potentialities, since the inner self has the unexercised capacity to demonstrate a range of *virtue* greater than any experienced situation could afford, or demand of it." Ideally, the discovery of such truths should "lead to an intenser enlargement of life and not to a constricted compass of response and possibilities for the qualification of motives" (San Juan, 138–39). But the grotesque, obsessed "by a mannerism, an idea, or an interest to the point where he ceases to be Man in the ideal sense," discovers instead that "the world is complex, that evil and good are inseparable . . . that their simple ideals are inadequate . . . [and that] what appears on the surface, what is commonly described, is not the true and inward reality" (Walcutt, 227, 234).

Anderson's grotesque is no social anachronism. Just as realism and naturalism grew out of the social and moral climate of the second half of the nineteenth century, the loneliness and solitude of the grotesque were by-products of the materialism and industrialism of the end of that century and the early decades of the twentieth. The grotesque represents the idea that "the 'vague thoughts' of the truth [are] a precious secret essence . . . that society, and more particularly industrial society, threatens these essences; that the old good values of life have been destroyed by the industrial dispensation; that people have been cut off from each other and even from themselves."[8]

In the foreword to his volume of short poems, *Mid-American Chants* (1918), Anderson meditates on this threat:

> In Middle America men are awakening. Like awkward and untrained boys we begin to turn toward maturity and with our awakening we hunger for sun. But in our towns and fields there are few memory haunted places. Here we stand in roaring city streets, on steaming coal heaps, in the shadow of factories from which come only the grinding roar of machines. We do not sing but mutter in the darkness. Our lips are cracked with dust and with the heat of furnaces. We but mutter and feel our way toward the promise of song.[9]

The entire volume of poems underscores the effect of urbanization and industrialization on the people of America. "Manhattan" is a "new place" one goes to "From the place of the cornfields" (*MAC*, 29), only to return to the cornfields to laugh and sing. In "Mid-American Prayer" there is singing and dreaming and suckling "face downward in the black earth of [the] western cornland" (*MAC*, 69); a "Hosanna" may be delivered because "The cornfields shall be the mothers of men," not the cold streets of Chicago (*MAC*, 67).

In "Godliness" (Part 1) Anderson describes the encroachment of industrialization:

> It will perhaps be somewhat difficult for the men and women of a later day to understand Jesse Bentley. In the last fifty years a vast change has taken place in the lives of our people. A revolution has in fact taken place. The coming of industrialism, attended by all the roar and rattle of affairs, the shrill cries of millions of new voices that have come among us from overseas, the going and coming of trains, the growth of cities, the building of the interurban car lines that weave in and out of towns and past farmhouses, and now in these later days the coming of the automobiles has worked a tremendous change in the lives and the habits of thought of our people of Mid-America. (*CW*, 3:65)

Personalities as well as towns were inevitably touched by the new industrialism. Jesse Bentley "had grown into maturity in America in the years after the Civil War and he, like all men of his time, had been touched by the deep influences that were at work in the country during those years when modern industrialism was being born. He began to buy machines that would permit him to do the work of the farms while employing fewer men and he sometimes thought that if he were a younger man he would give up farming altogether and start a factory in Winesburg for the making of machinery." Just as Jesse Bentley represents "all the men of his time," Louise Bentley is "one of the race of over-sensitive women that in later days industrialism was to bring in such great numbers into the world" (*CW*, 3:79, 88). With the influx of machines, there was also a widespread dissemination of words:

> Books, badly imagined and written though they may be in the hurry of [the] times, [were] in every household, magazines circulate[d] by the millions of copies, newspapers [were] everywhere. In our day a farmer standing by the stove in the store in his village has his mind filled to overflowing with the words of other men. The newspapers and the magazines have pumped him full. Much of the old brutal ignorance that had in it also a kind of beautiful childlike innocence is gone forever. The farmer by the stove is brother to the men of the cities, and if you listen you will find him talking as glibly and as senselessly as the best city man of us all. (*CW*, 3:65–66)

The point is made well and ironically: at a time when the printed word was proliferating, people had no words to express their ideas and feelings to each other. They became the "mere peddlers of words" that Winesburg's Helen White cautions George Willard not to become. He must instead learn "what people are thinking about, not what they say" (*CW*, 3:192).

Anderson's Prose Style—A Representative Story

Anderson's new short-story form, new themes, and new concept of character and incident are well represented in the story that begins *Winesburg, Ohio* (1919), "Hands." But the new style he developed is particularly transparent in this story, and what follows is an analysis of what could be termed Anderson's representative stylistic technique.

Writing about "Hands," Waldo Frank recognized "the tragic ambivalence of hands, which is the fate of all the characters of Winesburg," and, indeed, the fate of all Anderson's characters. At the turn of the twentieth century, hands "were making machines, making all sorts of things; making the world that was unmaking the tender, sensitive, intimate lives of the folk in their villages and farms. Hands are made for loving; but hands making mechanical things grow callous, preoccupied . . . fail at love."[10]

This is precisely the dilemma that confronts Wing Biddlebaum in "Hands." At the school where he taught when he had his real name, Adolph Myers, a "half-witted boy . . . became enamored of the young master [and] imagined unspeakable things and [then] in the morning went forth to tell his dreams as facts." Biddlebaum was driven from the Pennsylvania town he had been teaching in. Though he has now lived in Winesburg for 20 years, he does not "think of himself as in any way a part of the life of the town" and is friends only with George Willard, with whom he attempts "to put into words the ideas that had been accumulated by his mind during long years of silence" (*CW,* 3:8, 9, 14). The story relies on the title image as it details Biddlebaum's isolation and loneliness. Because the story is "concretely, poetically realized, its symbolism is true . . . not intellectualized, not schematized" (Frank, 30).

The words *hand* and *hands* occur 30 times in a story of just over 2,350 words. Hands are more than simply a symbol of Biddlebaum's perplexity; besides giving the caresses that led to his expulsion from the Pennsylvania town, hands are also characterized as dragging, beating, picking berries, and caressing (*CW,* 3:7, 9, 10, 13, 14).

But the repetition of a symbol is not the most significant stylistic technique Anderson brought to the short-story genre. His prose is cleaner, more pristine and clipped, less cluttered with lengthy sentences and multisyllabic words, than that of Irving, Hawthorne, Poe, and other American writers to that time. Instead, Anderson used short, direct sentences, frequent modifications of nouns, series of prepositional phrases, and the repetition of phrases and ideas, which often depend on a structural circularity.

The opening sentence of "Hands" is a complex sentence whose subordinate clause comprises a series of prepositional phrases and an adjectival phrase. The independent clause introduces Wing Biddlebaum with a noun modified by several adjectives: "Upon the half decayed veranda of a small frame house that stood near the edge of a ravine near the town of Winesburg, Ohio, a fat little old man walked nervously up and down" (*CW*, 3:7). Stripped to its bare essentials, the sentence would read, "A man walked." Here we see Anderson's use of prepositional phrases to define and develop details about a character and his setting. It is important to recognize, however, that Anderson relied on prepositional phrases not to lengthen a sentence but to clarify its sense and give fuller meaning to his subject. When he modified a noun, it was generally to the same end. The description of Wing Biddlebaum as "fat," "little," and "old" emphasizes both his physical and mental conditions, which the remainder of the story will elaborate. The "half decayed" veranda of the "small frame" house he occupies is a metaphorical extension of the wasteland he occupies and defines Biddlebaum's dejection and his blighted predicament.

The opening paragraph of "Hands" also introduces Anderson's use of repetition for emphasis and impact. The image of hands and Biddlebaum's nervous habit of walking up and down on the veranda of the house immediately recur in the second paragraph, which ends with Biddlebaum "rubbing his hands together and looking up and down the road" as he "walked up and down on the veranda, his hands moving nervously about." These details appear one last time in the story's closing paragraph, which exemplifies all of Anderson's stylistic techniques—the series of prepositional phrases, the modified nouns, the direct sentences, and the repetitions. "Upon the veranda of his house by the ravine Wing Biddlebaum continued to walk up and down until the sun disappeared and the road beyond the field was lost in the grey shadows" (*CW*, 3:8, 16).

The concluding paragraph also intensifies the central meaning of the story by circling back to an image established in the fifth paragraph. Wing Biddlebaum's story is "a story of hands. Their restless activity, like unto the beating of the wings of an imprisoned bird, had given him his name" (*CW*, 3:9). ("The name of Biddlebaum he got from a box of goods seen at a freight station as he hurried through an eastern Ohio town" [*CW*, 3:15].)

As the story closes, Wing Biddlebaum, in "his loneliness and his waiting," prepares to go to sleep and notices a "few stray white bread crumbs . . . on the cleanly washed floor by the table; putting the lamp upon a low stool he began to pick up the crumbs, carrying them to his mouth one by one with unbelievable rapidity." This is the quick, frustrated motion of hands that, with their "slender expressive fingers," Wing Biddlebaum is "forever striving to conceal . . . in his pockets or behind his back" in order to not betray his loneliness and his waiting (*CW*, 3:9, 16). The story ends still resonating with the poignancy and clarity created by Anderson's prose style.

First Stories

Six Sherwood Anderson short stories precede the collected stories of *Winesburg, Ohio*—"The Rabbit Pen" (1914), "Sister" (1915), "The Story Writers" (1916), "Vibrant Life" (1916), "Blackfoot's Masterpiece" (1916), and "The White Streak" (1918). Totaling less than 50 pages, these stories are significant in the Anderson canon because they establish many of the motifs and techniques developed more fully in his later stories. Here the reader meets the Anderson narrators and characters who are writers and artists, businesspeople and lawyers, and encounters what would be his lifelong themes: lost lives, loneliness, and the emotional bankruptcy of most people's lives. His tone in these stories ranges from ironic to sardonic as he goes from black comedy to tales of baroque injustice.

"The Rabbit Pen"

Sherwood Anderson's first published short story, "The Rabbit Pen," was written in 1913 and published in 1914.[11] It lay the foundation for much of his later short fiction.

According to Anderson, the story "had been written in answer to a kind of challenge."[12] During a visit from his former teacher at Wittenberg College, Miss Trilena White, they discussed the merits of William Dean Howells and his editing of *Harper's* magazine. Anderson criticized Howells, as well as Twain and Hawthorne, for being "too much afraid. . . . In all their writing there is too much of life left out." Anderson was specifically alluding to sex; he believed these writers were afraid of its influence on their lives. Anderson observed that sex "twisted people, beat upon them, often distorted and destroyed their lives"; nevertheless, fiction should "put down whatever is in men and women's lives, making the picture whole." Anderson boasted that "I myself can write a story that *Harper's* will print" (*SAM*, 334–35). While White and Anderson were drinking and arguing in the Andersons' backyard, "a buck rabbit killed some baby rabbits in a rabbit pen with blows of its hind feet." Anderson observed to White that the incident "could be made to stand for 'life.'"[13]

Part 1

"The Rabbit Pen" opens with the same stylistic techniques used in the opening sentence of "Hands": a series of prepositional phrases and a number of modifiers. Reduced to a single subject-verb-object, the sentence reads, "Fordyce came upon a tragedy." Every other word in the sentence provides additional information about the setting, the situation, the characters, and the theme, and a suggestion of the conflict: "In a wire pen beside the gravel path, Fordyce, walking in the garden of his friend, Harkness, and imagining marriage, came upon a tragedy" (*CW*, 21:5).

The operative word thematically is *marriage;* the conflict is suggested in the important word *tragedy.* These two words are linked not just in this first short story but in all the short fiction Anderson went on to write, reflecting this attitude that marriage is a bond filled with conflict and dismay. Another key word in this opening sentence is *imagining;* the story's protagonist, Frank Fordyce, has written "two successful novels" but can create what he thinks a marriage is, should be, or could be only in his fantasies, not in his real life (*CW*, 21:5). His paradigm for marriage is his friend's, but the Harkness union is not a model arrangement of shared responsibilities and individual freedoms. The story contrasts the real life of Joe and Ruth Harkness with the romantic life Fordyce fantasizes them to have.

In the opening paragraph, the archetypal male-female conflict is played out with violence and brute force while Fordyce watches. In the rabbit pen, amid her litter of "blind . . . hairless . . . [and] blue-black" new-born babies, a "mother rabbit fought the father furiously." She rushes "at the huge fellow again and again . . . [a] wild fire . . . in her eyes" (*CW*, 21:5). If the incident is to "stand for life," it is life in its rawest, most unadulterated form—the bloody battle for dominance between the young and the old, the male and the female. The father of the rabbits, in the manner of other fathers and sons, is trying to kill all the babies; the mother, trying to protect her young, is guarding the body of one of the dead babies.

At the sight of this bloody encounter, Fordyce can do nothing. The imaginative, romantic writer cowers, rendered impotent; he fears for the mother rabbit but is unable to act. His hands shake, his lips grow white, and all he can do is cry out for help. In response to Fordyce's call, Gretchen, the housekeeper, intercedes. The human female prevails, just as the animal female dominates the conflict in the pen. Gretchen is described with strong verbs and vivid adjectives. She is "free-walking" and "straight-backed" as she rapidly heads for the pen.

With a strong grasp she drags the father rabbit out of the way of the hunkering female and flings him—significantly—from the pen into a child's playhouse in some shrubbery beside the gravel path. She removes the dead baby rabbit from the pen, picking it up with the child's shovel and heaving it beyond the shrubbery into a vegetable garden. She is the only character in control. In her "bold, quick way," Gretchen enlists Hans's additional aid (*CW*, 21:6).

Hans finishes "the righting of things" (*CW*, 21:6) in order to efface the tragedy of the rabbit pen. Together, Gretchen and Hans represent the unit that can restore order to the disrupted romantic idyll that Fordyce imagines for the ideal married couple. The irony, of course, is that Gretchen and Hans are not married, nor do they represent the values of the upper class. As servants they are closer to the earth and hold working-class values.

In telling the story of the incident to his host, Fordyce admires the housekeeper's "efficiency," wondering at her magnificence. Harkness's rejoinder recognizes the romantic fantasies of the innocent writer: "Same old sentimental, susceptible Frank . . . romancing about every woman you see, but keeping well clear of them, just the same" (*CW*, 21:7).

Anderson divided the story into four parts, separated only by line breaks. The first part is the opening dramatic scene at the rabbit pen. The second part finds Fordyce ruminating about marriage, family, and his life in general. Solitary, passive, and egotistical, Fordyce sits in the Harkness garden reading one of his own books and imagining "himself the proud husband of Gretchen." In his fantasy of marital bliss Gretchen is a Brunhild, "complete . . . [with a] fine face, crowned by thick, smooth hair . . . [and a] quiet, efficient manner . . . [that gives him] a thrill of pride." He sees himself getting off a train and walking home through the leafy avenues of a Chicago suburb, but at this point reality intrudes and fuses with the actual "wide emerald lawn" of Cottesbrooke, the Harkness home. The fantasy is further tainted by Fordyce's growing realization that Harkness's marriage is predicated on his wife's money; Joe is "married to pretty Ruth and her fortune"—a comment that also reflects Anderson's constant concern about financial security and the status that money provided (*CW*, 21:8).

This subtle transition to the realities of the Harknesses' lives is followed by a minor family crisis akin to the conflict in the rabbit pen outside. The Harkness children, disrupting household harmony, refuse to go to bed at their mother's request. Again it is Gretchen who must

intervene to restore peace and domestic tranquillity. As with the help-
less Fordyce in the rabbit-pen incident, the efficient housekeeper
overrides the parents in order to control the children. In response to
Gretchen's "firm and purposeful" German ("Schweig!"), the children
obey her. The "brown-eyed, soft-voiced" Ruth laments the fact that
she can do nothing with her own children; it is Gretchen who sets the
Harkness house in order (*CW*, 21:8, 9).

In the third part of the story the writer prolongs his sojourn at Cottesbrooke as he finishes his third book. With winter coming on, Gretchen
works at closing up the house; the Harknesses have already returned
to their city house. Alone with Gretchen, Fordyce discovers that she is
unhappy with the Harknesses. When she laments their lack of respect
for money, he begins to fantasize that he is Gretchen's "real husband"
who can console the "frugal woman." The thought hangs in the air like
one of the leaves about to fall from the trees, but Gretchen bids him
"Auf Wiedersehen!" and is out of his life. Disconsolate, his memory
flashes back in typical Andersonian prepositional phrases to "thinking
of the day in the green summer when he had stood in the gravel path
by the wire rabbit-pen, watching her straighten out the affair in the
family of the rabbits." Again, the writer cannot act and feels "impotent
and incapable" in the shadow of her decisiveness (*CW*, 21:11, 12).

In the fourth part a few months have passed and it is February. Fordyce has also returned to the city, where Harkness tells him a tale of
family life that underscores the irony of the entire story. All along Fordyce has thought that Harkness has the ideal married life—money,
children, an endearing wife, a city home, a country home, a stableman,
a housekeeper. But now he finds out about his friend's discordant,
threadbare emotional existence under the apparent order and domestic
harmony on the surface of his life.

The lengthy fourth part is nearly half of the story. Fordyce has decided to take a trip to Germany because he thinks he will learn there
what he could not learn at home—how to speak German and therefore
understand the communication between the housekeeper and the stableman. He is sure he has missed the whispered "secrets of life" (*CW*,
21:12) because he does not know their language. Before he leaves on
his journey he dines with Harkness, who reveals the shaky underpin-
nings of his married life. He admits to Fordyce that he has been
unhappy.

He explains that he engaged Gretchen to control the house; the children had been unruly and Ruth could not manage them. Under Gretchen's competent care, the boys are now studying regularly, their toys are properly stored, and they are quiet at the dinner table. But Ruth is not managing. At Christmas Ruth had overindulged the boys with expensive gifts, despite her agreement with her husband not to exchange costly items. It was Ruth's ruse to win the boys away from Gretchen, but it did not work. The boys recognized Gretchen as aunt and their mother was incensed. Harkness sees "under the surface of the lives" of the two women in the house: when Gretchen took the boys upstairs, Ruth was left standing alone in the center of the room, "lighted only by the little electric bulbs in the branches of the Christmas trees," her fate, like that of the lonely little dead rabbit, controlled by the housekeeper (*CW*, 21:15).

Suddenly Fordyce sees Harkness as he has never seen him before. He had seen Harkness "as a man in a safe harbor," moored by his wife's wealth. The writer still cannot fathom the reality of what has happened. Though Harkness has sent Gretchen back to Germany, Fordyce continues to fantasize about the efficient woman. He sees himself "walking up a gravel path to the door of a German house. The house would be in a village, and there would be formal flower-pots by the side of the gravel path" (*CW*, 21:16, 17). But his plans are shattered when Harkness informs him that Gretchen has gone back to Germany to marry the stableman Hans.

In short, nothing is as it seems on the surface of lives: Harkness is unhappy, Ruth is unhappy, Gretchen is unhappy. Only Fordyce is as he seems—unhappy, and hopelessly entrenched in his romantic fantasies of life.

"Sister"

"Sister," which is best read as a piece of Anderson ephemera, continues the theme of the isolated writer, alone in a room, trying to come to terms with himself and another person. It is a brief and episodic first-person narrative sketch in which the writer-narrator ruminates about his adolescent sister. They have a gossiping mother and a malingering father who falls ill after whipping his daughter; both the sister and the brother recognize the need to function independently of the family structure. The reader learns that the whipping occurred after the 15-year-old girl had announced to the family that she intended to begin an affair with a 16-year-old neighbor. The story is over before it starts but provides a brief sketch of the writer-narrator as an objective observer trying to understand and assess the lives of those around him.

"Vibrant Life"

Like "Sister," "Vibrant Life" is brief (four pages), but it introduces what would frequently be a key idea in Anderson stories. This black comedy about two adulterous relationships links unbridled human sexuality with the vitality and sexual vibrancy of horses. Seven years later, this subject would become a significant thematic and structural aspect of the collection of stories *Horses and Men* (1923).

Sitting wake beside the coffin of his brother, a 45-year-old lawyer encounters a nurse, a "magnificent blonde creature with white teeth," who is "in charge of the children of his second wife." The brother, himself an adulterer, was shot dead when he was discovered with a married woman. Now the lawyer's wife is asleep upstairs, and his brother sleeps forever in the coffin beside him—until the corpse is disturbed by the heated struggles of the lawyer and the nurse and falls out of the coffin onto the floor.

It was a picture of a stallion in a magazine that aroused the lawyer and prompted him to accost the nurse. The lawyer perceives the "great animal" as "all life, vibrant, magnificent life" and correlates the sexuality of the animal with the "men of our family [who] have that vibrant, conquering life in us" (*CW*, 21:39, 41).

"The Story Writers"

"The Story Writers" deals at some length with the efforts of two ersatz writers "seeking atmosphere" (*CW*, 21:23) that will translate into successful manuscripts. Albert Prindle, a young lawyer who wants to leave behind an "undying name," aspires to be a storyteller. Certain that what "makes a writing man . . . [is] going where the air is heavy with romance and mystery" he seeks "an atmosphere of adventure and of free, full living." He is so sure that such surroundings will provide him with the means for "real expression" that he begins to arrange his life according to the designs for a writer's workshop he has discovered in an arts and crafts magazine (*CW*, 21:22, 23). Along the way he encounters a kindred spirit, the grocery store owner Appleby. Together they rent a writing apartment. Thus begins their sardonic journey down the short road to writing disaster.

Prindle and Appleby can agree on nothing, including the decor of their writing studio. They resolve their dispute about writing tables by settling on one "long table with a row of dictionaries and standard classics to divide the two working ends" and encourage "individuality" (*CW*, 21:29, 28). Certain now that they have "caught the atmosphere of art" (*CW*, 21:29), the lawyer and the grocer seek out the resources for their fiction.

The irony, of course, is that neither Prindle nor Appleby can see the stories in front of them. Numerous incidents occur in their own lives and in the lives of the occupants of their apartment building, but Prindle and Appleby overlook those stories. The two writers manqué spend barely half an hour writing, usually no more than ten minutes at a time "bent silently over their work." The "glowing stove" makes the room too hot; street noises disconcert them; the life below passes them by, as do the possibilities for their short stories (*CW*, 21:33, 35).

"The Story Writers" is a tale of missed ambitions. In trying to be successful, each character follows the "rules" for writing. Appleby wonders if, like "other great writers," he should start his short story with a "quotation, you know a line or two from some famous poem." Oblivious to the subjects in the life around them, the would-be writers resolutely believe that they are living at the "dead level of life" where nothing important, significant, or worthy of a writer's observation even occurs. They are confounded at the dearth of "the big things, the romance, of life" (*CW*, 21:35, 37); in short, they cannot see what Sherwood Anderson saw and wrote about—the extraordinary and universal in the ordinary lives of ordinary people.

"Blackfoot's Masterpiece"

The third story published in 1916, "Blackfoot's Masterpiece," explores the baroque injustices of the art world when the creative artist must individually confront crass commercialism and conventionality. The poverty-stricken Blackfoot, who is ultimately "tucked away in some asylum" in upstate New York, has created one original canvas. It brought order out of disorder. The painting "had everything in it—balance, poise, movement . . . sheer lyrical beauty." It contained the "most damnably elusive of all things in a work of art": "sheer lyrical beauty." Determined to receive $1,200 for the painting, Blackfoot is reduced to accepting only $400 from the business-minded connoisseur and art dealer, Ramsey. Unable to deal with the denigration of his talent, Blackfoot raves and rambles and is found "alone in the silence" of his Greenwich Village garret, his wife and two daughters asleep, feeding the "bills given him by Ramsey one by one into the fire" (*CW*, 20:12, 13, 15). The narrator recounts the dark irony that not much later Blackfoot's masterpiece sells for $20,000.

"The White Streak"

"The White Streak" is another story of desperate unhappiness, of lost loves, lost lives, and limited horizons. It traces the lack of communication between a commission merchant, Bushnell, and his wife. Bushnell is a butter-and-egg man eking out a life and business in Evanston, Illinois. After marriage, he and his wife had found they "had little to say to each other." Romance and adventure enter Bushnell's life when his wife's cousin, a teacher from the East, comes to visit. He retreats into the guest's room, opens the closet, and finds a white dress worn by her. Like F. Scott Fitzgerald's Daisy Buchanan, he lays his cheek against "the soft cloth of the dress" and cries. Just as Gatsby's beautiful shirts represent to Daisy wealth and an unobtainable goal, the white dress evokes for Bushnell a sense of disillusionment and a lost goal. With a lyrical poignancy, Bushnell holds the white dress "tightly against his cheek [and] declare[s] his love for the silent woman who had worn it and would wear it again." For Bushnell, the white dress makes "a white streak in the darkness, just as the silent white-clad woman made a white streak in the darkness of his mind" (*CW*, 21:44, 46, 47).

That darkness of the mind is reinforced by the two-part organizational structure of the story. In part 1, the reader is introduced to Bushnell at age 25; in part 2 Bushnell is 60. His life in Evanston, a morass of unfulfilled passions, has not changed much. He has had to live with emotional loss and sexual repression.

One night, the 60-year-old Bushnell spots a boat "making a white streak in the darkness" of the Chicago River. The image reminds him of the white dress; Bushnell "wants to put his cheek against the sides of the boat as he once put his cheek against the white gown that had been worn by the woman." In that instant, recognizing his loneliness and unhappiness, Bushnell "decides to do something desperate to find and to declare his love for the woman in white, but when he gets into a lighted street and sees his reflection in a store window, his desperate mood passes away." Bushnell comes to recognize that the woman in white "is for him a white streak in the dark places of life, something far off and beautifully strange, something to dream of but not to be touched" (*CW*, 21:49, 51).

Winesburg, Ohio

The 23 short stories in *Winesburg, Ohio* combine to make an unusual book. It has been recognized as both a collection of short stories about lonely people and a bildungsroman about George Willard, the young *Winesburg Eagle* reporter to whom most of the characters ("grotesques") bring their stories.

The lyrical form of the narrative (Frank, 29) and the psychoanalytical aspect of the stories[14] have both received attention.[15] But the stories' recurring images, which give the work a thematic and structural unity, are key to an understanding of *Winesburg, Ohio*. These images are informed by Anderson's new concept of the short-story form: having abandoned the traditional novel form, Anderson unified the book by using recurring images to function as leitmotivs. The images accumulate meaning as the work proceeds, thereby gaining importance and becoming symbols.

It is as though Anderson leans "with the reader beyond the edge of words where there are meanings which both can feel but never completely express" (Hatcher, 170). A reader can finish the book having experienced a kind of accumulated wisdom. The collection of moments and images makes *Winesburg, Ohio* a history of life.

"The Book of the Grotesque" functions as a preface to the work, clarifying the idea of truth and pointing to an understanding of how the symbol becomes truth. The narrator recalls the "one central thought" of an unpublished book by an old writer: "That in the beginning when the world was young there were a great many thoughts but no such thing as a truth. Man made the truths himself and each truth was a composite of a great many vague thoughts. All about in the world were the truths and they were all beautiful." But when someone "took one of the truths to himself, called it his truth, and tried to live his life by it, he became a grotesque and the truth he embraced became a falsehood" (*CW*, 3:4, 5).

The recurring images in the book function in a similar way. One of them considered alone, studied as a separate entity, becomes a grotesque; studied together, seen as a coral-like accretion, they become not only symbols but symbols that represent all the beautiful truths that existed at the beginning of the world. The wholeness of the world is reestablished. Just as George Willard collects the separate truths of the people of Winesburg to produce his own worldview, the reader who recognizes how the recurring images work comes away from the book with the same sense of wholeness.

The theme of most of the images is fertility; Anderson "believed that women still could supply the secret knowledge that man had lost, that they held the key to the ultimate mysteries."[15] Fertility imagery is the single most common motif in the book, the one from which various other symbols are derived.

This imagery is introduced very early in the book, in "The Book of the Grotesque." It is also inextricably connected with another *Winesburg, Ohio* theme, and one seen in other Anderson stories—thwarted or unfulfilled potential. The old writer who has difficulty getting into bed has a young thing inside him so that he is "like a pregnant woman" (*CW*, 3:2). But the young thing is never born; the writer does not produce. In a very real sense the narrator must act as midwife to the old man, just as George Willard must draw out the stories of Winesburg.

The first short story in the book, "Hands," strikingly develops both the theme of thwarted potential and Anderson's concern with sexual repression. Wing Biddlebaum's career as a teacher is destroyed when rumors of sexual perversion whisper across the Pennsylvania town in which he has been teaching. The idea of a life lost is carefully fore-shadowed in the first paragraph of the story: a field "that had been seeded for clover . . . had produced only a dense crop of yellow mustard weeds."[16] The same paragraph also refers to what could be impure or passionate love among the berry pickers, who "laughed and shouted boisterously" (*CW*, 3:7). Their lusty bravado prefigures the regret of Seth Richmond ("The Thinker") that "he also could not laugh bois-terously, shout meaningless jokes and make of himself a figure in the endless stream of moving, giggling activity that went up and down the road" (*CW*, 3:145). Just as Seth senses his own inadequacy, Wing Bid-dlebaum finds that others do not trust his caresses. He finds himself exiled from "a green open country" to the "half decayed veranda of a small frame house" in Winesburg, Ohio (*CW*, 3:7, 11). Decay is an image that recurs in the book: Winesburg is "a wasteland ruled by dull, conventional people. . . . Rubbish and broken glass clutter the alleys and the streets of the village."[17] But most important, the reader realizes that if Wing Biddlebaum was pregnant with promise, there has been an abortion.

This idea of thwarted potentiality, of a kind of miscarriage, appears in nearly all the stories in *Winesburg, Ohio*. In Dr. Reefy ("Paper Pills") there "were the seeds of something very fine" (*CW*, 3:18–19). Elizabeth Willard, George's mother, had hoped to go on the stage ("Mother"), to join "some company and wander over the world, seeing always new faces and giving something of herself to all people" (*CW*, 3:33). Dr. Parcival ("The Philosopher") had studied to be a minister. George Willard himself hopes to be more than a journalist; he discovers that if his possibilities are to be realized he must leave Winesburg.

Even more important than the idea of unfulfilled promise are the images Anderson chooses to convey it. In "Hands" there is the field of yellow mustard seeds. In "The Untold Lie" it is a field that needs to be harvested. Hal Winters confides to Ray Pearson that he has "got Nell Gunther in trouble." Ray, himself a husband and father, begins to tell Hal not to marry Nell, to assure him that "she went into the woods with him because she wanted to go," but he reconsiders after thinking about his own life (*CW*, 3:248, 251). He decides that Hal must make his own mistakes.

Ray's philosophizing about avoiding marriage is similar to the ideas passed around by some of the town's residents in Ransom Surbeck's poolroom. George Willard affects sophistication: "He said that women should look out for themselves, that the fellow who went out with a girl was not responsible for what happened." Art Wilson, who is "learning the barber's trade in Cal Prouse's shop," gains the most attention because of his experiences at "a house of prostitution at the county seat" (*CW*, 3:217). For most of the men in the town, a woman is not so much a mystery as a means to an end. This attitude is held even by the minister, Curtis Hartman ("The Strength of God"), to whom "God has manifested himself . . . in the body of [the] woman" Kate Swift (*CW*, 3:182). That the woman is caught up in her own emotional problems is, ironically, no concern of the reverend's. But for Ray, who decides in favor of the untold lie, there is still the mystery, still the feminine mystique in even the curve of his own wife's back (*CW*, 3:250).

"The Untold Lie" takes place while Ray and Hal are "at work in a field on a day in late October. They were husking corn." The field is very different from the mustard-weeded one of "Hands." Heavy with crops, it carries its harvest like a pregnant woman. The setting becomes significant when Hal tells Ray of his predicament, at which point the narrative becomes profoundly static. The men stand "in the big empty field with the quiet corn shocks standing in rows behind them . . . they had suddenly become alive when they stood in the corn field staring into each other's eyes" (*CW*, 3:246–47, 248, 250–51).

The cornfield recurs as a fertility symbol in many of the stories of Winesburg. When George Willard takes Louise Trunnion out for an "adventure" ("Nobody Knows"), "they passed a row of vacant lots where corn grew. The corn was shoulder high and had been planted right down to the sidewalk" (*CW*, 3:51). The image suggests George's sexual potential. In "Sophistication," George and Helen White, the banker's daughter, pass a "field of corn that had not yet been cut" (*CW*, 3:297), presaging the "harvest" that George and Helen accomplish on the hillside near the fairground in the crucial closing sections of the book.

Several stories draw together all these images and ideas—fields, corn, potential, and woman as a primal force. Those that do it best are "Nobody Knows," "Adventure," "The Thinker," "Loneliness," and the climactic story, "Sophistication."

The setting for "Nobody Knows" is as important as the cornfields of "The Untold Lie." After George responds to Louise Trunnion's provocative note—"I'm yours if you want me"—he tries hard to assure the secrecy of their meeting. Like all the sexual encounters in *Winesburg, Ohio*, they meet in darkness. It is a "warm and cloudy" (*CW*, 3:49, 51) night when George leaves the *Winesburg Eagle* office and runs nervously into an alleyway; George and Louise stand "in the darkness with [a] fence between them"; they dare not talk "in the shadows by William's barn" (*CW*, 3:51, 52).

Another Louise, Louise Bentley ("Godliness [Part 3]"), writes a similar note to her anticipated love, John Hardy: "I want someone to love me and I want to love someone." She gives a reason for the darkness that surrounds all the sexual encounters in the book: "In the darkness it [is] easier to say things" (*CW*, 3:96, 97).

When Anderson explores the sexual encounter as a means of communication, it is apparent that the people of Winesburg are as inarticulate about sex as they are about everything else. Joe Welling ("A Man of Ideas") goes in darkness to court Sarah King. Alice Hindman ("Adventure") lies with Ned Currie "in the dim light" (*CW*, 3:125). Tom Foster ("Drink") is drunk and lecherous only during the night. George walks with Belle Carpenter under a new moon and whispers about "lust and night and women" (*CW*, 3:225). With the recurring image of darkness Anderson suggests that sexual fulfillment requires surreptitious behavior.

In "Nobody Knows" it begins to rain after George and Louise leave the field, suggesting that rain, like sexual intercourse, is also a generating force. Rain as an image of fertility is most dramatically explored in Alice Hindman's story, "Adventure." In a moment of exhilaration, Alice runs out into the rain with a "mad desire to run naked through the streets" (*CW*, 3:133).[18] She wants to flaunt her sexuality, to display her womanliness. The rain arouses her dormant senses.

But the story depends on more than the rain imagery for its major meaning. Before Alice realizes that "many people must live and die alone, even in Winesburg," the reader learns that she is another case of thwarted potential. There might have been a valuable love between Alice and Ned Currie, but now "she did not want Ned Currie or any other man. She wanted to be loved, to have something answer the call that was growing louder and louder within her." She carries the seeds of love within her, but there is no harvest. Alice realizes the cyclical pattern of life implied in the planting and harvesting of corn when "she stood looking out over the land" and thought about "never ceasing life as it expresses itself in the flow of seasons" (*CW*, 3:129, 132, 134). Once again, Anderson uses thwarted potential, darkness (she meets Ned on a moonlit evening), a cyclical pattern, and rain imagery to invest a story with truth.

"The Thinker" is one of the stories in which Anderson attributes to women a mystical awareness of life. Virginia Richmond, the mother of Seth Richmond, the young man who would be a berry picker if he could, is much like David Hardy's mother, Louise, in "Godliness (Part 2)." Having run away from home, David returns and finds his mother's voice to be "like rain falling on trees" (*CW*, 3:75). (Again the rain is a generative force connected with women as mothers.) When Seth returns from an adolescent escapade with "coal soot in his ears and about his eye," his mother discards the remonstrances she has memorized and bestows on him instead a "kiss . . . upon the forehead" (*CW*, 3:150). For David and Seth, woman's maternal impulses overrule the desire to punish.

The objective correlatives that have been working in the other stories during sexual experiences also appear in Seth's story. Although Seth will not tell Helen White that he loves her—will not articulate his inner emotion—he does "imagine himself lying on a summer evening, buried deep among the weeds beneath a tree. Beside him, in the scene built in his fancy, lay Helen White, her hand lying in his hand. A peculiar reluctance kept him from kissing her lips, but he felt he might have done that if he wished. Instead, he lay perfectly still" (*CW*, 3:162). Images of weeds and gardens in connection with sexual encounters and courtship recur; in "A Man of Ideas," Joe Welling carries weeds to Sarah King; "long grass, now stiff and frozen" (*CW*, 3:224), lies beneath George's feet as he strolls with Belle Carpenter toward what he hopes will be another sexual adventure ("An Awakening").

The corn, the darkness, the man, the woman, fruition, thwarted potential, indeed, the essence of *Winesburg, Ohio*, is contained in Enoch Robinson's story, "Loneliness." In addition to the basic Anderson images, this story also uses the room as a symbol for isolation. It is a room very similar to the one in which Mary Hardy ("Surrender [Part 3]"), "without words . . . [but] with the aid of the man who had come to spend the evening with her," brings to Louise Bentley "a knowledge of men and women" (*CW*, 3:96). The room becomes the only reality for Enoch, but it is destroyed by a woman whom Wash Williams ("Respectability") would no doubt label a bitch.

One of the most important passages in *Winesburg, Ohio* occurs in "Loneliness"; it fuses all the recurring themes and images. When Enoch tries to explain a painting to his friends, he is inarticulate, but what he wants to say is very important:

> The picture you see doesn't consist of the things you see and say words about. There is something else, something you don't see at all, something you aren't intended to see. Look at this one over here, by the door here, where the light from the window falls on it. The dark spot by the road that you might not notice at all is, you see, the beginning of everything. There is a clump of elders there . . . and in among the elders there is something hidden. It is a woman, that's what it is. She has been thrown from a horse and the horse has run away out of sight. Do you not see how the old man who drives a cart looks anxiously about? That is Thad Graybard who has a farm up the road. He is taking corn to Winesburg to be ground into meal at Comstock's Mill. He knows there is something in the elders, something hidden away, and yet he doesn't quite know.
>
> It's a woman you see, that's what it is! It's a woman and, oh, she is lovely! She is hurt and is suffering but she makes no sound. Don't you see how it is? She lies quite still, white and still, and the beauty

comes out from her and spreads over everything. It is in the sky back
there and all around everywhere. I didn't try to paint the woman, of
course. She is too beautiful to be painted. (*CW*, 3:200–201)

The passage not only includes most of the recurring images of *Winesburg, Ohio,* it also explicates the concept of the symbol as truth. The
woman, the eternal feminine, "white and still," the one who can di-
vulge all the mysteries to man as if she were the Delphic oracle, is the
key to the painting, yet she cannot be seen. She emerges from the
painting's dark spot, which is much like the dark spots that envelop
the sexual encounters in the other stories. And the man who might see
her, the one who realizes something is around but cannot uncover it,
is taking corn into town to be milled—that is, the potential of the harvested grain is about to be fulfilled.

Enoch notes that one is not expected to see the woman in the elders,
and yet, paradoxically, one must recognize that *some*thing is in the elders. That something, if the reader refers to the dedication of the book
is beneath the surface of things. Only after the recurring images and
themes are collected, only after the reader (like the most perceptive
viewer of the picture) recognizes the moon and the fields and the darkness and the corn and the rain as recurrent motifs, only then does a
significant pattern—of symbols invested with truths—emerge.

The collected symbols become the beautiful things that existed at
the beginning of the world. Just as Enoch notes that one must go beyond the surface of the painting, a reader must lean with Anderson
beyond the edge of words to discover the truths.

In Enoch Robinson's story, as in others, rain imagery signals a significant event. Just before Enoch tells George his story and the story
of the painting there has been a "drizzly wet October rain." Even
though "the fruition of the year had come and the night should have
been fine with a moon in the sky and the crisp sharp promise of frost
in the air . . . [i]t rained and little puddles of water shone under the
street lamps of Main Street." The gloomy atmosphere is alleviated,
however, by George's attitude: he "was glad that it rained," glad because Enoch's story, concerned as it is with the idea of mystery and
potential, reveals a significant direction in his own life (*CW*, 3:206,
207).

In George's stroll with Helen White along the hillside near the fairgrounds ("Sophistication"), we see once again all the book's major
ideas and images. In the previous story, "Death," Dr. Reefy defines

love to Elizabeth Willard as "a wind stirring the grass beneath trees on a black night." He insists that "you must not try to make love definite. It is the divine accident of life. If you try to be definite and sure about it and to live beneath the trees, where soft night winds blow, the long hot day of disappointment comes swiftly and the gritty dust from passing wagons gathers upon lips inflamed and made tender by kisses" (*CW*, 3:272).

George and Helen sit on the grass at night and find that their love does not need to be articulated, does not need to be made definite. In contrast to the wordless scene Louise Bentley sees played out in the Hardy house ("Godliness [Part 3]"), this wordless scene resounds with honest love. George and Helen need no words, for silence, too, is conversation. What becomes important is the substance of the thing felt, the fact that "I have come to this lonely place and here is the other." George and Helen have come to this place through not just *one* "field of corn that had not yet been cut" but rather through *many* fields and *many* evenings of many stories and many people (*CW*, 3:296, 297). When the instructor from the college, a guest of Helen's mother, utters banalities, Helen rushes off thinking "that the world was full of meaningless people saying words" (*CW*, 3:293). Shortly thereafter, she and George become, in their moments of silence, meaningful people who need say nothing.

The implications of George's departure from Winesburg in April certainly emerge from all that has gone before. April may indeed be the cruelest month, for "life and the beginnings of new life are fearful things, and the season that breaks from the 'security' of death reminds one cruelly that the cycle of living is to resume."[19] George leaves his own wasteland with the hope of fulfilling his potential as a writer. The reader has seen many thwarted lives in the 23 short stories that make up *Winesburg, Ohio*, but here is one life that may come to fruition. George leaves when "the east is pink with the dawn" (*CW*, 3:299) and darkness is not over the land.

For George Willard, Winesburg, Ohio, becomes "but a background on which to paint the dreams of his manhood" (*CW*, 3:303). For the reader who recognizes—through the imagery—Anderson's concern with fruition and fulfilled potential, Winesburg becomes a land heavy with truths.

Stories After *Winesburg, Ohio*

Anderson would publish three other collections of stories: *The Triumph of the Egg* (1921), *Horses and Men* (1923), and *Death in the Woods* (1933). Together with other stories he wrote—some of which were published—he produced a total of 68 short stories after *Winesburg, Ohio*.[20]

For the most part, quantity exceeds quality in this period. In fact, at least 7 of the short stories are not short at all, ranging from 29 pages ("Unlighted Lamps" [1921]) to 108 pages ("Unused" [1923]). They continue Anderson's concern with certain concepts and truths and arise from those same moments from which Anderson believed all tales come.

The later stories have the same kind of characters, the same grotesques, and are told with the same regard for humanity. They are told as Winesburg's Kate Swift would talk about subjects to her students: "Once she talked to the children of Charles Lamb and made up strange, intimate little stories concerning the life of the dead writer. The stories were told with the air of one who had lived in a house with Charles Lamb and knew all the secrets of his private life. The children were somewhat confused, thinking Charles Lamb must be someone who had once lived in Winesburg" (*CW*, 3:190). Anderson treats every character as though he or she were as significant as Charles Lamb.

The characters in Anderson's later stories are like the man and the two women in front of the cathedral at Chartres. Or they are like Mrs. Grimes in "Death in the Woods" (1933): "one of the nameless ones that hardly anyone knows," but one of those persons who can interest a writer and demand that her story be told, even though she is an old woman who is "nothing special" (*CW*, 11:42). Of all the stories Anderson wrote after *Winesburg, Ohio*, however, some are certainly more special and worthwhile than others.

As "Death in the Woods" displays Anderson's concern with the truths of people who are nothing special, "There She Is—She Is Taking Her Bath" (1933), in the same collection, demonstrates his concern with structural matters. "Hands" depends on the image of hands to give larger meaning to the story of Wing Biddlebaum; "There She Is" depends on the narrator's wife repeatedly being in the bathtub when he arrives home from another day at the office—where he has done no work and thinks himself "a fool, a man turned suddenly a little mad or a man whose honor has really been tampered with" (*CW*, 11:97).

Like Upham Brainerd Garrison and the nameless central figure in Theodore Dreiser's "The Old Neighborhood" (1927), the narrator of "There She Is" has a certain anonymity and is predisposed toward jealousy. His name, John Smith, sounds like an alias. The alias he gives to a detective he hires to follow his wife is another common name, Jones. Smith does not really want to learn the truth about the possibility of his wife's peccadilloes. He is one of those persons who "trap themselves by their hilarious persistence in evading the truth" (Burbank, 102). Although he has discovered a letter under the doorway of their apartment that is apparently from a lover, whom he has hired one detective to ferret out, he hires another detective to tell him his wife is innocent—the point being that nobody really "wants to know the truth about such things."[21]

Smith imagines betraying himself and his suspicions to his wife by spilling coffee on the tablecloth or upsetting the dessert. Then, one night at dinner, attempting "finesse" because "men must protect the integrity of our homes and our fireside," Smith does spill the dessert on the tablecloth. In the closing paragraph of the story, after *both* detectives have assured him of his wife's innocence, he again projects the idea of going home to dinner and spilling the dessert (*CW*, 11:104, 111, 118). Anderson was using an objective correlative to represent his character's innermost anxieties. In *Winesburg, Ohio*, he exploited "natural scenery as an objective fact whose emotive charge or connotativeness may act as an index or correlative key to the affective or psychic situation of the characters" (San Juan, 147); in "There She Is" an object and an action serve the same function. And Anderson again used repetition from the coffee and dessert image to the repeated words of the title. When Smith returns home at the opening of the story, he calls out to his wife: " 'My dear, what are you doing?' I asked. My voice sounded strange. 'I am taking a bath,' my wife answered" (*CW*, 11:98). Mrs. Smith is taking a bath seven other times during the course of the story. Once, Mr. Smith, certain he has lost control of his faculties, bumps his head on the bathtub when he stoops down to pick up a fallen shaving brush.

Exemplifying Anderson's superb characterization of minor characters is the carpet-sweeper salesman. On the day Smith finds the note, "signed Bill," he also finds a carpet-sweeper salesman in his apartment. In his jealousy he exaggerates the situation until he is certain that the salesman is Bill (that is, the lover) and that the guise of carpet-sweeper salesman is simply a ruse to distract him from discovering his wife's affair. As the salesman leaves the apartment, Smith thinks, "It is a pretty slick scheme, this carrying carpet sweepers with them, the young men of this generation have worked out, but we older men are not to have the wool pulled over our eyes." When he sees yet another young man carrying a carpet sweeper and coming from an upper floor, Smith "saw through everything at once. The second young man was a confederate and had been concealed in the hallway in order to warn the first young man of my approach." The first young man stops in front of the building long enough to feel something in his pocket, making Smith certain that he is his wife's lover (*CW,* 11:107, 108–9). And still Smith hires the detectives and wants to be assured that his wife is innocent.

"There She Is" is one of the rare humorous depictions by Anderson of the results of jealousy. Three other all-out humorous and satirical efforts are "The Persistent Liar" (1946), "A Ghost Story" (1927), and "That Sophistication" (1933).

In subject matter, "The Persistent Liar" is closest to "There She Is." Fred is a successful Chicago businessman having an affair with his secretary, Mabel. His wife, Carrie, discovers a note from Mabel on her dressing table, but Fred tears it into bits and flushes it down the toilet. He has convinced himself that "if a man lies and keeps on lying presently people will believe. . . . Persistence does it" (*CW,* 21:209). It takes him nearly two years of denying that the note existed; but he is certain that it did not, and Carrie no longer suspects that the affair ever took place. At the end, even Fred has begun to believe his own lie.

The other two stories poke fun at false sophistication, the "moderns," culture, and the hoi-polloi. "That Sophistication" is the more accomplished of the two. It is a sparkling satire on the *salon des artistes* à la Gertrude Stein and Alice B. Toklas, a world in which lies abound: "Americans from Cleveland pretending to themselves they were important people . . . guests pretending they were important. They, the guests, pretending they had important reasons for being in Paris. A little string of lies, each telling the other a lie" (*CW,* 11:174).

Harry Longman and his wife, from Cleveland, hold a salon in their Paris apartment, six flights up in the boulevard Raspail. "A crowd [was] always about—feeding people as they did, wining them." When the narrator and Mabel Cathers frequent the apartment, they compare it to Madam T's salon, which is frequented by a lot of "mannish women and womanly men" and where "there was a lot of—shall I [the narrator] say Krafft-Ebing-talk." Mabel, running "all around Paris, day and night . . . was getting culture, sophistication" but at the end "said the trouble was that the more sophistication she got the more she felt like Chicago" (*CW*, 11:166, 168, 171, 173, 175). She decides she would have gotten all the sophistication she needs if she had stayed there.

It is the ghost himself who seeks culture in "A Ghost Story." A low-brow manufacturer in his previous lifetime, he seeks the company of a widowed schoolteacher renting the haunted house he once inhabited. In her he discovers a kindred spirit who introduces him to all the "moderns" so he can become assimilated into the proper crowd in the hereafter. She has been a woman "intent on culture," but her husband was an uncultured plumber. In the ghost she is sure she has found a "mate in the world of culture." The poignant irony of the story is that the ghost finally does not appreciate the widow's role in his education and one spring night simply departs. She resolves that "it just shows how a woman comes out when she tries to do anything for a man. . . . 'You try to lift them up and make them something better than they are and then they quit you'" (*CW*, 21:53, 55, 59).

Discursive Narratives of Adolescence

Anderson depicts the special problems of youth in several major stories following *Winesburg, Ohio*. Four of them—"I Want to Know Why" (1921), "I'm a Fool" (1923), "The Man Who Became a Woman" (1923), and "The Sad Horn Blowers" (1923)—best exemplify Anderson's belief that "in youth there are always two forces in conflict: the warm, unthinking little animal, and the thing that reflects and remembers, that is, the sophisticated mind. The reflective force reduces one to stasis in which the will is inert until the moment of liberation when sensations regenerate the spirit" (San Juan, 153–54).

The discursive nature of these four stories is especially deceptive. Rambling and elusive, they may seem to lack control or form. On the contrary, these stories are as carefully structured and controlled as any others in the Anderson canon. In each story Anderson chose for his youthful narrator a "puzzled and baffled spectator standing in awe of all the mysteries of life" (Geismar, xiv), an adolescent who questions and has no fixed answers yet but who, with time and experience, may find them.

It is the kind of answer found by the young narrator of "Death in the Woods" when he recalls the day he went with the men into the woods to see the body of Mrs. Grimes. Only years later is he able to sort out the sense and the meaning of the experience: "The scene in the forest had become for me, without my knowing it, the foundation for the real story I am now trying to tell. The fragments, you see, had to be picked up slowly, long afterward" (*CW,* 11:60). Mary Grey in "Brother Death" (1933) also realizes that "it takes time to understand things that happen in life. Life unfolds slowly to the mind . . . [and] knowledge comes slowly" (*CW,* 11:331, 335).

Of these four stories of adolescence, only "The Sad Horn Blowers" does not take place at a racetrack or around horses. For Anderson, horses and horse racing were "the symbol of the pagan and plenary state, the natural life which industrialization, science and finance capitalism had all conspired to deform or destroy" (Geismar, xvii). And one aspect of the "natural life" is, of course, sex. "I Want to Know Why" explores the identification between a whore in a "rummy farm house" (*CW,* 9:17) with the horses the narrator knows and loves and understands, though he cannot understand the liking of his fellow "swipes" for women. "I'm a Fool" makes a similar identification between sex and horses, but the narrator is a little older and finally becomes aware that his braggadocio has lost him a young woman who might have paid attention to him even without his lies. "The Man Who Became a Woman" details the visionary experience of a young man who so closely identifies girls with horses that he wishes one horse were a girl, or he himself were a girl and the horse a man. The story depends on just such a transformation when the narrator believes he has become a woman during a night of debauchery at the track.

"I Want to Know Why" reverberates with the shivers of recognition of the presexual adolescent mind. The story throbs with often confused, often undefined sexuality, but it definitely draws a direct connection between horses, men, women, and sexuality. Each of three horses—Middlestride, Sunstreak, and Strident—comes to represent a key personality trait and sexual profile of the narrator and other characters. Middlestride and Sunstreak are both the kind of horse that makes the narrator's "throat hurt to see." Middlestride is a gelding, Sunstreak a stallion. Middlestride is "long and looks awkward"; Sunstreak is "nervous and belongs on the biggest farm we've got in our country." Though Sunstreak is a stallion, he is compared to "a girl you think about sometime but never see"; he is also "hard all over and lovely too." Such ambisexuality is a significant theme in the story. Sunstreak's name implies that he is fast, clear, bright, and hot; Middlestride's name suggests a slow, muddled, lumbering, tepid horse. One of the prostitutes at the farmhouse is "like the gelding Middlestride, but not clean like him, but with a hard ugly mouth" (*CW*, 9:13–14, 18).

The narrator is trying to find his position between Middlestride and Sunstreak, between being a gelding and being a stallion. He is trying to find out how he is going to run in life once he gets his chance. Early in the story he observes that "any thoroughbred, that is sired right and out of a good mare and trained by a man that knows how, can run." At that point the boy cannot run like the thoroughbred. By the end of the story, however, the boy is like Strident, "a new colt [that] . . . will lay them all out" (*CW*, 9:11, 19). This is, in fact, his future destiny—to "lay them all out" once he sorts out the confusing information about sex.

The nearly 16-year-old first-person narrator recounts the tale of what happened on a trip to the racetrack at Saratoga, New York, about a year earlier, when he had just turned 15. He and two Beckersville friends, Hanley Turner and Bildad Johnson, "with the true instinct of Kentucky boys" hop the freight train "not just to Lexington or Louisville [but] to the big eastern track" they have always heard the Beckersville men talk about (*CW*, 9:5, 6).

Once he arrives at Saratoga, the narrator is enthralled by the trappings of the racetrack and by the incipient sexuality of its atmosphere. The story is about the preknowledge of sexuality when the boy is not yet a man. The central episode in "I Want to Know Why" is the visit to a brothel on the outskirts of Saratoga by the narrator, the horse trainer Jerry Tillford, and a few other men. It is Jerry who trains Sunstreak; Jerry is also responsible for what the narrator sees as a personal betrayal.

The narrator is confused by Jerry, whom he has seen as a soul mate in their shared love and understanding of horses. He feels betrayed when Jerry, playing cock of the walk, struts his stuff at the brothel and lays claim to Sunstreak's success: "He said that he made that horse, that it was him that won the race and made the record." Earlier in the day the narrator and Jerry had established through eye contact a mutual understanding that was also laden with sexual meaning. The narrator had "looked up and then that man and I looked into each other's eyes. Something happened to me. I guess I loved the man as much as I did the horse because he knew what I knew. . . . It was the first time I ever felt for a man like that" (*CW*, 9:15, 16, 18).

Later, however, "things are different . . . because a man like Jerry Tillford, who knows what he does, could see a horse like Sunstreak run, and kiss a woman like that the same day." A woman "like that" is a "tall rotten looking woman [who] was between us just as Sunstreak was in the paddocks in the afternoon" when the eye contact had been made (*CW*, 9:19). The woman has already been likened to Middlestride but now she is compared to Sunstreak. Just as the sexual proclivity of the stallion stood between the man and the boy in the afternoon, now the sexual sterility of the gelding separates them. The boy's loss of innocence is the epiphanic moment of the story. What was meant to be an out-of-town lark turns into an adventure of still undefined sexual awakening. Almost a year later the 16-year-old narrator is still confused and upset by the episode and thinks about it at night (*CW*, 9:12).

The narrator of "I'm a Fool" was 19 when he received his "hard jolt" (*CW*, 10:3). After getting a job as a swipe, he leaves town with two horses, full of exuberance and glee for his new life. As in "I Want to Know Why," this narrator recounts a past experience. Sitting in the grandstand, at the racetrack in Sandusky, Ohio, feeling "grand" and "important," he catches the eye of "a peach" (*CW*, 10:8), Miss Lucy Wessen of Tiffin, Ohio. As with a number of other Anderson characters, it is a lie that catches him out and brings him to his ironic epiphany.

His lie is built on a series of small truths. Wanting to impress Lucy, he says he is Walter Mathers, the son of the wealthy Mr. Mathers from Marietta, Ohio. One of the Matherses' horses, "About Ben Ahem," or "something like that," is racing that day. The boy describes the Matherses' stables and "grand brick house" from his memory of one short visit he and his friend Burt once made there. But once the lie starts, it grows until the narrator "went the whole hog" (*CW*, 10:10, 13). He tells himself it might be the liquor talking, but he also realizes that he has made a fool of himself. Nevertheless, he prolongs the charade and continues the brief romance.

The narrator, Lucy, her brother Wilbur Wessen, and Miss Elinor Woodbury go to the park and the beach at Cedar Point. There the narrator finds himself more involved with Lucy than he had thought possible. But now he cannot get himself out of the trap he has gotten himself into; he cannot "get . . . [him]self on the square" (*CW*, 10:15). He gives Lucy a quick kiss, promises to exchange letters, and hastily departs.

Now the narrator must face the consequences of his actions. Lucy will send Walter Mathers a letter in Marietta, Ohio. The irony, of course, is that she will be sending the letter to someone who does not exist. The narrator has ruined all his chances by lying. He sees himself as a "boob" (*CW*, 10:18) done in by his innocent deceptions that arose out of his adolescent lack of experience.

"The Man Who Became a Woman" bears a number of superficial resemblances to both "I Want to Know Why" and "I'm a Fool." All three stories have a discursive narrative structure. In "I'm a Fool" the threads pulling the story together are often annoyingly obvious and distracting. When the narrator realizes that he has departed from the story line he says, "But that isn't what I want to tell my story about"; or he tries to excuse his ramblings with the interjective, "But never mind that." And then there are those "gee whizzes" sprinkled throughout. Finally, he tries to assure the reader and himself that "I'm only telling you to get everything straight" (*CW*, 10:6, 9, 11).

Herman Dudley, the narrator of "The Man Who Became a Woman," is also trying to sort things out and get everything straight. Although this narrative is just as digressive as "I'm a Fool" and "I Want to Know Why," it is different in two significant ways. First, the narrator is not a late adolescent, even though the experience he recounts is about that time in his life. Unlike the boy narrators of the other two stories, Herman is more than a year older and has gained some distance on his experience. Now an adult, he was once a druggist's clerk and a wandering tramp before marrying and settling down. He says he "can think this whole thing out fairly now, sitting here in my own house and writing, and with my wife Jessie in the kitchen making a pie or something" (*CW*, 10:219).

The narrative distance in this story is crucial to the second difference: the narration often goes "round and round," but it is not like the rambling, protestative narration of "I'm a Fool." Here the reader functions as a lay psychologist to Herman's self-proclaimed "confession." Directly addressing the reader, Herman reveals, "I'm just trying to make you understand some things about me, as I would like to understand some things about you, or anyone, if I had the chance." Like the boy narrators in the other two stories, what Herman is trying to understand is his sexual identity as it was defined by an experience in his youth. It is clear that even as an adult Herman does not understand any more about himself than he did then. He finally says, "It's over my head" (*CW*, 10:190, 199, 208, 223).

Once again the youthful experience involves sex, horses, men, and women. The confusions are compounded for this narrator because, as the title indicates, he believes that he did in fact become a woman. He is sure that much of his confusion about his sexual identity came from being a virgin at 19: "I think it was all because I had got to be almost a man and had never been with a woman" (*CW*, 10:195).

Herman loves horses as much as the boys in the other two stories. He also identifies them with women and is confused about their sexuality. He is like the boy in "I Want to Know Why," who sees a stallion as both male and female, as "a girl you think about sometimes but never see," and as "hard all over and lovely too." As an adolescent Herman had wished that his horse Pick-it-boy "was a girl sometimes or that I was a girl and he was a man." He wants to run his fingers all over the body of a horse "just because I loved the feel of him and as sometimes, to tell the plain truth, I've felt about touching with my hands the body of a woman I've seen and who I thought was lovely too" (*CW*, 10:200, 217).

Early in the story Herman describes the intimate experience of walking a horse. His description becomes explicitly sexual when he says: "You walk and walk and walk, around a little circle, and your horse's head is right by your shoulder, and all around you the life of the place you are in is going on, and in a queer way you get so you aren't really a part of it at all. Perhaps no one ever gets as I was then, except boys that aren't quite men yet and who like me have never been with girls or women—to really be with them, up to the hilt, I mean" (*CW*, 10:198).

One cold, rainy Saturday evening on the track circuit in a small western Pennsylvania town, a lonely Herman wanders into a saloon. When he looks up into the "old cracked looking-glass" at the back of the bar, he does not see his own male face but instead, "the face of a woman. It was a girl's face, that's what I mean. That's what it was. It was a girl's face, and a lonesome and scared girl too. She was just a kid at that." No one else in the bar notices this transformation; the other patrons are too involved with the brawl that ensues when some miners malign a customer who is there with his small son. Shocked by the brutality of the encounter, "thinking how mean and low and all balled-up and twisted-up human beings can become," Herman leaves and wanders back to the fairground and the familiar comfort of the stalls and Pick-it-boy, the horse he had wished were a girl. Herman takes off his clothes, which have been soaked wet from the rain and settles in naked among the horse blankets. It becomes more of a "mixed-up night" for Herman: he gets "another wallop" when two drunken black swipes attack and attempt to rape him. Herman is certain they think he is a woman, his "body being pretty white and slender then, like a young girl's body I suppose" (*CW*, 10:207, 215, 220, 218, 219).

The attempted rape does, of course, reinforce the earlier experience at the saloon. The frightened boy invents "a kind of princess with black hair and a slender willowy body. . . . And now I was that woman, or something like her, myself." He reacts to the two drunken men the way he thinks a young girl might react: he "gave a kind of wriggle, like a fish, you have just taken off the hook. . . . I was caught and I squirmed, that's all" (*CW*, 10:221).

Herman escapes into the final episode of what has become a night of gothic horror. Running from the stables and the track, he comes to a field where there is a slaughterhouse. He stumbles, falls, and pitches forward into the skeletal remains of a horse. This terrifying encounter is a pivotal and metaphorical one. Herman must finally confront himself and attempt to discover who he is. This charnel experience has carnal implications.

Herman realizes that it "doesn't make any difference what the horse has been, that's the way he usually ends up." He seems to understand that it also happens to men when he says, "A lot of other good fast ones I've seen and known have ended that way" (*CW*, 10:224). In the belly of the beast, Herman discovers a "new terror," one that

seemed to go down to the very bottom of me, to the bottom of the inside of me, I mean. . . . It was a terror like a big wave that hits you when you are walking on a seashore, maybe. You see it coming and you try to run and get away but when you start to run inshore there is a stone cliff you can't climb. So the wave comes high as a mountain, and there it is, right in front of you and nothing in all this world can stop it. And now it had knocked you down and rolled and tumbled you over and over and washed you clean, clean, but dead maybe. And that's the way I felt—I seemed to myself dead with

> blind terror. It was a feeling like the finger of God running down
> your back and burning you clean, I mean. It burned all that silly
> nonsense about being a girl right out of me. (*CW*, 10:225)

The boy who wishes his horse "was a girl sometimes," or that he
"was a girl" so that his horse could be a man, who thinks he has been
a woman, finds himself in the carcass of a sexless horse and rediscovers
his own sex. After the traumatic encounter, he crawls out "from among
the pile of bones, and then I stood on my own feet again and I wasn't
a woman, or a young girl any more but a man and my own self, and as
far as I know I've been that way ever since" (*CW*, 10:225).[22]

Seventeen-year-old Will Appleton of "The Sad Horn Blowers" must
deal with the confusing concept of maturity after tragedy hits his family. His mother dies suddenly. His father burns himself with coffee just
as they are about to get a house-painting job that would have seen them
through the winter. Will leaves their farm in Bidwell, Ohio, his father,
his brother, and his 20-year-old sister Kate, for a factory job in Erie,
Pennsylvania. On the train he encounters an old man who, like his
father, is a longtime cornet player. Will agrees to go back with him to
his wife's boardinghouse. Once there, Will is uncertain when two
voices begin speaking to him—the old voice in Bidwell and the new
voice at the boardinghouse. He wonders if the old voice is "trying to
taunt him, trying to tell him that now he was a thing swinging in the
air, that there was no place to put down his feet." He knows he is afraid
but is not sure of what. He "had wanted so much to be a man, to stand
on his own feet and now what was the matter with him? Was he afraid
of manhood?" (*CW*, 10:266).

Will wanders the shore of Lake Erie knowing there "was something
to be settled with himself, something to be faced." He knows he is on
the edge of maturity, but the "life Will was now to lead alone, had
become a strange, a vast terrifying thing. Perhaps all life was like that,
a vastness and emptiness" (*CW*, 10:276, 277).

While Will is not being particularly successful in starting a new life,
his sister has gone on with her own. She writes to say she has met
someone and is planning to be married. To Will it is "evident [that]
Kate had got hold of something," and because of that, Will feels he is
no longer a boy. He thinks that a "boy is, quite naturally, and without
his having anything to do with the matter, connected with something—
and now that connection had been cut. He had been pushed out of the
nest. . . . The difficulty was that, while he was no longer a boy, he

had not yet become a man." He again perceives himself as "a thing swinging in space. There was no place to put down his feet." He stood "face to face with manhood now. . . . If only [he] could get [his] feet down upon something, could get over this feeling of falling through space, through a vast emptiness" (*CW*, 10:278–79, 280).

For Will, "the word [*manhood*] had a queer sound in the head. What did it mean?" He is uncertain it is not measured by the loudest noises or by adventures in brothels. At the end of the story, when he returns to the boardinghouse, he recognizes that the old man with his cornet is "a man who was after all not a man. He was a child as Will was too really, had always been such a child, would always be such a child." He takes the cornet but cannot play it like the old man exhorts him to, or like his father did in the Bidwell Silver Cornet Band. Instead, he "blew two or three notes, softly" (*CW*, 10:279, 282, 283).

"The Sad Horn Blowers" describes the poignancy of the discovery of self waiting at the threshold of maturity. The story plays for us the still, sad music of humanity in the soft, quiet notes of a cornet.

The Dark Vistas of Childhood

In three stories he wrote after *Winesburg, Ohio* Anderson explores the mortifyingly dark vistas of childhood. "The Egg" (1921), "Death in the Woods" (1933), and "Brother Death" (1933) reveal once again his insights into not only characters who lead lives of quiet desperation but the social forces affecting those lives. "The Egg" and "Death in the Woods" are told from the first-person perspective of an adult recollecting memories of childhood in disturbed tranquillity. The foreboding story "Brother Death" is told from a resolved third-person distance. Each story is told in the somber tones of a sad memory or dream.

Except for the stories in *Winesburg, Ohio* taken as a whole, "The Egg" is Anderson's most accomplished and significant short story. Like many other Anderson stories, it is about the tragedy of unlived lives. The ambitions of its characters are thwarted by shattered dreams based on false hopes. Nevertheless, the adult narrator reflects on his past with some measure of maturity in what is a final futile attempt to explain "many unexplainable things" (*CW*, 9:57). The narrator recalls an incident that involved him, his father, and his mother when he was nine. He lays the groundwork for this pivotal narrative event by detailing his parents' past and their common hope for the future.

The parents' contrasting personalities lead to the ultimate conflict.

His father, perhaps "intended by nature to be a cheerful, kindly man," had "no notion of trying to rise in the world" and was content with the farmhand's life of Saturday evening singing and beer drinking. But when at the age of 35 he met his future wife, a schoolteacher with high hopes, "something happened to the two people. They became ambitious. The American passion for getting up in the world took possession of them" (*CW*, 9:46).

Two business endeavors, a chicken farm, and a restaurant, lead to the family's downfall, the father's embarrassment, and the narrator's lifelong attempt to understand what life is all about. The first business supplies the story's controlling metaphor. Raising chickens is directly compared to raising children and the ultimate destinies of adulthood: "One unversed in such matters can have no notion of the many and tragic things that can happen to a chicken. It is born out of an egg, lives for a few weeks as a tiny fluffy thing such as you will see pictured on Easter cards, then becomes hideously naked, eats quantities of corn and meal bought by the sweat of your father's brow, gets diseases called pip, cholera, and other names, stands looking with stupid eyes at the sun, becomes sick and dies" (*CW*, 9:47–48).

The narrator observes that "one hopes for so much from a chicken and is so dreadfully disillusioned. Small chickens, just setting out on the journey of life, look so bright and alert and they are in fact so dreadfully stupid." He is certain that they "are so much like people they mix one up in one's judgment of life." The narrator cannot come to this recognition, however, until he grows up. It is being raised on the chicken farm that makes the narrator's first impressions of life "impressions of disaster." He grows up to be "a gloomy man inclined to see the darker side of life" (*CW*, 9:47, 48).

His memory of the second family business is no more positive. His "incurably ambitious" mother has "the idea that [a] restaurant would be profitable." So the family, "a tiny caravan of hope looking for a new place from which to start on [its] upward journey through life," opens a restaurant in Bidwell, Ohio (*CW*, 9:47, 49, 53). The father, consumed by his obsession with being successful, hatches a scheme he is sure will bring customers to his restaurant, and fame and fortune to him.

He has preserved the "grotesques [that] are born out of eggs as out of people. . . . A chicken . . . that has four legs, two pairs of wings, two heads, or what not. The things do not live." He dreams of taking these deformities "about the county fairs and of growing rich by exhibiting [them] to other farmhands." He brings these bottled aberrations to the restaurant to entertain customers. He first tries to attract a customer, the young Joe Kane, with the trick of standing an egg on its end. When that fails, the father displays the "poultry monstrosities." Joe still does not pay attention, so the father, in a "spirit of desperate determination," attempts to heat an egg in a pan of vinegar and slide it into a bottle. When the egg breaks in his hand, Joe flees in laughter (*CW*, 51, 60, 61). The father is enraged; he seeks refuge and compassion in his wife's arms.

The narrator is not completely certain what happened in the restaurant and reconstructs the event in his imagination. He is sure that for "some unexplainable reason [he knew] the story as though [he] had been a witness to [his] father's discomfiture." It is one of the "many unexplainable things" that "one in time gets to know." But what the narrator does not resolve, either as a young boy or as a mature adult, is "why eggs had to be and why from the egg came the hen who again laid the egg." The question gets into his blood and stays there, "I imagine, because I am the son of my father." The generational mysteries are not resolved, but the endless natural cycle, which is the "final triumph of the egg," continues for the narrator (*CW*, 9:57, 63).

The narrator of "Death in the Woods" also tries to come to terms with his memories of a singular event from childhood. He feels "impelled to try to tell the simple story over again." The whole thing was "like music heard from far off. The notes had to be picked up slowly one at a time. Something had to be understood" (*CW*, 11:61, 62).

The simple story that the narrator reconstructs is understood only many years later because the "fragménts . . . had to be picked up slowly, long afterwards" (*CW*, 11:60). The memories accrue to provide the narrator with some meaning for the death he witnessed. The narrator's memory is often jogged until "it all comes back clearly now." What gradually emerges is a simple narrative of the life and death of Mrs. Grimes, "an old woman [who] lived on a farm near the town" where the narrator lived. There does not appear to be anything exceptional about her; all "country and small-town people have seen such old women." She is a kind who generally goes unnoticed; "people drive right down a road and never notice an old woman like that" (*CW*, 11:41, 42, 43). Yet the narrator knows she has some importance in his own life.

One winter day Mrs. Grimes goes into town with her usual companions, a group of four dogs, to trade a few eggs. Rushing to get back before darkness, she sits down to rest at the foot of a tree, setting her pack against the tree trunk, and falls asleep. The weather turns. It begins to snow. The dogs become hungry. The style of the narrator's imaginative reconstruction of what probably happened next is distinctive and haunting:

> The dogs in the clearing . . . had caught two or three rabbits and their immediate hunger had been satisfied. They began to play, running in circles in the clearing. Round and round they ran, each dog's nose at the tail of the next dog. In the clearing, under snow-laden trees and under the wintry moon they made a strange picture, running thus silently, in a circle their running had beaten in the soft snow. The dogs made no sound. They ran around and around in the circle. (*CW*, 11:53)

The narrator tells of his own experience being in "a woods in Illinois, on another Winter night," and seeing "a pack of dogs act just like that." He recounts that those "dogs were waiting for me to die as they had waited for the old woman that night when I was a child, but when it happened to me I was a young man and had no intention whatever of dying." The old woman does die, "softly and quietly," and the dogs ravish the pack, "the grain bag containing the piece of salt pork, the liver the butcher had given her, the dog-meat, the soup bones." They tear her dress "from her body clear to the hips," but they do not touch the body (*CW*, 11:54, 55).

The boy knows this because, along with a hunter, some townspeople, and his brother, he had seen the corpse against the tree. He had seen "the oval in the snow, like a miniature race-track, where the dogs had run, had seen how the men were mystified, had seen the white bare young-looking shoulders, had heard the whispered comments of the men." But being a boy, he is not sure what it means, or that it means anything at all to him. At the sight of the naked body, his "body trembled with some strange mystical feeling." In one of those distinctively styled Anderson sentences of prepositional phrases and adjectival clauses, a shiver goes through the reader: "In a woods, in the late afternoon, when the trees are all bare and there is white snow on the ground, when all is silent, something creepy steals over the mind and body" (*CW*, 11:57, 58–59).

What creeps over the mind of the boy grown to adulthood is the sudden understanding of what Mrs. Grimes's death has meant: the "woman who died was one destined to feed animal life . . . that is all

she ever did. She was feeding animal life before she was born, as a
child, as a young woman working on the farm of the German, after she
married, when she grew old and when she died. She fed animal life in
cows, in chickens, in pigs, in horses, in men. . . . On the night when
she died she was hurrying homeward, bearing on her body food for
animal life. She died in the clearing in the woods and even after her
death continued feeding animal life." This is not what the narrator
understands when he first sees the body of Mrs. Grimes; only later
does he realize that a "thing so complete has its own beauty" (*CW*,
11:61–62). The old woman's death becomes for him something rich
and meaningful.

The poignant tone of the title story in the collection *Death in the
Woods* is also fully realized in "Brother Death," the concluding story.
Like the cherry tree in Chekhov's orchard, "two oak stumps, knee
high to a not-too-tall man and cut quite squarely across," represent the
end of one era and the beginning of the next. John Grey, "a land man,"
cannot abide the oak trees at the back of his house because "they make
too much shade. The grass does not grow." If the grass cannot grow,
then the cattle cannot graze and John Grey cannot obtain more possessions, which to him represent power (*CW*, 11:309, 312, 329).

Grey, however, is alone in his desire to cut down the oak trees. In
his family many "silent battles [have been] secretly going on," and his
children know that "people in your own family are likely at any moment to do strange, sometimes hurtful things to you." The central silent battle in "Brother Death" concerns 11-year-old Ted Grey's weak
heart and the attempts of everybody in the family, except his 14-year-
old sister Mary to protect him from any experiences of life that would
speed his death. As a result of a childhood disease, Ted suffers from
"a heart likely at any moment to stop beating, leaving him dead, cut
down like a young tree." So the rest of the family is overprotective, not
allowing him to "learn to drive one of the two family cars, climb a tree
to find a bird's nest, run a race with Mary." Certainly he is forbidden
to "try his hand at breaking a colt" (*CW*, 11:311, 315, 316).

Once, however, Mary and Ted ignore the admonitions. They run
through the rain to the barns. When Mrs. Grey reprimands Ted, Mary
tells her mother she should have more sense. Because the mother is
an Aspinwahl and more sensitive than her husband—it is she who first
pleads that the oak trees not be cut down—she understands, and after
that moment "there was a new inclination in the family to keep hands
off the pair" (*CW*, 11:319).

The crucial scene in the story, the decision to cut down the oak trees, is a family confrontation in which the father apparently wins; but Mary discovers in retrospect that her father had not won at all. Her older brother Don is 18 when the classic confrontation of wills occurs between him and his father. It is a play for possession of power within the family and an attempt by Don to assert himself. The father and son are too much alike, both physically and psychologically—"the same lines about the jaws, the same eyes. . . . Already the young man walked like the father, slammed doors as did the father . . . both land lovers, possession lovers" (*CW*, 11:326). But Mary knows "long afterwards, when she was a grown woman . . . [that in] what happened in the yard that afternoon [there] was something, a driving destructive thing in life, in all relationships between people." She learns that "ownership . . . gave curious rights, dominances—fathers over children, men and women over lands, houses, factories in cities, fields" (*CW*, 11:324, 325, 326).

Don threatens to walk off the farm and never return if his father destroys the trees. Mary imagines the exchange between them: "'I possess' . . . 'I will possess.' The father wheeled and looked sharply at the son and then ignored him. . . . [There were] unspoken words flying back and forth. 'I possess. I am in command here. What do you mean by telling me that I won't?' 'Ha! So! You possess now but soon I will possess.' 'I'll see you in hell first.' 'You fool! Not yet! Not yet!' None of the words, set down above, was spoken at the moment, and afterwards the daughter Mary never did remember the exact words that had passed between the two men" (*CW*, 11:329).

Don leaves, but he returns a few days later, "Mary afterwards thought, rather sheepishly." If the father "felt triumphant, he did not show his feeling." He tells his son, "It [the farm] will be yours soon now. . . . You can be boss then." Mary is not certain what her father means; knowledge comes to her slowly. Eventually she understands her father to have been saying: "You will be in command, and for you, in your turn, it will be necessary to assert. Such men as we are cannot fool with delicate stuff. Some men are meant to command and others must obey. You can make them obey in your turn. There is a kind of death. Something in you must die before you can possess and command" (*CW*, 11:334, 335).

The adult Mary also discovers in retrospect that before Ted died ("during the night in his bed"), there had been "a curious sense of freedom, something that belonged to him that made it good, a great happiness, to be with him." Her final thoughts (the closing sentence of the story) are that "having to die his kind of death, he never had to make the surrender his brother had made—to be sure of possessions, success, his time to command—would never have to face the more subtle and terrible death that had come to his older brother" (*CW*, 11:335, 336).

Mary comes to understand that there is more than one kind of death. Don must continue to die little deaths every day for the rest of his life. The story ends with the sounds of Chekhov's broken harp string somewhere in the distance and the ax strokes far away in the orchard. In these echoes can be heard the music of life's telling moments that transcend mortality because they are universal and eternal.

Some Minor Stories

For the most part, the remainder of the later stories suffer by comparison with Anderson's best writing. Many are simply vignettes, fillips of prose that provide very brief glimpses into lives more fully developed in the more accomplished stories. Some are very long stories that introduce a great many characters and events that are overshadowed by the more memorable characters of other stories. But they continue to explore familiar Anderson territory: loneliness, unlived lives, writing, advertising, mountain people, obsession, murder, lies, family, marriage, sex.

One of the longest stories, "Unused: A Tale of Life in Ohio" (1923) links sex and loneliness to small-town family life. It also includes an episode that mocks the "poison plot." The tragic tale of May Edgley is told when word of the discovery of her drowned body reaches a doctor and his odd-jobs boy while they are fishing. For the boy, the first sight of death is an oxymoronic sensation: the "cold and chill" of the corpse is juxtaposed with the "rich warm comforting smell" (*CW*, 10:33) of the barn where it has been put. The boy feels his imagination awakened by the tale the doctor tells of the Edgley family.

The doctor's five-part tale is a ravaging story of hardship, toil, and turmoil. It is the story of three sisters whose fates become linked by sexual misadventures. Kate is a waitress who "on almost any evening might have been seen walking out with some traveling man" (*CW*, 10:40). Lillian is a prostitute "on the turf" who is often seen wearing "a huge hat with a white ostrich feather that fell down almost to her shoulder" (*CW*, 10:36, 67). May is the brightest of the three, but she is abused by her life in the Ohio town; she loses valedictorian honors at her high school graduation because a member of the school board sees to it that his son is awarded the prize. Out of loneliness, May has sex in the berry fields with Jerome Hadley, the town baseball pitcher and mail clerk. As a result of this sexual encounter, May resolves to build a tower of lies to protect herself from the truth. She convinces herself that sex is something dirty, something she must wash away. She finds a female confidante in Maud Welliver, whom she tells that she saved a man from murder by going into the woods with Jerome. This is the "poison plot" (*CW*, 10:61) that May devises to justify her sexual encounter with Jerome.

May is also certain she has an inner self that is being destroyed, that there "was a very tender delicate thing within her, many people had wanted to kill. . . . To kill the delicate thing within was a passion that obsessed mankind. All men and women tried to do it. First the man or woman killed the thing within himself, and then tried to kill it in others. Men and women were afraid to let the thing live" (*CW*, 10:76–77).

Along with the tower of lies, May begins to build a "tower of romance." To counteract a contrasting story of true romance that Maud tells about a grocer from Fort Wayne, Freeman Hunt, who is coming to pursue Maud, May invents another tale of murder, which includes a mercenary and a prince who wants to marry her. May obviously creates the tale to make her life more bearable. She knows what the town has done to her, and "what it would do again when the chance offered" (*CW*, 10:81, 107).

The twin towers of lies and romance begin to topple in the denouement of the story. When May agrees to go with Maud to a dance in Surrey, by coincidence six Bidwell men show up. One of them, Sid Gould, had been beaten up by the Edgleys when he had expressed an interest in Kate Edgley. Sid affronts May. She beats him with a piece of driftwood, thinking that "the thing that was happening was in some odd way connected with the affair in the wood with Jerome. It was the same affair. Sid Gould and Jerome were one man, they stood for the same thing, were the same thing." Frightened, May runs away and is not discovered until days later, drowned, clutching Lillian's white hat with the "huge ostrich feather sticking out of the top" (*CW*, 10:131, *HM*, 35).

"An Ohio Pagan" (1923) and "Out of Nowhere into Nothing" (1921) are two long stories in which we encounter once again sex, loneliness, the idea of the thing within that the world destroys, and the need for an affirmation of the self.

Mary Cochran figures in two stories about unlived lives, "Unlighted Lamps" (1921) and "The Door of the Trap" (1921). "Unlighted Lamps" is the more effective of the two. One Sunday evening in Huntersburg, Illinois, everything about a father and a daughter is revealed to each of them, but never to each other. The father, Dr. Cochran, suffers from a "disease of the heart" that is both physical and psychological. In all of Mary's life, she has never felt "anything warm and close" from her father. Even her mother, who had aspired to be an actress, thought of him as "the silent cold man." During a walk in the woods on that Sunday evening, Mary is accosted by Duke Yetter, who recalls town rumors that her mother had left her father for another man. The truth is that she left with her own father for a career in Chicago. Mary does not know this. Nor does she know that even as she is taking her walk and attempting to resolve some of the confusion in her life, her father has resolved to tell her "the whole story of his marriage and its failure" (*CW*, 9:66, 67, 82, 86).

Mary returns to her father's office, where she has decided to tell him she loves him. Her father is returning to his office after delivering the firstborn child of a farmer and his wife, having decided to tell Mary he loves her. Neither the parent nor the child had been able to express that love before; neither gets the chance this evening. Dr. Cochran dies of a heart attack as he is walking up the stairs to his office. The story ends with unresolved relationships and incompletely lived lives.

Mary is a secondary character in "The Door of the Trap," another story of unfulfilled love in an unsatisfactory marriage. Hugh Walker is a math teacher at a small college in Union Valley, Illinois. Married with three children, he often finds himself walking to "cure the restlessness in himself." One source of his restlessness is his attraction to Mary Cochran. Freed by the death of her father in "Unlighted Lamps," Mary has gone to college and taken up residence in the Walker house. It is a house of cards ready to collapse. Hugh sees himself as a house whose "shutters are loose." When he kisses Mary and then asks her to leave the house, she does so "weak with fright" (*CW*, 9:118, 128, 132). Hugh remains, trapped in what he sees as the prison of his marriage and the reality of his life.

More than a dozen of the later stories deal with writing and advertising; "I Get So I Can't Go On" (1933) is the most appealing of them.

Part 1

Frank Blandin, a copywriter, accompanies three other colleagues—Al from sales, Gil, another copywriter, and Bud, a commercial artist—to a restaurant in Chicago. The story is structured as Frank's revery in which he imagines marriage and books to be ways to "get away from yourself" (*CW*, 21:76).

The first-person narrator of "Alice" (1929) is a writer trying to define beauty. He notes that he and two other men are struck by the beauty of women. Finding himself blocked in his writing, he is given $1,000 by friends of Alice, a singer from eastern Tennessee, at her request. When Alice and the writer visit her home in the Adirondacks, she tells him her life story, and on their return from the mountains he is struck by her beauty.

Neither the writer in "The Lost Novel" (1929) nor the writer in "Milk Bottles" (1923) can recognize good writing when it is right in front of him. The British novelist in "The Lost Novel" is unable to write, marries, begins writing of his wife, but when she walks into the room, strikes her. She leaves, and the novel he writes becomes a success. A second novel "was inside him like an unborn child," and he is sure that "automatic writing" has given him his novel. But when he wakes up the next day, there are only blank pages and the novel is lost (*CW*, 11:25, 26).

In "Milk Bottles," as in "The Story Writers," a restless writer tries to find material for a story in the August heat of Chicago. His copywriter friend Ed wants to write "real stuff," never realizing that what he discards as unsatisfactory is actually his best work because, in a true lesson of writing, what he "expressed in what he wrote about the milk bottle could not be forgotten" (*CW*, 10:236, 241).

Conclusion—Two Tributes

Anderson's short stories give us a new understanding of those rare moments he believed were the source of the only true history of life. Charles Bukowski and Raymond Carver each wrote a poem that recognizes Anderson's contribution to writing and to the short-story form.

Carver's "Harley's Swans" pays homage to Anderson's voice, tone, and influence. An epigraph from an Anderson letter establishes the theme of the poem: "I'm trying again. A man has to begin over and over—to try to think and feel only in a very limited field, the house on the street, the man at the corner drug store." The poem is in the form of a revery. The speaker thinks of Anderson while he remembers loitering "in front of the drug store this afternoon," or his dad taking him to get haircuts, his mother helping to pick out school clothes. The speaker, in short, remembers the small moments of life that occur under the surface of things but reverberate down the years, throughout a person's lifetime. At the end of the poem, alone in a "house / quiet and empty," the speaker wants to "try again" and speaks to Anderson, knowing that he, "of all people . . . can understand."[23]

The Bukowski poem, "One for Sherwood Anderson," speaks directly to Anderson's appeal to the reader. Bukowski recognizes that "one felt space between his lines, air / and he told it so the lines remained / carved there." Some stories are "left [with] the meaning open / and sometimes he told meaning-less stories / because that was the way it was." Even if sometimes Anderson told "the same story again and again," he "never wrote a story / that was unreadable."[24]

Anderson thought short stories "should be so written that they flow towards their inevitable end as majestically and powerfully as the great river [the Mississippi] flows down to the gulf."[25] In short, Anderson never wrote a story a reader cannot finish. Our debt to Anderson, for his innovations in short-story form, style, and characterization, is remarkable and immeasurable.

Notes to Part 1

1. Sherwood Anderson, quoted in Alfred Kazin, *On Native Grounds* (New York: Reynal and Hitchcock, 1942), 213; hereafter cited in text as Kazin.

2. Sherwood Anderson, *A Story Teller's Story*, in *The Complete Works of Sherwood Anderson*, 21 vols., ed. Kichinosuke Ohashi (Kyoto, Japan: Rinsen, 1982), 12:352; hereafter cited in text as *CW*.

3. Charles Child Walcutt, *American Literary Naturalism: A Divided Stream* (Minneapolis: 1956), 224; hereafter cited in text as Walcutt.

4. Epifanio San Juan, "Vision and Reality: A Reconsideration of Sherwood Anderson's *Winesburg, Ohio*," *American Literature* 35 (May 1963) 141–42; hereafter cited in text as San Juan. The term "roundness" is discussed in E. M. Forster, *Aspects of the Novel* (New York: Harcourt, Brace & Co., 1927), 73–78.

5. Henry James, *The Art of Fiction and Other Essays*, ed. Morris Roberts (New York: Oxford University Press, 1948), 13; Virginia Woolf, "Mr. Bennett and Mrs. Brown," *The Hogarth Essays* (London: 1924; reprint: Garden City, N.Y.: 1928), 11.

6. See Anderson's poem "The Story Teller," *A New Testament* (New York: Boni and Liveright, 1926), 63–64; it is also the preface to *The Triumph of the Egg* (New York: B. W. Huebsch, 1921).

7. Sherwood Anderson, Dedication to *Winesburg, Ohio*, *CW*, 3.

8. Lionel Trilling, *The Liberal Imagination* (New York: Viking, 1950), 27.

9. Sherwood Anderson, Foreword to *Mid-American Chants* (New York: John Lane, 1923), 7; hereafter cited in text as *MAC*.

10. Waldo Frank, "*Winesburg, Ohio* after Twenty Years," *Story* 19 (September–October 1941): 30; hereafter cited in text as Frank.

11. *Harper's* 129 (July 1914): 207–10 (as "The Rabbit-pen"), reprinted in *CW*, 21:5–17.

12. *Sherwood Anderson's Memoirs*, ed. Ray Lewis White (Chapel Hill, N.C.: University of North Carolina Press, 1969), 334; hereafter cited in text as *SAM*.

13. Kim Townsend, *Sherwood Anderson* (Boston: Houghton Mifflin, 1987), 85.

14. Both Harlan Hatcher ("Sherwood Anderson," *Creating the Modern American Novel* [New York: Farrar and Rinehart, 1935], 155–71) and Frederick J. Hoffman ("Anderson—Psychoanalyst by Default," *Freudianism and the Literary Mind* [Baton Rouge: Louisiana State University Press, 1945], 230–55) (hereafter cited in text as Hatcher, and as Hoffman) deal with this approach to Anderson.

15. Robert Spiller, *The Cycle of American Literature* (New York: 1955), 258.

16. The passage recalls the biblical mustard seed: "The kingdom of heaven is like to a grain of mustard seed . . . which indeed is the least of all seeds: but when it is grown, it is the greatest among herbs" (Matt, 13:31). This is one of the first but not the only biblical allusion in *Winesburg, Ohio;* religion in one form or another appears in many of the stories. "Hands" concludes with the image of Wing Biddlebaum picking up bread crumbs from the floor and looking "like a priest engaged in some service of his church. The nervous expressive fingers, flashing in and out of the light, might well have been mistaken for the fingers of the devotee going swiftly through decade after decade of his rosary" (*CW*, 3:17). "The Philosopher" concludes with a similar idea; Dr. Parcival is certain "that everyone in the world is Christ and they are all crucified" (*CW*, 3:48). As Epifanio San Juan points out, Christ conveys the possibility of resurrection, renewal, and affirmation (140). All of "Godliness" depends on the biblical myths of "another Jesse" (*CW*, 3:64) and Abraham and Isaac. And the central figure of "The Strength of God" is Rev. Curtis Hartman, who wears his own sort of Hawthornean black veil as he lusts after Kate Swift.

In addition to the biblical subject matter and reference points, there is a great deal of biblical rhetoric in the style of many of the stories.

See also John J. McAleer, "Christ Symbolism in *Winesburg, Ohio,*" *Discourse* 4 (Summer 1961): 168–81.

17. Rex Burbank, *Sherwood Anderson* (New York: G. K. Hall, 1964), 73; hereafter cited in text as Burbank.

18. The same impulse takes the narrator of "The Man Who Became a Woman," *CW*, vol. 10.

19. Frederick J. Hoffman, *The Twenties* (New York: Viking, 1955), 292.

20. A group of 14 stories that were either unpublished or published only in magazines, are collected in *The Sherwood Anderson Reader,* ed. Paul Rosenfeld (Boston: Houghton Mifflin, 1947). Volume 21 of *Complete Works* includes 20 previously uncollected stories. "Moonshine" was first published in *Missouri Review* 12, no. 1, Found Text series (1989): 135–45.

21. Introduction to *Sherwood Anderson: Short Stories,* ed. Maxwell Geismar (New York: Hill and Wang, 1962), xix; hereafter cited in text as Geismar.

22. Irving Howe (*Sherwood Anderson* [Stanford, Calif.: Stanford University Press, 1966], 163) considers the elements of homosexual fantasy that this encounter conveys.

23. Raymond Carver, *Where Water Comes Together with Other Water* (New York: Random House, 1984), 83–84.

24. Charles, Bukowski, *Dangling in the Tournefortia* (Santa Clara, Calif.: Black Sparrow Press, 1989), 31; reprint.

25. Sherwood Anderson, *Sherwood Anderson's Notebook*, *CW*, 14:226.

Part 2

THE WRITER

Introduction

Readers seeking the Sherwood Anderson behind his short fiction are fortunate to have a range of materials available to them. Anderson's ideas about himself, his writing, his work, his family, and his friends appear in letters, diaries, journals, memoirs, autobiographies, and essays. The following selections from a number of those sources range from an informal 1930 rumination on being published to a wry address to storytellers from *The "Writer's Book"* (1975), an unfinished Anderson text on the craft of writing. The voluminous *Letters of Sherwood Anderson* (1953) reads like a novel, but the selections from it focus on the submission of *Winesburg, Ohio* to *Seven Arts* magazine, sex and repression, short-story writing in general, and advice to a young writer in particular. "Writing Stories" appears in the original edition of *Sherwood Anderson's Memoirs* (1942) as well as in volume 19 of *Complete Works*. The excerpt from *A Story Teller's Story* (1924) recounts the story of Anderson's departure from his unhappy business life. In two brief passages from *The Modern Writer* (1925), Anderson defines the "modern" person and gives his conception of the storyteller's response to that person's story as it needs to be told. And in the final selection, "A Note on Realism," from *Sherwood Anderson's Notebook* (1926), Anderson further considers the possibilities and responsibilities of fiction writing.

"On Being Published" (1930)

There must have been a few other things. I dare say I always scribble.
I was a copy man in an advertising agency in Chicago.

One day Mr. Cyrus Curtis came in. He had been attracted to something I wrote. He wanted to see the man who wrote it. It must have been something about business, I can't remember.

However, his being attracted to it helped me. Mr. Curtis was already a big man in that advertising world. I got a raise out of that.

In some of my books I have told about a certain factory I later owned in Ohio. The tale is in "A Story Teller's Story." The truth is the factory was about ready to go to pieces. I didn't attend to business, didn't want to. Things were ready for a break.

The break, when it came, went deep. All the life I had built up was ruined. I had been trying to be a "regular fellow." I belonged to clubs, went about with salesmen, business men, etc.

I was leading a double life. I went home to my house and into a room upstairs. Often I didn't come down to dinner. I wrote all night. I was strong. My body stood it all right.

About my nerves I don't know. I wrote hundreds of words in that room and threw the sheets away. My wife must have thought me crazy.

I am sure I did not have any great passion to be a writer. I haven't now.

I did seek something.

Perhaps I felt my own life, rather at the core, during that time.

I remember the scene from the window of that room. There were two gardens I could see into. One man went in for flowers, the other for vegetables. I couldn't decide which was the most beautiful.

Right now it seems to me I can see every flower, every vegetable, in those two gardens. I can see the gardens at the various stages of the seasons. I must have been writing like that madly, in that room for at least two years.

Reprinted from *Colophon* (February 1930), unpaginated. Sincere and repeated attempts to locate a copyright holder have been unsuccessful.

Both the gardeners, who were my neighbors, were orderly men. I had a passion for order in myself. I wanted some sort of rhythm, a swing to life—my life and other lives.

I never got it in fact.

I have approached it sometimes, on the printed page.

Being published made no great impression. At that time I was in hospital in Cleveland.

Well, I had walked away from my factory, from that room, that town, all my life there. Perhaps my brain had cracked a little. I was an uneducated man. Many people had told me I could not write.

My notions seemed immoral to all the people I knew. I knew no artists.

There had been this intense struggle, within myself. Perhaps if I had stayed there in that place and had attended to business I would have got rich.

I did not want that either nor did I want specially to be published. What of all that? There was already too much rot published.

I was in a hospital to be examined for mental disorder. They did examine me there. I had left that factory and that town and had wandered about the country for days.

I was trying to find some order, some sense, in my own life and in other lives. They picked me up and took me to the hospital.

They were very kind to me there. Everyone was very kind. I must have written that story in that room looking into the gardens. I don't remember writing it. I must have sent it to that magazine.

Someone brought the letter, accepting the story, or the magazine with it in, to my bed in the hospital.

Perhaps they felt it a proof of my mental unsoundness that I was not elated. I wasn't. As a matter of fact it would be better for the art of prose writing if all stories were published unsigned.

I knew I had not got at what I wanted a little to get at in that story.

It was published. Well, the thing I was after, am still after, was just as far away as it had been before.

"Prelude to a Story" (1975)

On a certain day, in the early summer, some years ago, I got a letter from my literary agent. It may be that I had been writing to him. He had certain stories I had sent him to sell.

"Can't you, sir, sell one of the stories to some magazine? I am needing money."

He answered my letter. He is a sensible man, knows his business.

"I admit that the stories you have sent me are good stories.

"But," he said, "you are always getting something into all of your stories that spoils the sale."

He did not go further but I knew what he meant.

"Look here," he once said to me, "why can't you, for the time at least, drop this rather intimate style of yours?"

He smiled when he said it and I also smiled.

"Let us say, now, that you are yourself the editor of one of our big American magazines. You have yourself been in business. When you first began to write, even after you had published some of your earlier books, *Winesburg* and others, you had to go on for years, working in an advertising place.

"You must know that all of our large American magazines are business ventures. It costs a great deal of money to print and distribute hundreds of thousands of magazines. Often, as you know, the price received for the magazine, when sold on the newsstand, does not pay for the paper on which it is printed."

"Yes, I know."

"They have to have stories that please people."

"Yes, I know."

We had stopped to have a drink at a bar. But a few weeks before he had written me a letter. "There is a certain large magazine that would like to have a story from you.

Excerpted from *The "Writer's Book,"* by *Sherwood Anderson*, ed. Martha M. Curry (Metuchen, N.J.: Scarecrow Press, 1975), 4–11. Reprinted by permission of Martha M. Curry.

"It should be, let us say, a story of about ten thousand words.

"Do not attempt to write the story. Make an outline, I should say a three or four page outline.

"I can sell the story for you."

I had made the outline and had sent it to him. "It is splendid," he wrote. "Now you can go ahead. I can get such and such a sum."

"Oho!" The sum mentioned would get me out of my difficulties. "I will get busy," I said to myself. "In a week I will dash off this story." Some two or three weeks before a man friend had come to me one evening. He is a man to whom I am deeply attached.

"Come and walk with me," he said, and we set out afoot, leaving the town where he lived. I had gone to the town to see him but when I got to his town there was a sudden illness in his house. The man has children and two of them were in bed with a contagious disease.

I stayed at a hotel. He came there. We walked beyond the town, got into a dirt road, passed farm houses, dogs barked at us. We got into a moonlit meadow.

We had walked for a long time in silence. At the hotel I had noticed that my friend was in a tense excited mood.

"You are in some sort of trouble. Is it the children? Has the disease taken a turn for the worst?"

"No," he said. "The children are better. They are all right."

We were in the moonlit meadow, standing by a fence, some sheep grazing nearby, and it was a delicious night of the early summer. "There is something I have to tell to someone," he said. "I wrote to you, begged you to come here."

My friend is a highly respected man in his town.

He began talking. He talked for hours. He told me a story of a secret life he had been living.

My friend is a man of fifty. He is a scientist. He is employed, as an experimental scientist, by a large manufacturing company.

But, I might as well confess at once that I am, as you the reader may have guessed, covering the trail of my friend. I am a man rather fortunate in life. I have a good many men friends. If I make this one an experimental scientist, working for a large manufacturing company, it will do.

His story was, on the whole, strange. It was like so many stories, not

59

invented but came directly out of life. It was a story having in it certain so-called sordid touches, strange impulses come to a man of fifty, himself in the grip of an odd passion.

"I have been doing this.

"I have been doing that.

"I have to unload, to tell someone.

"I have been suffering."

My friend did unload his story, getting a certain relief, and I went home.

The letter came from the agent. I made the outline of the story that was pronounced splendidly by my agent.

But what rough places I had smoothed out!

"No, I cannot say that such a figure, holding such a respectable place in my life, did that.

"There must not be anything unpleasant. There must be nothing that will remind readers of certain sordid moments, thoughts, passions, acts, in their own lives.

"If I am to get this money, and, oh, how I need it!"

I am no Shakespeare but did not even Shakespeare write a play he called *As You Like It?*

"When you are writing, to please people, you must not touch certain secret, often dark, little recesses that are in all humans.

"Keep in the clear, man. Go gayly along.

"It will be all right to startle them a little.

"You must get a certain dramatic force into your story."

But that night the man, upon whose story I have based the story I am about to write, was, as he talked, simply broken. He even put his face down upon the top rail of the fence, there in that moonlit meadow, and cried, and I went to him. I put my arms about his shoulders, said words to him.

"This passion, that has come to you at this time in your life, that now threatens to tear down all you have so carefully built up, that threatens to destroy the lives of others you love, will pass.

"At our age everything passes."

I do not remember just what I did say to him.

But I was at my desk.

"Never mind him. Use, of the story he told you, only so much as will perhaps a little startle, without too much shocking, your readers. "You know very well how badly you need this money." These the sentences I had begun saying to myself.

And so I began to write, but alas!

Our difficulty is that as we write we become interested, absorbed, often a little in love with these characters of our stories, that seem to be growing here, under our hand.

I have begun this story, taking off, as it were, from the story told me in the meadow by my friend but now, as I write, he has disappeared.

There is a new man, coming to life, here, on this paper, under my hand. He seems to be here, in this room where I work.

"You must do me right now," he seems to be saying to me.

"There is a certain morality involved," he says.

"Now you must tell everything, put it all down."

"Do not hesitate. I want it all put down."

And so, there is all of that money I so needed, gone out of the window.

There is a series of letters, concerning a story to be written, that lie here on my desk. I have had them brought to me from my files.

"If you are to write the story for us it would be well for you to keep certain things in mind.

"The story should be concerned with the lives of people who are in what might be called comfortable circumstances.

"Above all, it should not be too gloomy.

"We want you to understand that we do not wish, in any way, to dictate to you."

I sit at my desk, reading over the above letter. "It is true," I say to myself, "that I was once in business." For years I was employed as a writer of advertisements, in an advertising agency. Having been born into and having lived, through boyhood and into my young manhood, in a very poor family, I had for a long time what I presume might be called "the American dream." I dreamed of getting rich, or at least well-to-do, of living in a big house, having an assured income. I had spent the years of my early young manhood working as a laborer, had been a farm laborer, a factory hand, lived as such men do in little rooms, often in cheerless enough streets. As I sit here this morning writing, scenes, smells, sights of that time in my own life come back to me. I see myself in a room in a house in a street in a factory town. I am sitting at my window looking out. I have got, at a second-hand furniture store, an old kitchen table and at a stationery store some tablets of white paper. Even at that time, and although I had not then begun to think of myself as a writer, such a thing as authorship being seemingly as far away from me as the stars in the sky at night, I had nevertheless this passion for writing. Like my man of the story of certain phases of a human life I have here written, in this book, I took it out in writing letters. I used to get names out of newspapers or out of books, borrowed at the public libraries. I began a letter, "Dear Cecelia."

I wanted to tell Cecelia of certain impressions, certain feelings about life, I had been having.

But who was Cecelia? How old was she? What did she look like?

It was not difficult for me to evoke the figure of Cecelia. Although, as a young workman, not skilled in any one trade and therefore never very well paid, I was compelled to live always in some poorer section of the town or city where I was employed, I did, usually, have one good suit of clothes, a presentable hat, presentable shoes, I could put on for a Sunday afternoon's or an evening's walk.

I walked in some rich or well-to-do series of town and there, on a wide street, under trees, I had seen a young woman walking.

She was tall and slender. She walked with easy grace. She had a somewhat dark, so-called "olive" skin—not the green but the ripe olive—but not that either—

"Her skin is of the color of the soil, in a certain field, seen from a distance, from a freight train, on which I was once bumming my way to a new town and a new job," I told myself.

She had dark eyes and very fine glistening black hair.

So I wrote to her. I called her Cecelia. I began to tell her stories of workmen beside whom I worked, of dreams that came, of people seen, of the hours of sleepless loneliness that sometimes came at night.

Of the noises at night in the rooming house, where I had my room.

I always made my Cecelias a bit older than myself. Let us say I had reached the age of twenty-four. I made her a woman of thirty.

It is true that these thoughts of Cecelia led sometimes into lascivious thoughts. What young man has not had them about some imagined woman? I stopped thinking of her eyes, the broad forehead, the finely shaped nose and chin, her graceful stride as she walked under the trees and thought instead [of] holding her two shapely breasts in the palms of my hands, of her lips, of her shapely thighs.

Then I could not write to her. I could not sleep. Sometimes, when such thoughts came, I had to leave my room. I walked for hours in the street. I went into saloons and drank. I wanted to get drunk. "I'd better get drunk," I told myself.

Four Letters (1916–1939)

MR. WALDO FRANK, *Seven Arts* MAGAZINE, NEW YORK
My dear Mr. Frank: I sent you a little thing the other day that I believe you will like. Here is a suggestion.

I made last year a series of intensive studies of people of my home town, Clyde, Ohio. In the book I called the town Winesburg, Ohio. Some of the studies you may think pretty raw, and there is a sad note running through them. One or two of them get pretty closely down to ugly things of life. However, I put a good deal into the writing of them, and I believe they, as a whole, come a long step toward achieving what you are asking for in the article you ran in *Seven Arts*.

Some of these things have been used. *Masses* ran a story called "Hands" from this series.[1] Two or three also appeared in a little magazine out here called the *Little Review*.[2] The story called "Queer" you are using in December[3] is one of them.

This thought occurs to me. There are or will be seventeen of these studies. Fifteen are, I believe, completed. If you have the time and the inclination, I might send the lot to you to be looked over.

It is my own idea that when these studies are published in book form, they will suggest the real environment out of which present-day American youth is coming. Very truly yours

RICHMOND, VIRGINIA [NOVEMBER, 1929]
TO ROBERT ANDERSON [SHERWOOD ANDERSON'S SON]
Dear Bob: I am comfortably placed here at the Westmoreland Club, not at all expensive. They put me in a tiny room, but I am moving this afternoon to a large room on the second floor where there is a good-sized room in which to work.

It seems a bit silly of me sometimes, not to be there with you, but this whole thing has done me good.

Excerpted from *The Letters of Sherwood Anderson*, ed. Howard Mumford Jones and Walter B. Rideout (Boston: Little, Brown, 1953), 4–5; 196–199; 403–407; 447–449. Reprinted by permission of Harold Ober Associates Incorporated. Copyright 1953 by Eleanor Anderson. Renewed 1981 by Eleanor Copenhaver Anderson.

I think what happened to me was rather strange and amusing.

I guess you do not know, and perhaps never will know, the underlying basic difference between your generation and mine. In my generation, as you know—you kids of mine had partly to pay for it—I was a rebel.

Could there be anything more strange than what has happened to me?

I wanted for people, quite frankly, many things my generation did not have. I fought for it in my life and in my work.

Then the War came. The War did more than anything I or my kind could have done to make people face life.

For example, the old battleground was sex. That led naturally to an emphasis on sex. We all saw, everyone saw, the effect of repressions.

I and my kind told the story of repressed life. I have never thought of myself as a profound thinker. I was the storyteller; I took my color from the life about me. You know that for a long time after I began writing I was condemned on all sides. That is pretty much forgotten now. My *Winesburg, Ohio,* was condemned as a sex-server. How strange that notion seems now.

And then came the Great War. Never mind what the War was. It was terrific in its physical aspects—bodies mangled, the young manhood of England, Germany and France blown away or bled white, a great nation like Germany humiliated in the end.

Never mind all that. That is past.

But something else got blown up in that war too: the repressions, the strange fear of sex, the resultant underestimate and overestimate of sex as a force of life got blown up too.

It may be that what happened in the Great War, because of it, was a truer estimate of life. The young men who went into it got, must have got, a profound sense of life's cheapness.

You, my son, did not get into the War. You were too young. You just escaped it. Just the same you are not at all the man you would have been but for the War.

Of course there came other forces at work—the flowering of the industrial age, speeded up, no doubt, by the War.

Thousand[s] of men, everywhere, jerked out of the old individualistic life—plenty of machinery to jerk them out fast, machinery to kill them in masses like cattle—hurled into a new mass life.

The old individualist—the man of the pre-War period, who was a young man then, who got his sharp impressions then (most of us continue all our lives to live in the impressions of youth; the men, the young men who got their sharp impressions of life in the War will probably continue to live in those impressions the rest of their lives)—the old individualist type of man—well, you see where he was.

Why talk of sex repressions now? Apparently there aren't any.

I remember, son, a certain woman who fought long and bitterly for woman's suffrage. The women got what they fought for.

But this particular woman couldn't quit fighting for woman suffrage. She kept right on. One day I was walking with a young woman, and we saw this older woman. As she knew me, she stopped. "What are you doing now?" I asked.

She began again on the rights of women. They had got some things but not enough. The words she was saying would have been glowing words twenty years ago. I shall never forget the puzzled look in the younger woman's eyes. She was a post-War kid. "Rights of women? What the devil is the old girl talking about?" she asked.

Well, you see where I am, son—or at least have been these last five years. I had a world, and it slipped away from me. The War blew up more than the bodies of men, as I have already suggested.

It blew ideas away—

Love

God

Romance.

I am working on a book. I call it *No God*.[4] I could just as well call it *No Love*. It is not without significance that Gauguin is your favorite modern painter while my favorite is Van Gogh. I remember what Gauguin said of love. "If I were to say the word, it would crack the teeth out of my mouth," he said.

As regards this transition, this sweeping change that has come in the whole underlying conceptions of life, it is a profound one.

If I were a bit older, it would not make any difference to me. The old are old.

As a man, as a writer, I had to ask myself which road I wanted to take. I could simply have been old, not to have tried to understand you and your brother and sister.

I fought against you for a long time. Who has cried out more sharply than myself against the coming of industrialism, the death of individualism, the modern world?

Well, I had already told the story of the man crying in the wilderness. I have been going about for four or five years now saying to myself, "To hell with that."

I want to say to you now that I would very likely have lost this little private battle of mine, that concerns no one vitally but myself, but for you kids of mine.

It would have meant kindly tolerance on your part, "The old man's all right." You know, that sort of thing.

In *No God*, the novel on which I am now at work, I am telling the story of a man having his roots in the pre-War life, accepting the present-day post-War life.

That is my man's story. He is a man who has had marriage in the old way—memories of it cling to him—and then he comes to accept a woman who is the product of the new world.

No God—No Love—in the old sense. That is what it means.

As for the woman, well, I see her every day on the street. I've a notion that she doesn't want and wouldn't take what men used to give women, calling it love. I hope I am right about her. She is the young female kid of today. She has had sex experience and will have more, when she wants it.

I look at her as my man in the book *No God* looks at her—glad of her, certainly all for her.

Writing about her and of my man's acceptance of her is fun. It is refreshing. It is good for me.

There is certainly plenty of the old pre-War thing in men, the fear of the new life that has constantly to be put down.

[TROUTDALE, VIRGINIA] AUGUST 27, 1938
TO GEORGE FREITAG[5]

Dear George Freitag: It sometimes seems to me that I should prepare a book designed to be read by other and younger writers. This not because of accomplishment on my own part, but because of the experiences, the particular experiences, I have had.

It is so difficult for most of us to realize how fully and completely commercialism enters into the arts. For example, how are you to know that really the opinion of the publisher or the magazine editor in regard to your work, what is a story and what isn't, means nothing? Some of my own stories, for example, that have now become almost American classics, that are put before students in our schools and colleges as

Part 2

examples of good storytelling, were, when first written, when submit-
ted to editors, and when seen by some of the so-called outstanding
American critics, declared not stories at all.

It is true they were not nice little packages, wrapped and labeled in
the O. Henry manner. They were obviously written by one who did
not know the answers. They were simple little tales of happenings,
things observed and felt. There were no cowboys or daring wild game
hunters. None of the people in the tales got lost in burning deserts or
went seeking the North Pole. In my stories I simply stayed at home,
among my own people, wherever I happened to be, people in my own
street. I think I must, very early, have realized that this was my milieu,
that is to say, common everyday American lives. The ordinary beliefs
of the people about me, that love lasted indefinitely, that success
meant happiness, simply did not seem true to me.

Things were always happening. My eyes began to see, my ears to
hear. Most of our American storytelling at that time had concerned only
the rich and the well-to-do. I was a storyteller but not yet a writer of
stories. As I came of a poor family, older men were always repeating to
me the old saying.

"Get money. Money makes the mare go."

For a time I was a laborer. As I had a passion for fast trotting and
pacing horses, I worked about race tracks. I became a soldier, I got into
business.

I knew, often quite intensively, Negro swipes about race tracks,
small gamblers, prize fighters, common laboring men and women.
There was a violent, dangerous man, said to be a killer. One night he
walked and talked to me and became suddenly tender. I was forced to
realize that all sorts of emotions went on in all sorts of people. A young
man who seemed outwardly a very clod suddenly began to run wildly
in the moonlight. Once I was walking in a wood and heard the sound
of a man weeping. I stopped, looked, and listened. There was a farmer
who, because of ill luck, bad weather, and perhaps even poor manage-
ment, had lost his farm. He had gone to work in a factory in town, but,
having a day off, had returned secretly to the fields he loved. He was
on his knees by a low fence, looking across the fields in which he had
worked from boyhood. He and I were employed at the time in the
same factory, and in the factory he was a quiet, smiling man, seemingly
satisfied with his lot.

I began to gather these impressions. There was a thing called happiness toward which men were striving. They never got to it. All of

68

life was amazingly accidental. Love, moments of tenderness and despair, came to the poor and the miserable as to the rich and successful.

It began to seem to me that what was most wanted by all people was love, understanding. Our writers, our storytellers, in wrapping life up into neat little packages were only betraying life. It began to seem to me that what I wanted for myself most of all, rather than so-called success, acclaim, to be praised by publishers and editors, was to try to develop, to the top of my bent, my own capacity to feel, see, taste, smell, hear. I wanted, as all men must want, to be a free man, proud of my own manhood, always more and more aware of earth, people, streets, houses, towns, cities. I wanted to take all into myself, digest what I could.

I could not give the answers, and so for a long time when my stories began to appear, at first only in little highbrow magazines, I was almost universally condemned by the critics. My stories, it seemed, had no definite ends. They were not conclusive and did not give the answers, and so I was called vague. "Groping" was a favorite term. It seems I could not get a formula and stick to it. I could not be smart about life. When I wrote my Winesburg stories—for the whole series I got eighty-five dollars—such critics as Mr. Floyd Dell and Henry Mencken, having read them, declared they were not stories. They were merely, it seemed, sketches. They were too vague, too groping. Some ten or fifteen years after Mr. Mencken told me they were not stories, he wrote, telling of how, when he first saw them, he realized their strength and beauty. An imagined conversation between us, that never took place, was spoken about.

And for this I did not blame Mr. Mencken. He thought he had said what he now thinks he said.

There was a time when Mr. Dell was, in a way, my literary father. He and Mr. Waldo Frank had been the first critics to praise some of my earlier work. He was generous and warm. He, with Mr. Theodore Dreiser, was instrumental in getting my first book published. When he saw the Winesburg stories, he, however, condemned them heartily. He was at that time, I believe, deeply under the influence of Maupassant. He advised me to throw the Winesburg stories away. They had no form. They were not stories. A story, he said, must be sharply definite. There must be a beginning and an end. I remember very clearly our conversation. "If you plan to go somewhere on a train and start for the station, but loiter along the way, so that the train comes into the station, stops to discharge and take on passengers, and then goes on its way, and you miss it, don't blame the locomotive engineer," I said. I daresay it was an arrogant saying, but arrogance is also needed.

And so I had written, let us say, the Winesburg stories. The publisher who had already published two of my early novels refused them, but at last I found a publisher. The stories were called unclean, dirty, filthy, but they did grow into the American consciousness, and presently the same critic who had condemned them began asking why I did not write more Winesburg stories.

I am telling you all of this, I assure you, not out of bitterness. I have had a good life, a full, rich life. I am still having a full, rich life. I tell it only to point out to you, a young writer, filled as I am made aware by your letter to me, of tenderness for life, I tell it simply to suggest to you plainly what you are up against. For ten or fifteen years after I had written and published the Winesburg stories, I was compelled to make my living outside of the field of writing. You will find none of my stories even yet in the great popular magazines that pay high prices to writers.

I do not blame the publishers or the editors. Once I was in the editorial rooms of a great magazine. They had asked me in for an editorial conference.

Would it not be possible for them to begin publishing my stories?

I advised against it. "If I were you, I would let Sherwood Anderson alone."

I had been for a long time an employee of a big advertising agency. I wrote the kind of advertisements on which great magazines live.

But I had no illusions about advertising, could have none. I was an advertising writer too long. The men employed with me, the businessmen, many of them successful and even rich, were like the laborers, gamblers, soldiers, race track swipes I had formerly known. Their guards down, often over drinks, they told me the same stories of tangled, thwarted lives.

How could I throw a glamour over such lives? I couldn't.

The Winesburg stories, when first published, were bitterly condemned. They were thrown out of libraries. In one New England town, where three copies of the book had been bought, they were publicly burned in the public square of the town. I remember a letter I once received from a woman. She had been seated beside me at the table of a friend. "Having sat beside you and having read your stories,

I feel that I shall never be clean again," she wrote. I got many such letters.

Then a change came. The book found its way into schools and colleges. Critics who had ignored or condemned the book now praised it. "It's Anderson's best work. It is the height of his genius. He will never again do such work."

People constantly came to me, all saying the same thing.

"But what else of mine have you read since?"

A blank look upon faces.

They had read nothing else of mine. For the most part they were simply repeating, over and over, an old phrase picked up.

Now, I do not think all of this matters. I am one of the fortunate ones. In years when I have been unable to make a living with my pen, there have always been friends ready and willing to help me. There was one man who came to me in a year when I felt, when I knew, that I had done some of my best and truest work, but when, no money coming in, I was trying to sell my house to get money to live.

He wanted, he said, one of my manuscripts. "I will lend you five thousand dollars." He did lend it, knowing I could never return his money, but he did not deceive me. He had an affection for me as I had for him. He wanted me to continue to live in freedom. I have found this sort of thing among the rich as well as the poor. My house where I live is filled with beautiful things, all given to me. I live well enough. I have no quarrel with life.

And I am only writing all of this to you to prepare you. In a world controlled by business why should we not expect businessmen to think first of business?

And do bear in mind that publishers of books, of magazines, of newspapers are, first of all, businessmen. They are compelled to be.

And do not blame them when they do not buy your stories. Do not be romantic. There is no golden key that unlocks all doors. There is only the joy of living as richly as you can, always feeling more, absorbing more, and, if you are by nature a teller of tales, the realization that by faking, trying to give people what they think they want, you are in danger of dulling and in the end quite destroying what may be your own road into life.

There will remain for you, to be sure, the matter of making a living, and I am sorry to say to you that in the solution of that problem, for you and other young writers, I am not interested. That, alas, is your own problem. I am interested only in what you may be able to contribute to the advancement of our mutual craft.

But why not call it an art? That is what it is.

Did you ever hear of an artist who had an easy road to travel in life?

[TROUTDALE, VIRGINIA] SEPTEMBER 19, 1939
MRS. HARRIET MARTIN, COLLINSVILLE, ILLINOIS

Dear Mrs. Harriet Martin: When your brother Mike was over here last Sunday, I told him that while I would be very glad to read your stories, I felt that the probabilities were strong that I could be of very little help to you. I rather got it from Mike that what you are after principally was to do what is called "crashing the magazine market," and I have never much had this aim, nor have I ever been to much extent a magazine writer. I rather came into writing by the back door. Writing seemed to give me more satisfaction than anything else I could do, and what reputation I have got is rather, I think, a literary rather than a popular one.

I will not try to go into a detailed discussion of your stories, because I feel I am incapable of doing so, but it does seem to me, from my point of view, that yours is wrong.

I have read with a good deal of interest the letters to you from the man Uzzell,[6] and it seems to me that when the characters of stories are taken from this point of view—a character in one of your stories, for example, who is a farmer, suddenly turned into a lawyer, a doctor, or something else in order to fit into some plot—there isn't much left of the character. It does not seem to me that it is right or fair to people to push them about in this way. A farmer is a farmer, a lawyer a lawyer, a doctor a doctor. It seems to me that the duty of the storyteller is to study people as they are and try to find the real drama of life just as people live and experience it. In other words, I feel that the obligation to imagined characters is exactly the same as the obligation to real characters in real life.

If I were advising a young writer who really wanted to get any satisfaction out of writing and who was willing to rather give up the idea of immediate success, I would certainly tell them to spend their time studying people and in not trying to think out plots. It seems to me that the stories and the drama of the stories should come out of the real lives of people, and that there is something false and wrong in this shoving imagined people around in this way; but, as I tried to tell Mike, any success coming to a writer out of this kind of work is likely to come slowly. You will have to get what satisfaction you get out of the work itself.

Now, I am very sorry that I cannot go at your stories as a Mr. Uzzell would do, for to tell you the truth, I do not much believe in the Uzzells of the writing world. I tried to tell Mike that, but am afraid I did not make myself very clear, and perhaps I am not making myself clear to you.

If I were a young writer, also it seems to me I would study, not the work of the tricky, flashy magazine writers, but of the masters of the craft. I would read the stories of Chekhov, such books as [Turgenev's] *Annals of a Sportsman*, and books of that kind. If you are interested in my own work, read *Winesburg, Ohio*, *Triumph of the Egg*, etc.

As suggested, I realize that the suggestions I am giving are not suggestions likely to lead you to any quick success, but they are the only kind of suggestions I feel able to make you. I am sorry that I cannot be of more definite help. Very truly yours

[P.S.] Stories returned under separate cover.

Notes

1. "Hands," *Masses*, VIII, 1 (March, 1916). This magazine, founded in 1911, was edited by Max Eastman from 1912 until late 1917. Devoted to radicalism in politics and the new freedom in literature, it numbered among its contributors John Reed and Floyd Dell.

2. Among Anderson's contributions to the *Little Review* only "The Philosopher" (III, 7–9 [June–July, 1916]) was gathered into *Winesburg, Ohio*, though he contributed six other items before that date to this magazine.

The *Little Review*, the creation of Margaret C. Anderson, began publication in Chicago in March, 1914, removed to New York in 1917, and to Paris later, where it expired in 1929.

3. "Queer," *Seven Arts*, I, 97–108 (December, 1916), was reprinted in the *Winesburg* volume.

4. This title was abandoned after Horace Liveright protested in a telegram of November 11, 1929, that the phrase would be misinterpreted.

5. George Freitag of Canton, Ohio, entered into correspondence with Anderson in the summer of 1938 on problems of the young writer. He published "The Transaction" in the *Atlantic* for August, 1938.

6. Thomas H. Uzzell (1884–), "professional adviser and instructor of American writers since 1920."

"Writing Stories" (1942)

I have seldom written a story, long or short, that I did not have to write and rewrite. There are single short stories of mine that have taken me ten or twelve years to get written. It isn't that I have lingered over sentences, being one of the sort of writers who say . . . "Oh, to write the perfect sentence." It is true that Gertrude Stein once declared I was one of the few American writers who could write a sentence. Very well. I am always pleased with any sort of flattery. I love it. I eat it up. For years I have had my wife go over all criticisms of my work. "I can make myself miserable enough," I have said to her. "I do not want others to make me miserable about my work." I have asked her to show me only the more favorable criticisms. There are enough days of misery, of black gloom.

However this has leaked through to me. There is the general notion, among those who make a business of literary criticism and who have done me the honor to follow me more or less closely in my efforts, that I am best at the short story.

And I do not refer here to those who constantly come to me saying, "*Winesburg* contains your best work," and who, when questioned, admit they have never read anything else. I refer instead to the opinion that is no doubt sound.

The short story is the result of a sudden passion. It is an idea grasped whole as one would pick an apple in an orchard. All of my own short stories have been written at one sitting, many of them under strange enough circumstances. There are these glorious moments, these pregnant hours and I remember such hours as a man remembers the first kiss got from a woman loved.

I was in the little town of Harrodsburg in Kentucky . . . this when I was still a writer of advertisements. It was evening and I was at a railroad station—a tiny station as I remember it and all day had been writ-

Excerpted from *Sherwood Anderson's Memoirs*, vol. 19 of *The Complete Works of Sherwood Anderson*, ed. Kichinosuke Ohashi (Kyoto: Rinsen Book Co., 1982), 341–345. Reprinted by permission of Harold Ober Associates Incorporated. Copyright 1942 by Eleanor Anderson. Renewed 1969 by Eleanor Copenhaver Anderson.

ing advertisements of farm implements. A hunch had come to me and I had bought a yellow tablet of paper at a drug store as I walked to the station. I began writing on a truck on the station platform . . . I stood by the truck writing. There were men standing about and they stared at me.

It did not matter. The great passion had come upon me and the men standing about, small town men, loitering about the station, now and then walking past me . . . the train must have been late but it was a summer night and the light lasted. . . .

There were crates of live chickens at the other end of the truck on which I rested my tablet. There is this curious absorption that at the same time permits a great awareness. You are, as you are not at other times, aware of all going on about you, of the color and shapes of the clouds in the sky, of happenings along a street, of people passing, the expression of faces, clothes people wear . . . all of your senses curiously awake. . . .

At the same time an intense concentration on the matter in hand.

Oh that I could live all of my life so. Once I wrote a poem about a strange land few of us ever enter. I called it the land of the Now.

How rapidly they march. How the words and sentences flow, how they march.

It is strange, but, now that I try to remember which of my stories I began, standing by the truck at the little railroad station at Harrodsburg, Kentucky, and finished riding in the day coach of the train on my way to Louisville, I can remember only the station, each board of the station wall, the places where the boards of the station wall had pulled loose, nails pulled half out. The tail feather of a rooster stuck out of one of the crates. Once later I made love to a woman in the moonlight in a field. We had gone into the field for that purpose. There were some white flowers, field daisies, and she plucked one of them. "I am going to keep it to remember this moment," she said.

So also did I pluck a feather from the tail of a rooster at the railroad station at Harrodsburg. I put it in my hat. "I will wear it for this moment, for this glorious peep I am having into the land of Now," I said to myself. I do not remember which of my stories I wrote that evening but I remember a young girl sitting on the porch of a house across a roadway.

She also was wondering what I was up to. She kept looking across at me. When I raised my eyes from the paper on which I wrote so rapidly, she smiled at me. The girl . . . she couldn't have been more than sixteen . . . was something of a flirt. She had on a soiled yellow dress. She had thick red hair. In such moments as I am here trying to describe the eyes see more clearly. They see everything. The ears hear every little sound. The very smell of the roots, of seeds and grass buried down under the earth, seem to come up into your nostrils.

The girl sitting on the porch of the house across the road from the railroad station, had heavy sleepy blue eyes. She was full of sensuality. "She would be a pushover," I thought. "If I were not writing this story I could walk over to her.

"Come," I could say to her. "What woman could resist such a man as I am now, at this moment?"

I am trying to give, in this broken way, an impression of a man, a writer in one of the rich moments of his life. I am trying to sing in these words, put down here the more glorious moments in a writer's life.

My mind moves on to other such moments. I was in a big business office, surrounded by many people. Clerks and other fellow workers in the office where I was employed walked up and down past my desk.

They stopped to speak to me. They gave me orders, discussed with me the work in which I was engaged, or rather the work in which I was presumed to be engaged.

I had been for days in a blue funk. I had been drinking. "Here I am condemned day after day to write advertising. I am sick of it." I had been filled with self-pity. No one would buy the stories I wrote. "I will have to spend all of my life in some such place as this. I am a man of talent and they will not let me practice the art I love." I had begun hating the men and women about me, my fellow employees. I hated my work. I had been on a drunk. For several days I stayed half drunk.

I sat at my desk in the crowded busy place and wrote the story, "I'm a Fool." It is a very beautiful story. Can it be possible that I am right, that the thoughts I now am having, looking back upon the two or three hours when I wrote this story in that crowded busy place, have any foundation in fact? It seems to me, looking back, on that particular morning as I sat at my desk in a long room where there were many other desks, that a curious hush fell over the place, that the men and women engaged in the writing of advertisements in the room, advertisements of patent medicines, of toilet soaps, of farm tractors, that they all suddenly began to speak with lowered voices, that men passing in and out of the room walked more softly. There was a man who came to my desk to speak to me about some work I was to do, a series of advertisements to be written, but he did not speak.

He stood before me for a moment. He began speaking. He stopped. He went silently away.

Do I just imagine all of this? Is it but a fairy tale I am telling myself? The moments, the hours in a writer's life of which I am here trying to speak, seem very real to me. I am, to be sure, speaking only of the writing of short stories. The writing of the long story, the novel, is another matter. I had intended when I began to write to speak of the great gulf that separates the two arts, but I have been carried away by this remembering of the glorious times in the life of the writer of short tales.

There was the day, in New York City, when I was walking in a street and the passion came upon me. I have spoken of how long it sometimes takes to really write a story. You have the theme, you try and try but it does not come off.

And then, one day, at some unexpected moment it comes clearly and sweetly. It is in your brain, in your arms, your legs, your whole body.

I was in a street in New York City and, as it happened, was near the apartment of a friend.

The friend was Stark Young and I rang his bell.

It was in the early morning and he was going out.

"May I sit in your place?"

I tried to explain to him. "I have had a seizure." I tried to tell him something of my story.

"There is this tale, Stark, that I have for years been trying to write. At the moment it seems quite clear in my mind. I want to write. Give me paper and ink and go away."

He did go away. He seemed to understand. "Here is paper. And here is a bottle."

He must have left with me a bottle of whiskey for I remember that as I wrote that day, hour after hour, sitting by a window, very conscious of everything going on in the street below, of a little cigar store on a corner, men going on in and coming out, feeling all the time that, were I not at the moment engaged with a particular story I could write a story of any man or woman who went along the city street, feeling half a god who knew all, felt all, saw all . . . I remember that, as I wrote hour after hour in Mr. Young's apartment, when my hand began to tremble from weariness, I drank from the bottle.

It was a long short story. It was a story I called "The Man's Story." For three, four, five years I had been trying to write it. I wrote until the bottle before me was empty. The drink had no effect upon me until I had finished the story.

That was in the late afternoon and I staggered to a bed. When I had finished the story, I went and threw myself on the bed. There were sheets of my story thrown about the room. Fortunately I had numbered the pages. There were sheets under the bed, in the bedroom into which I went, blown there by a wind from the open window by which I had been sitting. There were sheets in Mr. Young's kitchen.

I am trying as I have said to give an impression of moments that bring glory into the life of the writer. What nonsense to mourn that we do not grow rich, get fame. Do we not have these moments, these hours? It is time something is said of such times. I have long been wanting to write of these moments, of these visits a writer sometimes makes into the land of the Now.

On the particular occasion here spoken of I was on the bed in Stark Young's apartment when in the late afternoon he came home.

He had brought a friend with him and the two men stood beside the bed on which I lay. It may have been that I was pale. Stark may have thought that I was ill. He began pulling at my coat. He aroused me.

"What has happened?" he asked.

"I have just written a beautiful, a significant story and now I am drunk," I replied.

As it happens I have not re-read the story for years. But I have a kind of faith that something of the half mystic wonder of my day in that apartment still lingers in it.

From *A Story Teller's Story* (1924)

[I]

On an evening of the late summer I got off a train at a growing Ohio industrial town where I had once lived. I was rapidly becoming a middle-aged man. Two years before I had left the place in disgrace. There I had tried to be a manufacturer, a money-maker, and had failed, and I had been trying and failing ever since. In the town some thousands of dollars had been lost for others. An effort to conform to the standard dreams of the men of my times had failed and in the midst of my disgrace and generally hopeless outlook, as regards making a living, I had been filled with joy at coming to the end of it all. One morning I had left the place afoot, leaving my poor little factory, like an illegitimate child, on another man's doorstep. I had left, merely taking what money was in my pocket, some eight or ten dollars.

What a moment that leaving had been! To one of the European artists I afterward came to know the situation would have been unbelievably grotesque. Such a man could not have believed in my earnestness about it all and would have thought my feelings of the moment a worked-up thing. I can in fancy hear one of the Frenchmen, Italians or Russians I later knew laughing at me. "Well, but why get so worked up? A factory is a factory, is it not? Why may not one break it like an empty bottle? You have lost some money for others? See the light on that field over there. These others, for whom you lost money, were they compelled to beg in the streets, were their children torn by wolves? What is it you Americans get so excited about when a little money is lost?"

A European artist may not understand but an American will understand. The devil! It is not a question of money. No men are so careless and free with money as the Americans. There is another matter involved.

It strikes rather deeply at the roots of our beings. Childish as it all

Part 2

may have seemed to an older and more sophisticated world, we Americans, from the beginning, have been up to something, or we have wanted to think we were up to something. We came here, or our fathers or grandfathers came here, from a hundred diverse places—and you may be sure it was not the artists who came. Artists do not want to cut down trees, root stumps out of the ground, build towns and railroads. The artist wants to sit with a strip of canvas before him, face an open space on a wall, carve a bit of wood, make combinations of words and sentences, as I am doing now—and try to express to others some thought or feeling of his own. He wants to dream of color, to lay hold of form, free the sensual in himself, live more fully and freely in his contact with the materials before him than he can possibly live in life. He seeks a kind of controlled ecstasy and is a man with a passion, a "nut," as we love to say in America. And very often, when he is not in actual contact with his materials, he is a much more vain and disagreeable ass than any man, not an artist, could possibly be. As a living man he is almost always a pest. It is only when dead he begins to have value.

The simple truth is that in a European country the artist is more freely accepted than he is among us, and only because he has been longer about. They know how harmless he really is—or rather do not know how subtly dangerous he can be—and accept him only as one might accept a hybrid cross between a dog and a cat that went growling mewing barking and spitting about the house. One might want to kill the first of such strange beasts one sees but after one has seen a dozen and has realized that, like the mule, they cannot breed their own kind one laughs and lets them live, paying no more attention to them than modern France for example pays to its artists.

But in America things are somewhat different. Here something went wrong in the beginning. We pretended to so much and were going to do such great things here. This vast land was to be a refuge for all the outlawed brave foolish folk of the world. The declaration of the rights of man was to have a new hearing in a new place. The devil! We did get ourselves into a bad hole. We were going to be superhuman and it turned out we were sons of men who were not such devilish fellows after all. You cannot blame us that we are somewhat reluctant about finding out the very human things concerning ourselves. One does so hate to come down off the perch.

We are now losing our former feeling of inherent virtue, are permitting ourselves occasionally to laugh at ourselves for our pretensions, but there was a time here when we were sincerely in earnest about all this American business, "the land of the free and the home of the brave." We actually meant it and no one will ever understand present-day America or Americans who does not concede that we meant it and that while we were building all of our big ugly hurriedly thrown-together towns, creating our great industrial system, growing always more huge and prosperous, we were as much in earnest about what we thought we were up to as were the French of the thirteenth century when they built the cathedral of Chartres to the glory of God.

They built the cathedral of Chartres to the glory of God and we really intended building here a land to the glory of Man, and thought we were doing it too. That was our intention and the affair only blew up in the process, or got perverted, because Man, even the brave and the free Man, is somewhat a less worthy object of glorification than God. This we might have found out long ago but that we did not know each other. We came from too many different places to know each other well, had been promised too much, wanted too much. We were afraid to know each other.

Oh, how Americans have wanted heroes, wanted brave simple fine men! And how sincerely and deeply we Americans have been afraid to understand and love one another, fearing to find ourselves at the end no more brave heroic and fine than the people of almost any other part of the world.

I however disagree. What I am trying to do is to give the processes of my own mind at two distinct moments of my own life. First, the moment when after many years of effort to conform to an unstated and but dimly understood American dream by making myself a successful man in the material world I threw all overboard and then at another moment when, having come back to the same spot where I passed through the first moment, I attempted to confront myself with myself with a somewhat changed point of view.

As for the first of these moments, it was melodramatic and even silly enough. The struggle centred itself at the last within the walls of a particular moment and within the walls of a particular room.

I sat in the room with a woman who was my secretary. For several years I had been sitting there, dictating to her regarding the goods I had made in my factory and that I was attempting to sell. The attempt to sell the goods had become a sort of madness in me. There were certain thousands or perhaps hundreds of thousands of men living in towns or on farms in many states of my country who might possibly

buy the goods I had made rather than the goods made in another factory by another man. How I had wheedled! How I had schemed! In
some years I gave myself quite fully to the matter in hand and the
dollars trickled in. Well, I was about to become rich. It was a possibility. After a good day or week, when many dollars had come, I went to
walk and when I had got into a quiet place where I was unobserved I
threw back my shoulders and strutted. During the year I had made for
myself so many dollars. Next year I would make so many more, and
the next year so many more. But my thoughts of the matter did not
express themselves in the dollars. It never does to the American man.
Who calls the American a dollar-lover is foolish. My factory was of a
certain size—it was really a poor haphazardly enough run place—but
after a time I would build a great factory and after that a greater and
greater. Like a true American, I thought in size.

My fancy played with the matter of factories as a child would play
with a toy. There would be a great factory with walls going up and up
and a little open place for a lawn at the front, shower baths for the
workers with perhaps a fountain playing on a lawn, and up before the
door of this place I would drive in a large automobile.

Oh, how I would be respected by all, how I would be looked up to
by all! I walked in a little dark street, throwing back my shoulders.
How grand and glorious I felt!

The houses along the street in which I walked were small and ugly
and dirty-faced children played in the yards. I wondered. Having
walked, dreaming my dream for a long time I returned to the neighborhood of my factory and opening my office went in to sit at my desk
smoking a cigarette. The night watchman came in. He was an old man
who had once been a school-teacher but, as he said, his eyes had gone
back on him.

When I had walked alone I had been able to make myself feel somewhat as I fancied a prince might have felt but when anyone came near
me something exploded inside. I was a deflated balloon. Well, in fancy,
I had a thousand workmen under me. They were children and I was
their father and would look out for them. Perhaps I would build them
model houses to live in, a town of model houses built about my great
factory, eh? The workmen would be my children and I would look out
for my children. "Land of the free—home of the brave."

But I was back in my factory now and the night watchman sat smoking with me. Sometimes we talked far into the night. The devil! He
was a fellow like myself, having the same problems as myself. How

could I be his father? The thought was absurd. Once, when he was a younger man, he had dreamed of being a scholar but his eyes had gone back on him. What had he wanted to do? He spoke of it for a time. He had wanted to be a scholar and I had myself spent those earlier years eagerly reading books. "I would really like to have been a learned monk, one of those fellows such as appeared in the Middle Ages, one of the fellows who went off and lived by himself and gave himself up wholly to learning, one who believed in learning, who spent his life humbly seeking new truths—but I got married and my wife had kids, and then, you see, my eyes went back on me." He spoke of the matter philosophically. One did not let oneself get too much excited. After a time one got over any feeling of bitterness. The night watchman had a boy, a lad of fifteen, who also loved books. "He is pretty lucky, can get all the books he wants at the public library. In the afternoon after school is out and before I come down here to my job he reads aloud to me."

Men and women, many men and many women! There were men and women working in my factory, men and women walking in streets with me, many men and women scattered far and wide over the country to whom I wanted to sell my goods. I sent men, salesmen, to see them—I wrote letters; how many thousands of letters, all to the same purpose! "Will you buy my goods?" And again, "Will you buy my goods?"

What were the other men thinking about? What was I myself thinking about? Suppose it were possible to know something of the men and women, to know something of oneself, too. The devil! These were not thoughts that would help me to sell my goods to all the others. What were all the others like? What was I myself like? Did I want a large factory with a little lawn and a fountain in front and with a model town built about it?

Days of endlessly writing letters to men, nights of walking in strange quiet streets. What had happened to me? "I shall go get drunk," I said to myself and I did go and get drunk. Taking a train to a near-by city I drank until a kind of joy came to me and with some man I had found and who had joined in my carousal I walked in streets, shouting at other men, singing songs, going sometimes into strange houses to laugh with people, to talk with people I found there.

Here was something I liked and something the others liked too. When I had come to people in strange houses, half drunk, released, they were not afraid of me. "Well, he wants to talk," they seemed to be saying to themselves. "That's fine!" There was something broken down between us, a wall broken down. We talked of outlandish things for Anglo-Saxon trained people to speak of, of love between men and women, of what children's coming meant. Food was brought forth. Often in a single evening of this sort I got more from people than I could get from weeks of ordinary intercourse. The people were a little excited by the strangeness of two unknown men in their houses. With my companion I went boldly to the door and knocked. Laughter. "Hello, the house!" It might be the house of a laborer or that of a well-to-do merchant. I had hold of my new-found friend's arm and explained our presence as well as I could. "We are a little drunk and we are travelers. We just want to sit and visit with you a while."

There was a kind of terror in people's eyes, and a kind of gladness too. An old workman showed us a relic he had brought home with him from the Civil War while his wife ran into a bedroom and changed her dress. Then a child awoke in a near-by room and began to cry and was permitted to come in in her nightgown and lie in my arms or in the arms of the new-found friend who had got drunk with me. The talk swept over strange intimate subjects. What were men up to? What were women up to? There was a kind of deep taking of breath, as though we had all been holding something back from one another and had suddenly decided to let go. Once or twice we stayed all night in the house to which we had gone.

And then back to the writing of letters—to sell my goods. In the city to which I had gone to carouse I had seen many women of the streets, standing at corners, looking furtively about. My thoughts got fixed upon prostitution. Was I a prostitute? Was I prostituting my life?

What thoughts in the mind! There was a note due and payable at the bank. "Now here, you man, attend to your affairs. You have induced others to put money into your enterprise. If you are to build a great enterprise here you must be up and at it."

How often in after years I have laughed at myself for the thoughts and emotions of that time. There is a thought I have had that is very delicious. It is this, and I dare say it will be an unwelcome thought to many, "I am the American man. I think there is no doubt of it. I am just the mixture, the cold, moral man of the North into whose body has come the warm pagan blood of the South. I love and am afraid to love. Behold in me the American man striving to become an artist, to become conscious of himself, filled with wonder concerning himself and others, trying to have a good time and not fake a good time. I am not English Italian Jew German Frenchman Russian. What am I? I am tremendously serious about it all but at the same time I laugh constantly at myself for my own seriousness. Like all real American men of our day I wander constantly from place to place striving to put down roots into the American soil and not quite doing it. If you say the real American man is not yet born, you lie. I am the type of the fellow."

This is somewhat of a joke on me but it is a greater joke on the reader. As respectable and conventional a man as Calvin Coolidge has me in him—and I have him in myself? Do not doubt it. I have him in me and Eugene Debs in me and the crazy political idealists of the Western States and Mr. Gary of the Steel Trust and the whole crew. I accept them all as part of myself. Would to God they would thus accept me!

And being this thing I have tried to describe I return now to myself sitting between the walls of a certain room and between the walls of a certain moment too. Just why was that moment so pregnant? I will never quite know.

It came with a rush, the feeling that I must quit buying and selling, the overwhelming feeling of uncleanliness. I was in my whole nature a tale-teller. My father had been one and his not knowing had destroyed him. The tale-teller cannot bother with buying and selling. To do so will destroy him. No class of men I have ever known are so dull and cheerless as the writers of glad sentimental romances, the painters of glad pretty pictures. The corrupt unspeakable thing that had happened to tale-telling in America was all concerned with this matter of buying and selling. The horse cannot sing like a canary bird nor the canary bird pull a plow like a horse and either of them attempting it becomes something ridiculous.

[II]

There was a door leading out from my office to the street. How many steps to the door? I counted them, "five, six, seven." "Suppose," I asked myself, "I could take those five, six, seven steps to the door, pass out at the door, go along that railroad track out there, disappear into the far horizon beyond. Where was I to go? In the town where my factory was located I had still the reputation of being a bright young business man. In my first years there I had been filled with shrewd vast schemes. I had been admired, looked up to. Since that time I had gone down and down as a bright young man but no one yet knew how far I had gone. I was still respected in the town, my word was still good at the bank. I was a respectable man.

Did I want to do something not respectable, not decent? I am trying to give you the history of a moment and as a tale-teller I have come to think that the true history of life is but a history of moments. It is only at rare moments we live. I wanted to walk out at a door and go away into the distance. The American is still a wanderer, a migrating bird not yet ready to build a nest. All our cities are built temporarily as are the houses in which we live. We are on the way—toward what? There have been other times in the history of the world when many strange peoples came together in a new strange land. To assume that we have made an America, even materially, seems to me now but telling ourselves fairy tales in the night. We have not even made it materially yet and the American man has only gone in for money-making on a large scale to quiet his own restlessness, as the monk of old days was given the Regula of Augustine to quiet him and still the lusts in himself. For the monk, kept occupied with the saying of prayers and the doing of many little sacred offices, there was no time for the lusts of the world to enter in and for the American to be perpetually busy with his affairs, with his automobiles, with his movies, there is no time for unquiet thoughts.

On that day in the office at my factory I looked at myself and laughed. The whole struggle I am trying to describe and that I am confident will be closer to the understanding of most Americans than anything else I have ever written was accompanied by a kind of mocking laughter at myself and my own seriousness about it all.

Very well, then, I wanted to go out of the door and never come back. How many Americans want to go—but where do they want to go? I wanted to accept for myself all the little restless thoughts of which myself and the others had been so afraid and you, who are Americans, will understand the necessity of my continually laughing at myself and at all things dear to me. I must laugh at the thing I love the more intensely because of my love. Any American will understand that.

It was a trying moment for me. There was the woman, my secretary, now looking at me. What did she represent? What did she not represent? Would I dare be honest with her? It was quite apparent to me I would not. I had got to my feet and we stood looking at each other. "It is now or never," I said to myself, and I remember that I kept smiling. I had stopped dictating to her in the midst of a sentence. "The goods about which you have inquired are the best of their kind made in the—"

I stood and she sat and we were looking at each other intently. "What's the matter?" she asked. She was an intelligent woman, more intelligent I am sure than myself, just because she was a woman and good, while I have never been good, do not know how to be good. Could I explain all to her? The words of a fancied explanation marched through my mind: "My dear young woman, it is all very silly but I have decided to no longer concern myself with this buying and selling. It may be all right for others but for me it is poison. There is this factory. You may have it if it please you. It is of little value I dare say. Perhaps it is money ahead and then again it may well be it is money behind. I am uncertain about it all and now I am going away. Now, at this moment, with the letter I have been dictating, with the very sentence you have been writing left unfinished, I am going out that door and never come back. What am I going to do? Well now, that I don't know. I am going to wander about. I am going to sit with people, listen to words, tell tales of people, what they are thinking, what they are feeling. The devil! It may even be I am going forth in search of myself."

The woman was looking into my eyes the while I looked into hers. Perhaps I had grown a little pale and now she grew pale. "You're sick," she said and her words gave me an idea. There was wanted a justification of myself, not to myself but to the others. A crafty thought came. Was the thought crafty or was I, at the moment, a little insane, a "nut," as every American so loves to say of every man who does something a little out of the groove.

I had grown pale and it may be I was ill but nevertheless I was laughing—the American laugh. Had I suddenly become a little insane? What a comfort that thought would be, not to myself but to the others. My leaving the place I was then in would tear up roots that had gone down a little into the ground. The ground I did not think would support the tree that was myself and that I thought wanted to grow.

My mind dwelt on the matter of roots and I looked at my feet. The whole question with which I was at the moment concerned became a matter of feet. I had two feet that could take me out of the life I was then in and that, to do so, would need but take three or four steps to a door. When I had reached the door and had stepped out of my little factory office everything would be quite simplified, I was sure. I had to lift myself out. Others would have to tackle the job of getting me back, once I had stepped over that threshold.

Whether at the moment I merely became shrewd and crafty or whether I really became temporarily insane I shall never quite know. What I did was to step very close to the woman and looking directly into her eyes I laughed gayly. Others besides herself would, I knew, hear the words I was now speaking. I looked at my feet. "I have been wading in a long river and my feet are wet," I said.

Again I laughed as I walked lightly toward the door and out of a long and tangled phase of my life, out of the door of buying and selling, out of the door of affairs.

"They want me to be a 'nut,' will love to think of me as a 'nut,' and why not? It may just be that's what I am," I thought gayly and at the same time turned and said a final confusing sentence to the woman who now stared at me in speechless amazement. "My feet are cold wet and heavy from long wading in a river. Now I shall go walk on dry land," I said, and as I passed out at the door a delicious thought came. "Oh, you little tricky words, you are my brothers. It is you, not myself, have lifted me over this threshold. It is you who have dared give me a hand. For the rest of my life I will be a servant to you," I whispered to myself as I went along a spur of railroad track, over a bridge, out of a town and out of that phase of my life.

From *The Modern Writer* (1925)

Men and women are seeking expression for their lives in new and bolder ways and everywhere among writers the Modern is but the man who is trying to give expression to the newer impulses of our lives in books, in song, in painting and in all the others of the seven arts.

. . . Anything may happen in life. We all know that. People hardly ever do as we think they should. There are no plot short stories in life. All the clever tricks by which effects are to be got on the printed page are in reality a selling of ourselves. If it is your purpose to live in a pasteboard world you have got to avoid storms. There is always that huge, comfortable, self-satisfied American audience made up of all kinds of people with little prejudices, hates and fears that must not be offended. To know men and women, to be in the least sympathetic with them in their actual trials and struggles is a handicap. If it is your desire to be that kind of a writer, to grow rich and be successful by writing and if you have a natural talent that can be made to serve your purpose, stay just as far away as possible from any real thinking or feeling about actual men and women. Stay in the pasteboard world.

Excerpted from *The Modern Writer* (San Francisco: Lantern Press, 1925), 11, 23. Sincere and repeated attempts to locate a copyright holder have been unsuccessful.

"A Note on Realism" (1924)

There is something very confusing to both readers and writers about the notion of realism in fiction. As generally understood it is akin to what is called "representation" in painting. The fact is before you and you put it down, adding a high spot here and there, to be sure. No man can quite make himself a camera. Even the most realistic worker pays some tribute to what is called "art." Where does representation end and art begin? The location of the line is often as confusing to practicing artists as it is to the public.

Recently a young writer came to talk with me about our mutual craft. He spoke with enthusiastic admiration of a certain book—very popular a year or two ago. "It is the very life. So closely observed. It is the sort of thing I should like to do. I should like to bring life itself within the pages of a book. If I could do that I would be happy."

I wondered. The book in question had only seemed to me good in spots and the spots had been far apart. There was too much dependence upon the notebook. The writer had seemed to me to have very little to give out of himself. What had happened, I thought, was that the writer of the book had confused the life of reality with the life of the fancy. Easy enough to get a thrill out of people with reality. A man struck by an automobile, a child falling out at the window of a city office building. Such things stir the emotions. No one, however, confuses them with art.

This confusion of the life of the imagination with the life of reality is a trap into which most of our critics seem to me to fall about a dozen times each year. Do the trick over and over and in they tumble. "It is life," they say. "Another great artist has been discovered."

What never seems to come quite clear is the simple fact that art is art. It is not life.

The life of the imagination will always remain separated from the

Excerpted from *Sherwood Anderson's Notebook*, vol. 14 of *The Complete Works of Sherwood Anderson*, ed. Kichinosuke Ohashi (Kyoto: Rinsen Book Co., 1982), 71–78. Reprinted by permission of Harold Ober Associates Incorporated. Copyright 1926 by Boni R. Liveright. Renewed 1954 by Eleanor Anderson.

life of reality. It feeds upon the life of reality, but it is not that life—cannot be. Mr. John Marin painting Brooklyn Bridge, Henry Fielding writing *Tom Jones*, are not trying in the novel and the painting to give us reality. They are striving for a realization in art of something out of their own imaginative experiences, fed to be sure upon the life immediately about. A quite different matter from making an actual picture of what they see before them.

And here arises a confusion. For some reason—I myself have never exactly understood very clearly—the imagination must constantly feed upon reality or starve. Separate yourself too much from life and you may at moments be a lyrical poet, but you are not an artist. Something within dries up, starves for the want of food. Upon the fact in nature the imagination must constantly feed in order that the imaginative life remain significant. The workman who lets his imagination drift off into some experience altogether disconnected with reality, the attempt of the American to depict life in Europe, the New Englander writing of cowboy life—all that sort of thing—in ninety-nine cases out of a hundred ends in the work of such a man becoming at once full of holes and bad spots. The intelligent reader, tricked often enough by the technical skill displayed in hiding the holes, never in the end accepts it as good work. The imagination of the workman has become confused. He has had to depend altogether upon tricks. The whole job is a fake.

The difficulty, I fancy, is that so few workmen in the arts will accept their own limitations. It is only when the limitation is fully accepted that it ceases to be a limitation. Such men scold at the life immediately about. "It's too dull and commonplace to make good material," they declare. Off they sail in fancy to the South Seas, to Africa, to China. What they cannot realize is their own dullness. Life is never dull except to the dull.

The writer who sets himself down to write a tale has undertaken something. He has undertaken to conduct his readers on a trip through the world of his fancy. If he is a novelist his imaginative world is filled with people and events. If he have any sense of decency as a workman he can no more tell lies about his imagined people, fake them, than he can sell out real people in real life. The thing is constantly done but no man I have ever met, having done such a trick, has felt very clean about the matter afterward.

On the other hand, when the writer is rather intensely true to the people of his imaginative world, when he has set them down truly, when he does not fake, another confusion arises. Being square with your people in the imaginative world does not mean lifting them over into life, into reality. There is a very subtle distinction to be made and upon the writer's ability to make this distinction will in the long run depend his standing as a workman.

Having lifted the reader out of the reality of daily life it is entirely possible for the writer to do his job so well that the imaginative life becomes to the reader for the time real life. Little real touches are added. The people of the town—that never existed except in the fancy—eat food, live in houses, suffer, have moments of happiness and die. To the writer, as he works, they are very real. The imaginative world in which he is for the time living has become for him more alive than the world of reality ever can become. His very sincerity confuses. Being unversed in the matter of making the delicate distinction, that the writer himself sometimes has such a hard time making, they call him a realist. The notion shocks him. "The deuce, I am nothing of the kind," he says. "But such a thing could not have happened in a Vermont town." "Why not? Have you not learned that anything can happen anywhere? If a thing can happen in my imaginative world it can of course happen in the flesh and blood world. Upon what do you fancy my imagination feeds?"

My own belief is that the writer with a notebook in his hand is always a bad workman, a man who distrusts his own imagination. Such a man describes actual scenes accurately, he puts down actual conversation.

But people do not converse in the book world as they do in life. Scenes of the imaginative world are not real scenes.

The life of reality is confused, disorderly, almost always without apparent purpose, whereas in the artist's imaginative life there is purpose. There is determination to give the tale, the song, the painting Form— to make it true and real to the theme, not to life. Often the better the job is done the greater the confusion.

I myself remember with what a shock I heard people say that one of my own books, *Winesburg, Ohio*, was an exact picture of Ohio village life. The book was written in a crowded tenement district of Chicago. The hint for almost every character was taken from my fellow-lodgers in a large rooming house, many of whom had never lived in a village. The confusion arises out of the fact that others besides practicing artists have imaginations. But most people are afraid to trust their imaginations and the artist is not.

Would it not be better to have it understood that realism, in so far as the word means reality to life, is always bad art—although it may possibly be very good journalism?

Which is but another way of saying that all of the so-called great realists were not realists at all and never intended being. Madame Bovary did not exist in fact. She existed in the imaginative life of Flaubert and he managed to make her exist also in the imaginative life of his readers.

I have been writing a story. A man is walking in a street and suddenly turns out of the street into an alleyway. There he meets another man and a hurried whispered conversation takes place. In real life they may be but a pair of rather small bootleggers, but they are not that to me.

When I began writing, the physical aspect of one of the men, the one who walked in the street, was taken rather literally from life. He looked strikingly like a man I once knew, so much like him in fact that there was a confusion. A matter easy enough to correct.

A stroke of my pen saves me from realism. The man I knew in life had red hair; he was tall and thin.

With a few words I have changed him completely. Now he has black hair and a black mustache. He is short and has broad shoulders. And now he no longer lives in the world of reality. He is a denizen of my own imaginative world. He can now begin a life having nothing at all to do with the life of the red-haired man.

If I am to succeed in making him real in this new world he, like hundreds of other men and women who live only in my own fanciful world, must live and move within the scope of the story or novel into which I have cast him. If I do tricks with him in the imaginative world, sell him out, I become merely a romancer. If, however, I have the courage to let him really live he will, perhaps, show me the way to a fine story or novel.

But the story or novel will not be a picture of life. I will never have had any intention of making it that.

Part 3

THE CRITICS

Introduction

The five selections in this section introduce the reader to the critical responses to Sherwood Anderson in a number of ways.

Robert Morss Lovett's essay from the *New Republic* (1936) is a contemporary's analysis of Anderson's growing prominence in American literature. It touches on a number of subjects, including Anderson's consideration of sexual repression and its relation to the separateness of individuals, his concern for the social scene in his novels and short fiction, and the evolution of his literary theory.

Anderson's short-story method is examined more fully in Frank Gado's "The Form of Things Concealed," the Introduction to his *Sherwood Anderson: The Teller's Tales* (1983). Walter B. Rideout's "'I Want to Know Why' as Biography and Fiction" elucidates the biographical relationship between that particular short story and Anderson's life in 1919, the year *Winesburg, Ohio* was published.

Glen A. Love's "Horses or Men: Primitive and Pastoral Elements in Sherwood Anderson" (1976) discusses Anderson's depiction of the individual's search for a meaningful life in the midst of encroaching urbanization. Finally, Mary Anne Ferguson's cogent essay "Sherwood Anderson's *Death in the Woods:* Toward a New Realism" discusses the organization of that book and analyzes Anderson's later writing methods.

Robert Morss Lovett

A revaluation of Sherwood Anderson must necessarily take account of the extraordinary impact that he made upon American literature almost at his appearance. In spite of the crudity of his first novels the impression was general that an original and distinguished talent was to be reckoned with. This recognition extended to European critics, among whom M. Fay committed himself to the statement in the Revue de Paris: "I believe that Sherwood Anderson is one of the greatest writers of the contemporary world, and the best in America." This verdict may be accounted for by Anderson's possession, in truer balance than any other of his contemporaries, of three qualities marked by Maeterlinck as requisites for great literature: a sure touch upon the world of our senses; a profound intimation of the mystery that surrounds this island of our consciousness; and the literary technique comprehended in the term style.

I first met Sherwood Anderson in 1913 at Ernestine Evans' studio in Chicago, whither he came to read a manuscript. He was in house painter's clothes, and seemed the proletarian writer for whom we were already on the lookout. His writing suggested Dreiser. It was minutely naturalistic, but of anything beyond this present scene, anything of grace of style, I now recall no trace. Floyd Dell, then literary editor of The Chicago Post, who lent his august presence to the occasion, saw with his usual discernment the promise in this attempt, and, I understand, recommended "Windy McPherson's Son" to John Lane in London, where it was received as a genuine American document. This it undoubtedly is in its first part, its substance drawn from Anderson's early life in the Middle West, but as in more than one of his novels, the point at which realism gives way to badly conceived romance is easily marked. The same verdict falls upon Anderson's second novel, "Marching Men." In the latter, however, there is an imaginative effort to transcend the actual, to embody the significance of the great union, symbolized by the march of the toilers. Already Anderson was writing the poetry which appeared the next year in "Mid-American Chants," and infusing his prose with the soaring rhythms that carry his fiction at times into a realm in which realistic criticism is irrelevant.

"Sherwood Anderson," *New Republic*, 25 November 1936, 103–5.

"Winesburg, Ohio," in 1919, marks an important date in American literary history, and in itself profited by an obvious timeliness. It was the year after the War, and readers stupefied by tales of its abominations needed to be reassured that peace hath its horrors no less worthy of renown. D. H. Lawrence had discovered sex as a source of incongruity of character. Katherine Mansfield had developed after Chekhov the story in which nothing happens but a sudden moment of illumination and awareness. The stream-of-consciousness method was a recent invention. Edgar Lee Masters in "The Spoon River Anthology" had assembled a community of people whose confessions revealed the deep places of human experience hidden by their provincial lives.

In "Winesburg, Ohio" Anderson shows perfect command of the small-town stuff familiar to him from his youth. True, he protests: "I myself remember with what a shock I heard people say that 'Winesburg, Ohio' was an exact picture of Ohio village life. The book was written in a crowded tenement district of Chicago. The hint for almost every character was taken from my fellow-lodgers in a crowded rooming house, many of whom had never lived in a village." Nevertheless, they live there now. In the process of transference from the crowded rooming house into an environment which Anderson controlled so completely that the reader takes it for granted, they have assumed an actuality that is not dependent on realism. They move among the material furnishings of the world with the deftness and precision of sleep walkers. If Anderson had left them in their rooming house he might have written another "Pot-Bouille." Instead he has made a character sketch of the rotten little town which has become as much a part of the American scene as Gopher Prairie or Muncie, Indiana. As a literary form, a group of tales adding up to a unit greater than the sum of its parts the book is a masterpiece. Mr. Cleveland B. Chase in his rather disparaging brochure on Anderson admits that it is "one of the most important products of the American literary renaissance, and has influenced writing in America more than any book published in the last decade."

"Winesburg, Ohio" represents the solution of the problem that Anderson consciously set himself. His own experience, unusually rich and varied, gave him his grip on the actual world in which he was to live so abundantly. He has borne testimony to this in his numerous autobiographical writings, but as an artist his aim was constantly to emerge from the chrysalis stage of realism into the winged career of imagination. "Imagination must feed upon reality or starve" is a sentence from his notes which in effect recurs again and again. Of the process of transubstantiation he has given explicit account in "A Story-Teller's Story." As a boy he listened to his father, a fantastic liar who had served in the Civil War and on the basis of that fact made himself the hero of a dozen campaigns to the delight of his audience. Sherwood inherited or learned the knack. "When I was a lad," he tells us, "I played with such fanciful scenes as other boys played with brightly colored marbles. From the beginning there have been, as opposed to my actual life, these grotesque fancies. Later, to be sure, I did acquire more or less skill in bringing them more and more closely into the world of the actual."

In so doing he worked at this relation of material to imagination, and the projection of fact into fiction. Humble and sordid realities, the trivia of observed phenomena, bring to him an emotion which is the essence of poetry. In "A Story-Teller's Story" he recalls such a moment of inspiration. Looking from a window, he sees a man in the next yard picking bugs off potato vines. The man's wife comes to the door, scolding. He has forgotten to bring home the sugar. A quarrel follows. And for Anderson his own life and interests, his business, and his waiting dinner are forgotten. "A man and a woman in a garden have become the center of a universe about which it seemed to me I might think and feel in joy and wonder forever." It is in thus seizing on scraps of reality and projecting them beyond the small range controlled by the senses that Sherwood Anderson's imagination brings fiction to the enhancement of life, and enlarges his art beyond the limits of naturalism into expressionism. Not the fact, but the emotion with which the artist accepts it, is the essence of living.

"Winesburg, Ohio" is not only an instance of the evolution of a literary theory; it marks also Anderson's achievement of a craftsmanship which is an essential part of that theory. When, in his preface to "The Triumph of the Egg" he speaks of himself as a tailor, "weaving warm cloth out of the thread of thought" to clothe the tales which, born of experience and imagination, "are freezing on the doorstep of the house of my mind," he is using a figure that comes naturally to him. He was an artisan before he was an artist. His work as sign painter and mechanic gave him a sense of the relation of materials and tools. As a tailor of tales he finds excitement in pen or pencil and paper, thousands of sheets of it, waiting for his hand. The author's medium is words, which are to him what pigments are to the painter, or food stuffs to the cook.

One of his happiest sketches is that of Gertrude Stein bustling genially about her kitchen choosing the ingredients of her pastry. From her, it may be conjectured, Anderson gained something of the assurance that words have qualities inherent in them other than meaning. "Words have color, smell; one may sometimes feel them with the fingers as one touches the cheek of a child." It is through words that the experience of men and women in the actual world is communicated and shared.

For the communication of the immediate scene Sherwood Anderson has mastered his instrument. But, as he repeatedly asserts, mere realism is bad art. His peculiar quality resides in his intuition of something behind the scene, something "far more deeply interfused" whose dwelling is not for him "the light of setting suns" but rather "the heart of man." As Mr. Boynton remarks: "Anderson did not hit on this true note of his own until he reached the point where he became more interested in what was happening in the minds of his individuals than in what was going on outside their bodies." It is in states of consciousness which eventuate in moments when the unconscious wells up and overwhelms personality with a sense of completion in the larger unity of life that his creative power resides, and it is with such moments that his characteristic stories deal. A recurring theme in them is the effort of the character to break down the wall which confines the individual in isolation from this general life which he shares with his fellows. Sometimes this theme comes to explicit utterance, as in "The Man in the Brown Coat":

> I'll tell you what—sometimes the whole life of this world floats in a human face in my mind. The unconscious face of the world stops and stands still before me.
>
> Why do I not say a word out of myself to the others? Who, in all our life together, have I never been able to reach through the wall to my wife? Already I have written three hundred, four hundred thousand words. Are there no words that lead into life? Some day I shall speak to myself. Some day I shall make a testament unto myself.

Naturally in this pursuit of unity, in this breaking down of separateness, Anderson is much concerned with human relations and especially with sex. Through sex is maintained the great flow of the race of which each individual is but a drop. Sexual intercourse seems the most hope-

ful point of assault upon the wall which keeps each individual a prisoner. "The Egg," in his second series of tales, is concerned with a
desperate effort of a broken man to preserve some sort of human relationship through the performance of a trick, but the title gives an iron-
ical significance to the volume—"The Triumph of the Egg." Nearly
all the stories are concerned with sex, from the boy's view of its mystery in "I Want to Know Why," to the tragedies of frustration in
"Seeds," "Unlighted Lamps," "The Door of the Trap," "Out of Nowhere into Nothing." It is worth while to mention them, for each is a
triumph, a witness to Anderson's mastery of the short-story form. The
next series, "Horses and Men," continues the theme in "Unused." It
also reflects a love of horses, which in adolescence passes the love of
women.

Anderson's later novels bear an increasingly definite relation to the
social scene. For him, the Middle West reveals on a large scale the
restless striving, the frustration of unfulfilled purpose, which is so often
the theme of individual life treated in his short stories. "Poor White"
is an ambitious attempt in which, as in the earlier novels, a firmly
realized conception tends to lose its way in cloudy romance. Hugh
McVey is a boy in "a little hole of a town stuck on a mud bank on the
western shore of the Mississippi," where he follows his father listlessly
about, sweeping saloons, cleaning outhouses, or sleeping on the river
bank with the smell of fish upon him, and the flies. A New England
woman takes Hugh in hand and trains him, so that after her departure
his awakened will forces him into sustained activity. He becomes an
inventor, an industrial magnate. Like Sam McPherson and Beaut
McGregor in "Marching Men" the hero loses identity, but throughout
the mass of the book the symbolism is closely woven into the realism,
as warp and woof.

Hugh McVey, the physically overgrown, almost idiotic boy, is the
Middle West in the last decade of the century. When by sheer strength
of will he harnesses his mind to problems of mechanical invention and
solves them by a power he does not understand, he typifies the spirit
of industrial pioneering in all its crude force. Sarah Shepherd with her
school-mistressy formula, "Show them that you can do perfectly the
task given you to do, and you will be given a chance at a larger task,"
is the spirit of New England brooding on the vast abyss of the Middle
West and making it pregnant. Harley Parsons with his boast: "I have
been with a Chinese woman, and an Italian, and with one from South
America. I am going back and I am going to make a record. Before I

get through I am going to be with a woman of every nationality on earth, that's what I'm going to do"—what is he but an ironic incarnation of our national destiny? Joe Wainsworth, the harness-maker who in his hatred of machinery or machine-made goods kills his assistant, is the ghost of the horse-and-buggy age attacking the present. Smokey Pete, the blacksmith who shouts to the fields the scandal he dares not utter on Main Street, is the spirit of American prophesy, a Jeremiah of Ohio. Anderson has made his story a sort of Pilgrim's Progress of the Middle-Western life he knows so well.

The best of Anderson's novels is undoubtedly "Dark Laughter." It is not only a good novel in structure and movement, but more subtly than "Poor White" or "Many Marriages" it is of that thoughtful quality which entitles it to rank among the novels of ideas. The two themes which are woven together are leading ones with Anderson—freedom through craftsmanship, and through love. The hero, Bruce Dudley, walks out of his home and his job as a reporter and finds work in an Ohio village in Grey's carriage factory. There he meets Sponge Martin, who teaches him how to paint carriage wheels and how to live. His philosophy is that of art as a guide to life:

> Perhaps, if you got the thoughts and fancies organized, a little, made them work through your body, made thoughts and fancies part of yourself—they might be used then, perhaps as Sponge Martin used a brush. You might lay them on something as Sponge Martin would lay varnish on it. Suppose about one man in a million got things organized a little. What would that mean? What would such a man be? Would he be a Napoleon? A Caesar?

Bruce meets Aline Grey, the wife of his employer, and with her steps forth on the road to freedom. Meanwhile the Negro world which surrounds them, in its dark laughter, sounds an ironic chorus.

In his later novels Anderson has shifted his scene to the South. There the process of industrialization, going on more ruthlessly, fills him with horror. Scenes in the cotton mills recur with a kind of obsession. Rather timidly he puts forward his social remedy in "Perhaps Women," the result of "a growing conviction that modern man is losing his ability to retain his manhood, in the face of the modern way of utilizing the machine, and that what hope there is for him lies in women." "Beyond Desire" is an expression of the two elements—sex and industry—but it can scarcely be maintained that any essential relation between them is established. "Kit Brandon" is an example of that "assisted autobiography" in which the author enters into the experience of another person, in this case a bootlegger whose career is not without social implications. In form it is evidence of Anderson's ability to enforce his claim, "I write as I like"—but the reader finds himself sighing for the lucid simplicity of Moll Flanders.

Recently Anderson put forth a brief statement in Story Magazine which emphasizes what is true of his writing at its best, that in its fact and its imaginative penetration beyond fact, it is a phase of his experience:

> I think that writing or painting or making music . . . is merely a tool a man can sometimes use to get at this business of living. . . . It is all wrapped up in this other thing . . . a man's relationship . . . his handling of relationships, his striving, if you will, for the good life. Relationships, I should say, with the world of nature too, development of the eyes, ears, nose, fingers. It is even, I think, concerned with the way you touch things with your fingers.

Some years ago Anderson forsook the "solemn and perhaps even asinine business, this being what is called great, doing immortal work, influencing the younger generation, etc.," and engaged in the humble business of editing a small-town newspaper—two, in fact, for there were two in town, one Democratic and one Republican. In playing the parts appropriate to the several stock characters in the newspaper play, society reporter, sports reporter, editorial writer, etc., he found abundant opportunities for cultivating relationships and leading the good life. Whether we get masterpieces from him or not, he has given an indication of the sincerity of his profession that art is a part of experience, not something added thereto, and that an artist may be too interested in life to care overmuch about success in it.

Frank Gado

What Whitman had been to an American poetry searching for its own voice, Anderson was to the new American fiction in the period after

"The Form of Things Concealed," Introduction to *Sherwood Anderson: The Teller's Tales* (Schenectady, N.Y.: Union College Press, 1983), 1–20. Reprinted by permission of the author.

the First World War. Squads of young writers carried copies of *Winesburg, Ohio* as though it were the recognition badge of a new fraternal order, and most responded in some way to his influence while learning to resolve their particular visions. But if those engaged in "making it new" instinctively understood the revolutionary nature of his work, the scholars, assessing it after the fact, have disagreed over its significance and fundamentally distorted its motives.

Although Anderson occupies a prominent place in historical commentaries on the "Revolt from the Village" that scrutinized the small towns of the Mid-West, his differences from the writers identified by that rather omnibus classification are far more radical than the characteristics they share. When the topic is Realism, he is tied to such writers as Willa Cather and Ellen Glasgow, but Realism presumes the replication of reality by art, and although he draws from life, his art is not mimetic. His homage to Dreiser, coupled with his long line of characters buffeted by forces that neither understand nor control, has prompted some literary historians to insert him among the Naturalists; the objectivity and deterministic philosophy that are cardinal marks of Naturalism, however, are quite remote from his concerns. Often called "the American D. H. Lawrence," he was one of the first to deal openly with sex, but his interests in the subject are not essentially Laurentian—nor, despite the claims of observers seeking to demonstrate literature's response to the intellectual currents of the twenties, is his treatment of repressed desires Freudian, in any valid sense, in more than a few instances. Most commonly, those who regard the changed view of language itself as a prime sign of the century's new writing point to him as the bridge from Mark Twain to Faulkner and (with Gertrude Stein) to Hemingway; even so, his concept of words in the tracing of forms bespeaks an aesthetic engineering basically unlike theirs. All these attempts to fix him within a category exaggerate superficial or secondary attributes, and in so doing, miss the originality of his genius.

But the biographers and literary historians, even though they have skewed their reports, have at least tried to deal with Anderson; the critics, in contrast, have generally been chary of him. One reason may be that his works do not easily lend themselves to the methodologies successively fashionable in academe—from the New Criticism to the latest vogue from New Haven. A more persuasive explanation, however, resides in the fact that Anderson's talent lay principally in the short story.

If America did not invent the short story, it did transform the genre and dominate its modern development. Yet our critics have tended to slight its importance in American letters, perversely treating it as though it were a lower species of fiction. While studies of the art of the novel spread unrelentingly across library shelves, studies of the art of the short story remain few and quite inferior. Among those considered major writers, Poe alone has earned recognition primarily for his short fiction. Hawthorne's tales are often artistically and psychologically more complex than his novels—and more profoundly at the center of the American psyche—but it is Hawthorne the novelist who has drawn the greater attention. James preferred "the blest *nouvelle,*" but critical discussions of his works usually only allude to his short stories in the course of examining the novels. All that is of value in Hemingway can be found in his stories, which are genuinely in the front rank of this century's literature; his reputation, however, still rests on his novels—formally uninteresting performances that seem more mannered and pretentious with every rereading. If, as in the case of a Peter Taylor or a Grace Paley, a gifted writer chooses to be constant to the short story, critical neglect is virtually certain. Inversely, a well-established success in the novel can insure that the writer's stories will enjoy a popularity exceeding their intrinsic merit (e.g., Fitzgerald's stories—which, apart from scattered passages of brilliant prose, reflect a sophomoric mind and a technically clumsy composer).

This bias has been especially damaging to the perception of Anderson. He wrote novels because they held out hope of financial security (a will o' the wisp he chased throughout most of his career as an artist), not because he felt an affinity towards the genre. (*Poor White,* a valuable document reflecting America's painful emergence from its agrarian chrysalis, is the best realized of these efforts, but even here, he struggles unsuccessfully with novelistic practice in the setting, narrative advance, and, most conspicuously, form.) Yet, when the critic looks beyond *Winesburg,* his eye invariably trains on the novels, the province of fiction where Anderson is at his weakest—indeed, the predisposition is so strong that even *Winesburg* is treated as though it were a kind of novel, with almost all critical concern riveted to its continuing characters and themes rather than to the construction of the individual pieces. The reverse side of this prejudice, of course, is a crimped view of the short fiction. In his recent book on the short story, Walter Allen concedes, grudgingly, that Anderson is central to the American tradition of story writing, but he never bothers to explain why; more curious still, he confines his comments to *Winesburg*—which, although it looms over the rest of Anderson's books, contains neither his most representative nor his best short stories. Unfortunately, Allen's constricted vision is not atypical. When Allen calls him simplistic—"a *naif* and at times . . . a *faux naif*"—or Frederick J. Hoffman speaks of his words coming "together in an unconscious process of creative illiteracy," one hears the echo of attacks first mounted in the twenties and repeated with devastating effect by Lionel Trilling in 1941. Anderson, they claimed, lacked precision, aesthetic refinement, and intellectual depth; his fiction appealed to adolescent sensibilities and preferred easy solutions to complex problems. To be sure, the novels often warrant such disparagements, but his finest stories (and it is presumably the successes that reveal an artist's measure) most emphatically do not. Far from dealing in solutions, they reach for a heightened awareness of vital mysteries, and their constructions are intricate and often elegant.

In his most-quoted remark, Anderson blasted the contrived stories he called "the bastard children of de Maupassant, Poe, and O. Henry." There were, he insisted, "no plot short stories ever lived in any life"; consequently, there are no plots in Anderson's stories, either. But this does not mean that they are loose, aimless affairs. The short story has traditionally operated according to realistic assumptions: regardless of its type, from the so-called fairy tale to the Naturalists' "experiments," it implicitly claimed to reflect the world it postulated. That which defined the story—made beginning, middle, and end one piece—was the presentation of events in such a way that *the events themselves* became invested with meaning; plot, the nexus of elements described by movement in time, depended upon the author's selection and manipulation, but the story remained essentially a report from the world. Anderson overturned the conventions to liberate the fiction from the determinants of time and incident. In his scheme, the story resides not in events or even solely in the relationship between the teller and the thing narrated but in its being told. Although sequentiality is an inescapable quality of narrative, in Anderson the sequence of particulars responds to an urgency quite independent from the usual chronological impulse.

An equally important aspect of his departure from realism has to do with his concept of language. A passage in "Loneliness," one of the more autobiographical sections in *Winesburg*, comments directly on the relationship between the artist and the world he imitates. The story's central character (who, like the author himself, paints scenes of Winesburg) hears his work praised, but the admiration exasperates him because it has a false premise: "You don't get the point . . . the picture you see doesn't consist of the things you see and say words about." As with Anderson's stories, what it does "consist of" is a "hidden knowledge"—"the beginning of everything" that brings images into configuration but cannot itself be imaged. Concern with how the word evokes its referent was a preoccupation of expatriate literary circles, and Anderson's focus on what lies beneath the surface seems, initially, to anticipate Hemingway's "iceberg theory"—the idea that the eighth part that is visible in writing must be supported by the seven-eighths the writer knows and yet does not describe. Actually, however, the two take opposite positions. While Hemingway realized that an excess of words would blunt the reader's sensitivity, he nonetheless believed that presenting the essential would enable the reader to supply the missing details, and thus restore the writer's original perception in full. In Anderson, the hidden knowledge remains hidden (even from the author) because its ramifications and implications lie beyond language's power of containment; it excites the current of energy that flows from the story's source to its conclusion, but neither the source nor the conclusion—nor, even, the connecting material—can depict it. Whereas Hemingway condenses language to intensify what the early decades of the century fashionably called its *quiditas*, Anderson, stressing the irreducibility of the world to experience, allows it to expand, apparently uncontrolled, as though it were searching for its uncertain object.

Anderson's idiosyncratic conception of narrative emerges most clearly where he operates at the farthest remove from conventional structures. "In a Strange Town" is a prime example. Although the opening statement, "A morning in a country town in a strange place," seems nothing more than a simple stage direction establishing the setting, its actual purpose is to imply a question that will pulse through the rest of the story: Why does the narrator repeatedly leave his home to wander in unfamiliar surroundings? After several paragraphs in which he notes the chorus and dance of the living world, the narrator supplies a simple answer: being alone among strangers, he says, whets a sense of wonder that his rubbing against the familiar has dulled. But this assertion, the reader gradually realizes, masks as well as reveals, and the same compulsive garrulousness that betrays his reluctance to speak the whole truth also makes it difficult to surmise what that underlying urgency may be. (Indeed, Anderson's strategy of indirection misorients the reader into assuming this floatation of utterances is unmoored to authorial artifice.) Eventually, however, as if to slice through the confusion he has created, the narrator returns to the subject he had posed at the long monologue's start:

> A while ago I was speaking of a habit I have formed of going suddenly off like this to some strange place. "I have been doing it ever since it happened," I said. I used the expression "it happened."
> Well what happened?
> Not so very much.

"It," he then explains, was a car accident that killed a female student who used to visit the narrator, a philosophy professor, in his office. Although he insists "she was nothing special to me," the womanly girl had roused thoughts long stilled by his wife and the others who populate his days. Yet, on receiving the news of the accident, he showed no emotion—his only response was to ride a train into the countryside.

The solution to the puzzle introduced in the story's initial sentence has finally fallen into place. Contrary to what the reader may immediately infer when the "secret" is told, these ritual excursions do not express a form of mourning for the girl's death (which he deems "not so very much"), nor are they just the result of a naive wanderlust as he first suggests. Something else, related to both but different from either, is at work here: a need to recreate the stirring of vitality he felt in that brief moment when her life touched his. In this respect, the narrator's recitation of his curious adventures represents an act of affirmation; beginning with a celebration of life's fullness and concluding with the evocation of a friend's death, it is an elegy in which the usual order is reversed.

But if analyzing the story in this way reveals its formal outline, it does not constitute a paraphrase. Few of Anderson's stories lend themselves to such translation since their textual statements usually operate as refractions of the mind and the being submerged beneath the level of language. Typically, "In a Strange Town" makes this underlying reality manifest through the tensions among contrarieties, none of which is wholly true or false. The narrator describes his trips as baths in life, yet, relishing being alone among strangers, he scarcely immerses himself in their lives. He claims to like people's thinking him odd because it will stimulate "a little current" of curiosity; yet his suppression of his own curiosity about the inhabitants of the mysterious house on his street also shows that he is intimidated by the label. He preaches against the false faces human beings show to each other; yet, as a stranger intruding into the rhythm of life in the town, he associates himself with someone who passed bad checks among its citizens. Paradoxically, he knows "too much and not enough" about those he observes; although he seeks communion with them by expanding his knowledge of their inner experience, he also admits that what he knows blunts his interest in them. The most significant of the many contradictions, however, involves the presumptive accumulated meaning of the story itself. The narrator proclaims his love of life while he repeatedly sneers at the importance accorded death by those who lead unquickened lives. Yet a careful reading discloses his own preoccupation with death and his haunting awareness that he is "no longer young"; moreover, far from exhibiting a celebrant in the mass of humanity, his almost furtive demeanor in the strange towns attests a crabbed and frightened psyche. Anderson's purpose is not to establish his narrator's "unreliability"; rather, it is to array statement against itself, to reveal the narrator—our deputy—as life's fool.

If any one coupling of theme and structure in Anderson's short fiction is paradigmatic, it is this progress to a culminative moment in which the reader emphatically perceives a character's utter vulnerability and confusion. Anderson employs various strategies toward this end, but behind each lies the universal nightmare of the self discovering its nakedness before the world.

As "I Want to Know Why" shows, this nightmarish quality often arises from a sexual context. The story seems another instance of the initiation motif that is so characteristic of the period's fiction; indeed, one recognizes a number of conventions in its movement from the narrator's expressions of his unwitting wish to remain a child, to a climactic event that simultaneously confirms his innocent intuition and prefigures its inevitable loss, to his bewilderment on discovering his surrogate father's "rottenness." Even so, Anderson departs from the usual pattern: the narrator does not actually become an initiate (none of Anderson's narrators is ever truly initiated into the secrets of the tribe), nor is this adolescent's attainment of sexual sophistication quite the point. Almost by definition, the initiation story proceeds from ignorance to knowledge; here, in contrast, the narrator begins with an account of his sure moral judgment and ends with a confession of his uncertainty. A critical approach to "I Want to Know Why" virtually requires consideration of the reasons for this inversion.

The implications of the conclusion appear self-evident: in kissing the prostitute, Jerry Tillford has shown himself to be just another adult, thereby betraying the narrator's trust in his mentor's moral superiority; furthermore, since Jerry also functions as an older alter-ego, his fall from grace anticipates the narrator's encounter with his own "rottenness" as he advances into manhood. (Thus, it is not only Jerry but also life that betrays the adolescent's innocent faith.) Nothing in the ending violates the reader's expectations; in fact, Anderson has specifically foreshadowed it by having the narrator, early in the story, complain about a trick played on him. An adult had said that eating half a cigar would stunt his growth, but the foul-tasting remedy "did no good. I kept right on growing. It was a joke." The same elements—anger at the treachery of adults, despair over the inability to halt biological change, and fear of not fitting into a mysterious scheme of life—recur in the ending; in effect, it is the joke's complement.

But to see *merely* how this specific joke operates within the story is not enough. The more significant observation, bearing directly on Anderson's unorthodox practice, is that the dynamics of the story itself are joke-like. Humor in general deals figuratively with anxiety, and jokes in particular manifest this anxiety not only in their subject matter but also in their structure. The joke trades in subversion, especially in the punch line's upsetting of assumptions; its action proceeds along a double course that simultaneously confirms and violates its own logic. Although the result is scarcely funny, in "I Want to Know Why," the story develops toward a similar state of contradiction. The narrator urgently wants to "know why," yet, just as urgently, he tries to retreat from that knowledge. The reader immediately knows the "why's" that cause the narrator's distress, yet, from a farther remove, the more profound questions raised about human behavior remain unanswered—and unanswerable. On the one hand, the conclusion implies the reassurance that the narrator's confusion will disappear when, inevitably, he attains the reader's level of sophistication; on the other, it induces a longing for return to innocence.

Although critics commonly speak of Anderson's "ambiguity," the term is seldom appropriate. His characters are often frustrated in their efforts to unriddle their circumstances, but the stories themselves neither turn on the possibility of alternative interpretations nor show their author to be equivocal or unsteady in his purpose. What is mislabeled ambiguity might better be described as a method of "*anti*guity." In "There She Is—She Is Taking Her Bath," for example, John Smith, the troubled husband who narrates the story, has hired a detective to collect evidence of his wife's infidelity; then, afraid of being forced to act when the proof will be delivered, he has returned to the agency pretending to be his wife's lover and bribed the detective's partner to falsify the report. The initial motive underlying the story's action drives toward certainty; the second reverses direction to re-establish uncertainty. But the sum of the action is zero only in respect to the husband's question about his wife's chastity, and contrary to first impressions and at least one critic's inference,[1] the story is not about whether Mrs. Smith is unfaithful but about her husband's insistence that life conform to codes of behavior. Smith admires "men who, like myself, . . . keep the world going"; as a paragon of those "of some account in the world," he cites an expert on the rules of whist. Rules are very important to Smith; in fact, it is not jealousy that stirs him but the thought that his wife believes she can *cheat* with impunity—and, still worse, with a "young squirt" who flouts the work ethic and thus makes fools of those who shoulder their responsibilities. That she should be casually taking a bath (instead of trembling with a guilty conscience) when he is about to confront her with his justified suspicions shakes his faith in an invisible order that governs all existence. Furthermore, Smith's tenuous hold on self-esteem depends upon his membership in what he conceives to be the great confraternity of men, a lodge of "insiders" possessing the secret knowledge of how things are done. The closed bathroom door behind which his wife insouciantly bathes while his world is tottering defines him as an outsider, feckless before the greater mystery of woman.

Woman's power to expose the male as a fool often recurs as a theme in Anderson's fiction. Contemplating remarriage, the doctor in "Another Wife" vacillates between fear and desire. The woman is ten years his junior, yet, he imagines, she is far more experienced sexually; consequently, he sees himself in her eyes as at once an unattractive old man and a fumbling boy. He clings to the memory of his undemanding first wife as though it were an amulet; however, he also recalls somewhat ruefully that she had never excited him. To earn the new woman's respect, he feels he must rekindle his ambition, strive for professional success; at the same time, he yearns for rest from life's race. He wants to kiss her, but he is also afraid she wants to be kissed in order to trap him. This mental dance finally ends when, on returning to his cabin (presumably after proposing to her), he says, "Oh Lord— I've got me a wife, another wife, a new one." But if, in Aristotelian terms, this completes the action, it does not resolve the confusion within the doctor's psyche—which is the story's true subject. The last two sentences, significantly, consist of an exclamation of mixed emotion and a question: "How glad and foolish and frightened he still felt! Would he get over it after a time?" The same two sentences could serve as the conclusion to "The Other Woman," which focusses on the mind of a narrator who is torn between his attraction to a lower-class woman (with whom he feels sexually free) and his love for his bride (a "respectable woman" who asks him to delay consummation of their marriage until she has overcome her inhibitions). Clearly, the narrator's unsorted feelings toward these two women are similar to the doctor's abashment in "Another Wife" (particularly in respect to his two wives); in addition, the story's final image parallels that of "There She Is— She Is Taking Her Bath": although here it is an uncrossed *open* door that separates the narrator from his wife, the effect is almost the same.

Still another story that may be included in this group (despite differences in the manner in which it addresses its content) is "Daughters." Anderson repeatedly juxtaposes John Shepard's annoyance with his daughter Wave—whom he sees as wayward, headstrong, inconsiderate, and unfeminine—and his loving concern for her dutiful, mild, self-sacrificing sister Kate. Continuing throughout the recitation of Shepard's decline in fortunes, these comparisons seem tediously predictable and all-too-obviously foreshadow a violent outburst, directed at once against Wave and the injustice of life. Just such an explosion does occur at the close: after eavesdropping on the sharing of physical intimacies between Wave and a male boarder the family has taken in, the father almost chokes her to death. But the expected conclusion then develops an entirely unexpected signification. Shepard, the reader suddenly realizes, has subconsciously identified himself with the boarder, whom he had hoped might marry Kate—just the kind of woman he says he would have chosen for a wife. When the father sees this alter-ego fondling Wave, the implications are devastating: beneath the puritanical rage, and beneath the exacting of vengeance for what he construes to be a slight suffered by the "good" daughter, lies the far more powerful emotional storm roiled by the lust within him that Wave has aroused and he has repressed for years. Deepening the psychological dimension of this scene, Anderson describes it as though it were a dream that has become real. (If one stops short of pronouncing this lust incestual, it must at least be recognized as an unacknowledged desire for such unbridled, passionate women as Wave represents.) Then, finally, the author gives the screw yet another turn. While the father tries to fall asleep, he hears both daughters whispering and laughing behind the closed door of their room—perhaps about him. "There was something incomprehensible": their easy comradeship suggests that he has misread them, that Kate is really no different from Wave, that all women are alike in their harboring a luminous secret, and that its light exposes him as a fool.

Despite variations, the stories from "I Want to Know Why" to "Daughters" travel similar orbits and arrive at similar destinations. The most striking correspondence is in their concern with the sexual relationship between men and women and their use of that relationship as a mirror revealing the problematic nature of the self. What aggregates them as a constellation, however, is not subject or theme but a conception of structure that moves toward nullification rather than completion. Not all of Anderson's stories, of course, operate on the same principle (if they did, he would have been violating one of his favorite counsels for young writers: to avoid formulas of any sort.) Even so, his insistence on avoiding the "mechanical" in the composition of fiction fostered the development of anti-mechanical formulations that, although of different kinds, almost become conventions of their own. Thus, alongside a class of stories that rely on an "antiguous" structure, we find a group in which the antiguity inheres in a central symbol.

Perhaps the simplest exchange of this sort (if one can speak of simplicity in such an artfully complex performance) is "Milk Bottles." Superficially, the half-empty bottles of the milk that has been transported from the country to the city, where, in unrefrigerated apartments, it spoils in the summer heat, represent the lives of the people. Spiritually isolated from each other, these immigrants from the farms are "souring" in their struggle for success in Chicago. The reader soon perceives, however, that the symbolism is multistable. In each of the seven instances in which the bottles are mentioned, the signification changes. An even more pronounced shift occurs in the values revolving about the "milk" itself. Inspired by the bottles-of-sour-milk theme, the narrator's friend, an ad man, has written an account of a couple he took to be lovers until he heard them quarreling over money. When the narrator reads the crumpled pages of the story his friend has thrown away, he recognizes its worth as genuine literature, but to the ad man, it is trash that has served its purpose in priming the pump for his writing the "real stuff"—an over-blown piece of boosterism about "a coolheaded, brave people, marching forward to some spiritual triumph, the promise of which was inherent in the physical aspects of the town." The paradox is self-evident: the truth about the city dwellers, which is foul, is beautiful; the lie, which is beautiful, is foul. And wrapped around this paradox is another: the narrator appreciates the beauty in his friend's life, even though its conduct is based on delusion. The story manifestly celebrates the human, but in doing so, it undermines its own logic.

"The Egg," one of Anderson's three greatest works and a classic of American literature, also utilizes a multistable symbol which, as in "Milk Bottles," is indicated by the title. Clearly, the egg symbolizes life, but this identification scarcely settles the issue of its meaning, for life itself eludes meaning—which in turn *is* the story's "meaning." A symbol, by definition, implies relationship to a referent, yet in this context, the quest for the significance of the referents leads only back to the symbol. Initially, the egg suggests the folly of ambition and the absurdity of life. Next, it is associated with the narrator's father, marked as unmistakably ovoid by his bald head; the victim of his previous attempt to realize his ambitions (he is, in Anderson's idiosyncratic use of the word, a "grotesque"), the father now seeks to make up for his failure by opening a restaurant, where, on a shelf behind the counter, he exhibits bottles containing the grotesque accidents of nature that sometimes hatch from eggs. The saddest *lusus naturae* behind the counter, however, is really himself. Here, the egg develops still another implication. Misunderstanding the point of the anecdote about Columbus and the egg, the failing restaurant owner brands the discoverer of the New World a cheat and announces that he will make an egg stand on end without trickery. If there is justice, he thinks, the feat will win him the approbation of the world—synecdochically represented by one lonely customer. The weight of the entire story bears on this desperate scene as the father struggles to justify his life (and to redeem his faith in justice). Of course, the egg breaks, and in his wrathful acknowledgment of the utter frustration of his ambitions, the father hurls another egg at the customer, who is fleeing this drama of absurdity. The progression has come full circle.

But the joke is not yet played out. Shortly after beginning his account, the narrator had cautioned himself to tell the tale correctly, so that "it will center on the egg," not the hen. At the end, he reminds the reader that "from the egg came the hen who again laid the egg," and then states, "I am the son of my father." The significance in this combination of otherwise empty truisms is patent. Given that the course of the narrative corresponds to the cycle of egg and hen and egg, the egg now represents the son, and the story, "correctly told," finds the narrator at its center. "In the long nights when there was little to do, Father had time to think," he had commented midway through his tale. "That was his undoing." In the closing lines, it is the *son* who is thinking—and who is undone. When he was a child, he recalls, he had stared at an egg that lay on the table the night of the fiasco in the restaurant (and, perhaps, wondered why it could not be made to stand upright); in the final sentences, as an adult, he concedes that the problem of the egg, which "remains unsolved," has scored its "final triumph."

The crucial role of the narrator in "The Egg" illustrates a general principle that Anderson often preached to others and almost always followed in his own short fiction: form, he maintained, is a function of the *teller's* reaction to his materials. (His novels, it is worth noting, do not take their shape from this relationship—and thereby suffer egregiously from a failure of discipline.) More than any other trait or aesthetic practice, the tensions generated among the teller, the telling, and the content of the tale told are responsible for those qualities that are the hallmark of the Anderson short story. As one might therefore expect, most of his stories are written in first person, and even among the rest, many (e.g., "Another Wife" and "Daughters") employ a restrictive point of view that is virtually first person. The "I" is more important in some narratives than in others, however. Of the first person stories discussed above, all but two ("In a Strange Town" and "The Egg") *could* be rewritten in restrictive third person; although it would surely diminish their effectiveness, their essence would remain. But in the exceptions, the story actually consists in the act of telling. (Unlike the possibility of an "I Want to Know Why" ending with "He was puzzled," or of a "There She Is—She Is Taking Her Bath" that describes the husband in the park after walking away from the bathroom door, a recasting of "The Egg" concluding with a third person statement that the egg had finally triumphed in the protagonist's family is an impossibility.) Furthermore, it is in the telling of these quintessentially first person stories—which, in addition, also include "The Man Who Became a Woman" and "Death in the Woods"—that the peculiar Andersonian condition of antiquity is vested; the telling creates a form by "unresolving" what the content (i.e., the narrator's construction of an objective reality) seems to have resolved.

As the narrator explicitly states in the text, relating the central episode of "The Man Who Became a Woman" is his substitute for going to confession. Although he is now a married adult, Herman Dudley continues to be haunted by the memory of that tremulous moment in adolescence when the issue of a safe passage into manhood was very much in doubt. The theme of ambivalent sexuality indicated by the title first surfaces in the account of his feelings about his gelding, Pick-it-boy: "I wished he was a girl sometimes or that I was a girl and he was a man." In itself, the intimacy was reassuring, but the presence of a younger horse (a stallion named O My Man) signals the advent of a new stage in life when the very comfort provided by that relationship could prove dangerous. (The names of the horses are suggestive, as are the syllables of the narrator's own name: *her*, *man*, and *dud*.)

The story's next phase—set outside the fairgrounds in a grimy mining town, a "hellhole" that gives him "the fantods and the shivers" for reasons he cannot articulate but which the reader knows have to do with the subterranean recesses of his mind—illustrates the danger. Although he associates himself with men by entering in the town's saloon, it is a lonesome, frightened girl's face that stares back at him when he peers into the bar's cracked mirror. His reaction, not shame but fright that others may notice, is most revealing—and foreshadows the next event. The crowd's taunting of the "cracked" man and his "queer-looking kid" validate Herman's fears of what might happen if his own "crack" were noticed, and although he sympathizes with the victims, he resents being entrusted with the boy as though he were a member of this family. But the truly shattering moment comes when the cracked man stomps on his tormentors. The violence terrifies him, in part, it seems, because it manifests the possibility of a previously-undiscovered capacity within himself; slinking out "like a thief or a coward, which perhaps I am," Herman retreats to Pick-it-boy's stable and "the best and sweetest feelings I've ever had in my whole life."

This regression, a sexual fantasy in which boy and horse enjoy a nuptial relationship, proves to be another foreshadowing of the consequences of indulging the imagination when the two Negro swipes interrupt his dreams and proceed to treat him like a girl. Although he is "scared," his reactions are those of a virgin female, frightened and yet also submissive—as his thinking of himself as "a kind of princess" attests. Just when a fateful "deflowering" is about to decide the nature of his identity, however, he gives "a kind of wriggle" and, "as good luck would have it," slides through a hay hole. He has been reborn a man. Running "like a crazy man," he eventually stumbles into the skeleton of a horse that is lying in a boneyard on the skirts of the fairground. "A feeling like the finger of God running down your back and burning you clean" overcomes him. "It burned all that silly nonsense about being a girl right out of me. I screamed at last and the spell that was on me was broken." The next day, he makes his escape from the stables that represent his youth, "out of the race horse and the tramp life for the rest of my days."

The psychosexual implications of Herman's nightmarish experience are too obvious to ignore, of course, and the fact that its narration has a clearly demarcated beginning, middle, and end increases the temptation to regard the story solely in those terms. To yield to it, however, would be to miss half the story—and the more important half at that. One must bear in mind that the Herman Dudley who is *compelled* to tell his tale is an adult. If his perilous adventure had truly reached a safe conclusion, as the final line states, why does the urge to confess the tale still cause him to wake screaming? Why does he repeatedly mention his marriage to Jessie as proof that everything has turned out "all right"? And perhaps most significant of all, if only a full confession will exorcise his possession by the memory, why does he refuse to confront the truth (e.g., in his attempt to hide from the homosexual nature of the swipes' attack by advancing the most improbable claim that they either *mistook* him for a girl or were "maybe partly funning")? As Irving Howe points out: "Herman Dudley may even be, as he insists, a normal man, but to grant this somewhat desperate claim is to record the precariousness and internal ambiguity of adult normality itself. And this . . . is the particular achievement of the story, that through a recollection of adolescence it subtly portrays a complex state of adult emotion." Indeed, it may be even more complex than Howe realizes. If the bones into which Herman falls represent (in Howe's words) "the death of his adolescent [and homosexual] love," they also represent death itself; in this respect, the reader should note that the burning "finger of God" is a "new terror," making him seem "to myself dead." The told tale of one fearful passage *in* life suggests an untold tale of fear about the passage *from* life. This is not to say, of course, that "The Man Who Became a Woman" rests on a submerged allegory; rather, that the telling of the story, by undermining the resolution it asserts, displaces a specific fear with a general anxiety, and that herein lies the true seat of the terror generated by the tale.

The counterpoint of narrative act and object becomes more overt in "Death in the Woods," which, along with "The Egg" and "The Man Who Became a Woman," is usually recognized as the short story writer's outstanding work. That it was also Anderson's own favorite and that he labored over it longer than over any other story suggests as well that it best exemplifies his theory and practice of short fiction. Quite properly, anthologists have selected it to represent Anderson more often than any other tale. With all this attention, one would think that it has been clearly and widely understood; however, the contrary seems the case. The notes in one recent anthology, unfortunately all-too typically, state that it "packs the history of a nameless old woman into a series of incidents. By adopting the point of view of an impressionable young boy, Anderson endows his narrative with suspense and innocence. . . . The death of the old woman becomes a symbol of both waste and mercy." Aside from the questionable interpretation of the theme, the fact that the narrator is not a boy but a man, and the curious lapse in remembering that her name is Grimes, this description (quaintly subtending the heading "For Thought") commits the frequent misreading of the story as a synchronic presentation (albeit in piecemeal fashion) of Mrs. Grimes's life and death. Even so perceptive a critic as Howe entirely misses the mark when he states that "'Death in the Woods' has only one significant flaw: a clumsiness in perspective which forces the narrator to offer a weak explanation of how he could have known the precise circumstances of the old woman's death."

That the narrator does not know (and cannot have known) these precise circumstances is, precisely, the point—or, at least, the key to the point—of the story. The narrator was eyewitness only to the scene of her death, *after* her body had been removed and the dogs had returned to town. Although the story begins as though the narrator were reporting a series of facts about the woman, the presumption of certainty is steadily erased as the narrative proceeds, section by section. All the details are based either on hearsay or on inferences drawn from the lives of others; even his description of the discovery of the body is confected from what he has heard a hunter say—colored, further, by his listening to a report of that account by his brother (who, "it is likely," did not get the point).

Since Anderson's method is to have the tale ride on its own melting, it is the closing sentences of the last section, where the facticity of Mrs. Grimes's story has evanesced, that reveal its meaning:

> The whole thing, the story of the old woman's death, was to me as I grew older like music heard from far off. The notes had to be picked up slowly one at a time. Something had to be understood. . . .
> . . . A thing so complete has its own beauty.
> I shall not try to emphasize the point. I am only explaining why I was dissatisfied then and have been ever since. I speak of that only that you may understand why I have been impelled to try to tell the simple story over again.

The image of the woman—old and exhausted yet strangely young as she lies dead in the snow, circled by the running dogs that deputize for all the living creatures who have depended on her providing for them—has captured the narrator's imagination because of the beauty in its completeness. Mrs. Grimes has only precipitated that image, which, in its composition of contrarieties, represents the mystery of life. In the final sense, however, what the story is "about" is not the emblem but the need to retell the story, over and over again; not a meaning itself but the search for a means to understand it. The true story never ends; it is a figure that enlarges as it fills with the experience of one's life.

If the preceding short stories illustrate the body of Anderson's original genius in the genre, the last two stories in this collection, "Brother Death" and "The Corn Planting," stand as a coda. Not only in their structure and use of symbolism but even in their narrative conception, they adhere to the conventional; the etching of a statement supersedes the unfolding of an antiquity. Both of these stories are homiletic at their core, and although they are emotionally powerful and skillfully executed, they spring more from the preacher than from the artist.

"Brother Death" brings to mind the stories of another preacher, the Tolstoy of *Twenty-three Tales*. Essentially, it is a parable. John Grey cuts down the shade trees to break his son Don's resistance to his will: "Something in you must die before you can possess and command." When that "something" does die, Don is reborn as the father. The other son, Ted, is spared this rite because it is assumed that his weak heart will cause him to die before he reaches manhood. And indeed, a year or two after the beautiful oaks have been reduced to stumps, Ted does die. But: "having to die his kind of death, he never had to make the surrender his brother had made—to be sure of possessions, success, his time to command—would never have to face the more subtle and terrible death that had come to his older brother." In that final irony, the story's didactic meaning is fully resolved, and in the coincidence of the symbol of the two stumps with the action that ends in disclosure of the two brothers' contrasting fates, its design is closed.

"The Corn Planting," which retells Wordsworth's poem "Michael" in American terms, at first resembles "Milk Bottles" or "Death in the Woods" (with which it is often compared). But the narrator here functions simply as a reporter; his consciousness is in no way involved with the dynamics of the story as a figure of meaning. And, in a still more important difference, although all three stories focus on a symbol that alludes to the complex wonder of life, here, even though what the old couple "were up to in connection with the life in their field and the lost life in their son is something you can't very well make clear in words," the symbolism of that image is conclusive in regard to both the story's meaning and its form.

To say that neither "Brother Death" nor "The Corn Planting" evinces an idosyncratically Andersonian quality of storytelling is not, of course, to pronounce them *necessarily* inferior. On their own terms, they are engaging, well-wrought fictions, similar in several respects to the *Winesburg* stories he produced at the start of his literary career. (One cannot fail to notice the resemblance "Brother Death" bears to sections of the "Godliness" stories; and in its contraposing of urban dissoluteness to the telluric vitality of nature, "The Corn Planting" restates a theme that is interwoven throughout the *Winesburg* volume.) Nevertheless, the absence here of that special energy Anderson generates in his best work serves to accentuate his genius where it does achieve originality.

Note

1. In the introduction to his collection of Anderson's short stories, Maxwell Geismar reads the conclusion as saying: "Who wants to know about such things?"—i.e., that this is a tale designed with a caution against curiosity as its moral.

Walter B. Rideout

Sherwood Anderson's tale, "I Want to Know Why," written in August, 1919, had, as it were, a past, a present, and a future. For its past it reached back not only to Anderson's own boyhood, but to Mark Twain's great novel, *Huckleberry Finn*. For its present it incorporated a surprising amount of Anderson's 1919 experience. For its future it not only would have an immediate offspring in Ernest Hemingway's "My Old Man," but, in combination with *Winesburg, Ohio* and various other Anderson stories, would decisively influence later American fiction. "I Want to Know Why" helps to validate William Faulkner's generous and acute assessment of Sherwood Anderson as "the father of my generation of American writers and the tradition of American writing which our successors will carry on." In this paper I shall emphasize how "I Want to Know Why" incorporates Anderson's situation and attitudes in 1919, but I shall occasionally refer to the story's past and shall in conclusion suggest very briefly something of its future.

On May 8, 1919, the day *Winesburg, Ohio* was published, Anderson was leaving or about to leave Chicago on a business trip to Owensboro, Kentucky, going by way of Louisville, where at Churchill Downs on May 10 he watched the thoroughbred Sir Barton run a muddy track to victory in the Kentucky Derby. Over the next few weeks, as Anderson worked out an advertising campaign for the Owensboro Ditcher & Grader Company and then, back in Chicago, labored resentfully at his copywriting in the Critchfield office, Sir Barton went on to win the Preakness and the Belmont Stakes, thus becoming the first thoroughbred in history to win all three top races, a feat for which in 1950 he would be posthumously named the first Triple Crown Winner. My point here is not to show off my expertise on thoroughbreds, obtained, I confess, from three days' research in a library, but rather to suggest that the newspaper reports of Sir Barton's extraordinary performance would have helped keep Anderson actively aware of horse racing during the spring and summer of 1919.

July brought a respite from the daily selling of his brains to various Critchfield clients. During most of that month he and his wife, Ten-

"'I Want to Know Why' as Biography and Fiction," *Midwestern Miscellany* 12 (1984): 7–14. Reprinted by permission of the author.

nessee Mitchell, who had been in ill health for nearly a year, regained strength in the little resort town of Ephraim, Wisconsin, on the Green Bay side of the Door County peninsula. One afternoon late in July he climbed a cliff to a moss-covered ledge overlooking Green Bay. He felt renewed and at rest and wished that he could stay on at Ephraim alone for months, but almost symbolically factory smoke from a town miles across the Bay faintly discolored the sky. If he could only "give up the superficial battle for a living," he wrote a friend that evening, he would have the strength this coming year "to do things more subtle and difficult than anything I have ever done."

Chicago when he returned on August 1 made him psychically ill by contrast with the woods, hills, and harbor at Ephraim. The city people, even the children, looked old and weary to him; the lines of the buildings were ugly. For the five days just preceding, Chicago had in fact been convulsed with race riots during which gangs of marauding whites had invaded the Black Belt and thirty-three people, twenty black and thirteen white, had been killed and over three hundred injured. Even on this first day of sullen calm Anderson sensed tension and hatred still thick in the air. It remained risky for blacks to be in white neighborhoods, especially at night, and Sherwood, who had become acquainted with several black men who worked nearby, now out of revulsion at white violence gave them a key to his small apartment so that for some nights they could sleep on the floor of his living room, uncomfortable but at least safe. He had become acutely sensitized to pain by Tennessee's illness and even at Ephraim had seen pain "in the fishes taken from the sea, in the writhing of the worms by which the fishes were caught, in the eyes of cattle in the field, tortured by flies." Returning to the hate-filled city and to the demands of business was like being afflicted with a terrible disease.

Fortunately the practical demands on his time brought him through his initial days of shock; and as so often happened, he was able to snatch a few hours here and there for his writing, even when he was most harried by business, if some outer event or inner fancy precipitated a story. Such an event would seem to have been the news in the sports pages of August 10 that on the previous day the thoroughbred Sun Briar had won the Champlain Handicap at the races at Saratoga Springs, New York, and had set a new track record. Around the record-breaking winning of Saratoga's "Mullford Handicap" by a stallion named "Sunstreak" began to accrete in Anderson's mind one of his finest stories. It was to be told in the first person as a reminiscence by

Part 3

a fifteen-year-old boy from a small Kentucky town who, though the son of a lawyer, was crazy about race horses and had perhaps picked up from the people who worked with them, people outside conventional middle-class society, a mode of speech rather like Huck Finn's. The narrator recalls how the previous summer he and some other boys had stolen off by freight train to see the races at Saratoga, in the "East," had been taken care of there by a black race track cook named Bildad Johnson from their home town of Beckersville, had seen Sunstreak and the gelding Middlestride, both horses from farms around Beckersville, come in first and second in the Handicap, and had returned home to take the expected punishment from their parents, though the Boy's father understood his love of horses and barely scolded him. As the Boy is telling his adventure the following spring, however, he is still troubled by something he alone saw at Saratoga, the one thing he didn't tell even his father.

So with many digressions about his joy at watching thoroughbreds being worked out at the Beckersville training track early on spring mornings, about the beauty, honesty, and courage of the horses, about the superior decency of "niggers" over most white men where boys are concerned—digressions that both build up a world of rapture and reveal the Boy's reluctance to get to the event that destroyed it for him—after these digressions he tells how, with his gift for intuiting whether a horse is going to win, he watches Sunstreak being saddled for the Handicap, catches the eye of Jerry Tillford, the horse's trainer, and loves the man as much as the horse because he knows from Jerry's look that the trainer too has sensed Sunstreak's resolve to win. After Sunstreak's victory the Boy wants to stay close to Jerry and secretly follows him and some of the other men from Beckersville to a farmhouse where, he discovers, there are "ugly mean-looking women." Watching through an open window, he hears Jerry brag that Sunstreak had won only because he had trained him. Then when Jerry looks at one hard-mouthed whore in the same way he had looked at the Boy and Sunstreak at the saddling and kisses her, the Boy is enraged, creeps away, and persuades his friends to leave Saratoga for home. The repulsive fact that Jerry could watch Sunstreak run and could kiss a bad woman the same day had stuck in the Boy's mind for months and is now spoiling his joy in a new spring, in the laughter of the track Negroes, in the morning run of the thoroughbreds. Why, he wants to know, should such things have to be?

124

"I Want to Know Why" has been read in many ways—as a variation on the Genesis myth of the fall from innocence to experience, as a representation of the ambiguity of good and evil in the world, as a psychological study of a young male's concern over sexuality—but in the context of Anderson's emotional situation at the time he was writing the story in mid-August of 1919 an immediate, personal reading also emerges. Part of what he was transmuting into this fiction was his direct experience of the race track milieu, and bits of that assimilated reality stand out. Very possibly he had seen the thoroughbreds race at Saratoga in the August of 1916 or 1917 when he was not far away at Chateaugay Lake; but certainly he had learned all he needed to know about "Beckersville" from his occasional visits to Harrodsburg, Kentucky, where two other of his clients, David and Hanley Bohon, sons of a local banker, had become rich in the mail order business through schemes Anderson had suggested to them. Both Beckersville and Harrodsburg are near Lexington in the Blue Grass region, and in both there is, or was, a "Banker Bohon." For the lyrical descriptions of the morning sights, smells, and sounds of the training track Anderson had only to recall nostalgically his boyhood mornings at the track at the Clyde fairgrounds. The names and characteristics of the thoroughbreds required little invention. "Sun Briar" was readily converted into "Sunstreak," of course; and he could draw on his recent memory of watching Sir Barton's five-length win over Billy Kelly at the 1919 Derby for his conception of a horse that before a race was outwardly composed but was "a raging torrent inside." Yet he may have drawn as well on reports concerning a new two-year-old, Man o' War, who was driving the Saratoga fans wild that August with his speed, stamina, and utter will to win; for just as Sunstreak is owned by "Mr. Van Riddle of New York" who has "the biggest farm we've got in our country," so Man o' War was owned by Mr. Sam (Samuel D.) Riddle, a wealthy Pennsylvania textile manufacturer who had both the Glen Riddle Farm near Philadelphia and the huge Faraway Farm near Lexington. As for the awkward-looking but powerful gelding "Middlestride," Anderson had seen him win at Churchill Downs in 1918 under his real name Exterminator, a gelding well-known for his many victories and his gaunt, unprepossessing appearance, which gave him the affectionate nickname of "Old Bones." (Incidentally, Anderson may have adapted the name Middlestride from Midway, a thoroughbred who, the newspapers reported, had won the Kentucky Handicap at Churchill Downs back in late May, 1919.)

Horses and Negroes would have been much on Anderson's mind in
August of 1919, that month not only of the Saratoga thoroughbred
meets but also of the Grand Circuit harness races that were moving
from Ohio to the East and back to Ohio, carrying with them an intense
rivalry among three great drivers—Walter Cox, Tom Murphy, and Anderson's long-time favorite, Pop Geers, the Silent Man from Tennessee, who unlike Jerry Tillford never boasted that it was he, not his
trotter or pacer, who won a race. The horses themselves one could
depend on; they were embodiments of beautiful motion, courage, a
clean honest devotion to the challenge of the race. One could depend
too on some, if not all, of the men who worked with the thoroughbreds
and hence took on their best qualities. Especially one could depend
on the track "niggers" like Bildad Johnson, who intuitively understood
horses and horse-crazy boys, and of whom one could say, comparing
them with whites: "You can trust them. They are squarer with kids."
When "I Want to Know Why" was published in H. L. Mencken's *The
Smart Set* in November, 1919, after the terrible summer of race riots in
several American cities, it was as though Anderson were declaring publicly which side he had been on.

The praise of blacks might also have been prompted by some memory of Burt, the black groom Sherwood had known in Clyde; but the
chances are good that Bildad was in part suggested by Jim in *Huck Finn*,
for *Huck* would have been on Anderson's mind that August also. Off
and on for over a year he had been talking and corresponding about
Twain and his masterpiece with Van Wyck Brooks, who was at the
moment writing about that Westerner's ordeal in the East. A Huck
Finn cast to the Boy's speech—why else his use of the odd word "fantods"?—would be fitting, given a Bildad Johnson who, though allowed
only to cook at the tracks for the white men, is as admirable a figure
as Huck's black friend, and given too the picaresque atmosphere of the
race trace world, which is as much a refuge from conventional society
as was the raft on the Mississippi River. As much and no more, for just
as life on the raft was vulnerable to invasion by all sorts of human
ugliness, so is life at the track. Only a few weeks earlier in Ephraim,
Anderson had temporarily planned a group of children's tales, not the
usual "asinine sentimental nonsense," as Anderson put it and Twain
might have, but pictures of actual "country life at the edge of a middle-
western town"; and "I Want to Know Why," concerned with a boy only
a little beyond childhood, was not conceived as sentimental nonsense
either. Like Huck Finn of St. Petersburg, Missouri, the fifteen-year-

old Boy from Beckersville, Kentucky, is no innocent. He knows a good deal about adult nastiness already—a horse can be "pulled" in a race by a crooked jockey, one can hear "rotten talk" around a livery stable, a "bad woman house" can be found near any race track—but he can submerge such knowledge in his sheer joy at the thoroughbreds and the aura of dedication, beauty, and sensuous delight they cast around themselves. He can submerge it up to the point, that is, that the world of corruption breaks massively in on him.

Such a point is reached, of course, with Jerry Tillford's betrayal of Sunstreak and the communion which the horse created between Jerry and the Boy. The betrayal occurs in a sexual context; yet as happens so often in the Winesburg tales, something does not symbolize sex, sex symbolizes something. Fundamentally the Boy is right to question why things are as they disgustingly are. What he protests against is not adulthood, sexual or otherwise, not even moral ambiguity as the condition of existence. He (and his creator) already knows that some adults are "good," others "bad," most are a mixture of both. Although the father of one of the boys is a professional gambler, he alone refuses to enter the "rummy-looking farmhouse" where the women are as unbeautiful as they are unvirtuous; although the Boy's own father is middle-class by professional status, he understands his son and allows him his low-life associations. Rather, the Boy despairingly protests the degradation of a shared moment which, though he would not himself see the analogy, is equivalent in intensity and function to the artist's imaginative creation of an art work and to the observer's imaginative experience of it.

Such degradation, as Anderson knew on his pulses, comes from two directions. There is the corruption always threatened by the conventional world, represented here neither by the Boy's father nor by the professional gambler, but by those minor characters, some of them Beckersville citizens, all of them, incidentally, white, who follow the thoroughbreds but cannot intuit their inner natures and who view the racetrack as a milieu licensing the satisfaction of their lusts, for money or for sex, in no matter how squalid a fashion. One such person, to take a real-life example, might be Dave Bohon, businessman son of Banker Bohon of Harrodsburg, whose visits to Chicago required of Anderson and other Critchfield employees that they pander their brains for his advertising needs while Dave alternated an evening at the Chicago Symphony with sordid debauches of drink and women. More terrible even than the corruption from the outer world, however, is that which threatens degradation from within the self. Jerry Tillford shares the moment of communion at the saddling, yet debases it doubly—not so much through sex as through ugly sex, and not by ugly sex alone but specifically through speaking slander. He uses words to defame Sun-streak, the ultimate source of the shared moment; he uses words to lie with—as indeed Anderson with self-loathing felt himself doing daily in his advertising work and thereby defiling the material with which he should be building his art. Instead, words should be used as the Boy uses them, to tell truths no matter how bitter the truth or how embittering the telling of it—as indeed Anderson used words in this story. The personal meaning of "I Want to Know Why," then, is that it affirms the value of intuition and communion, which Anderson saw as the very ground and function of both art and life, but it simultaneously acknowledges the almost overwhelming destructive forces arrayed against them. The extreme unhappiness of the Boy is a measure of how, "more than ever before," as Anderson wrote his friend Marietta Finley, he felt and understood in that August of 1919 "the reality of pain."

As conclusion I suggest three aspects of what I called the future of this and other Anderson tales, their effect, that is, on later American writers. In the case of "I Want to Know Why" there is first the *voice* of the Boy narrator—a voice using common speech to convey intensity of feeling and, like *Huck Finn*, directing American fiction away from 19th-Century formal style. There is second the underlying *theme*—the pitting of the self by a sensitive person, and author, *against* encroaching ugliness and *for* some kind of intuitive human communion, a theme echoed in the education of Nick Adams and the repudiation of the McCaslin land by Uncle Ike, in such more recent works as Saul Bellow's *Seize the Day* and Alice Walker's *The Color Purple,* and in surely hundreds of fictions to be published from 1984 onwards, if we have an onwards. There is third the *form*—the way the Boy's long delaying digressions at the beginning of "I Want to Know Why" reveal an author creating a structure to carry meaning rather than imposing on his fiction some currently favored formula. *Voice, theme, form*—Anderson's new way of using them in 1919 was his bequest to American writers then, now, and to come.

Glen A. Love

Perhaps no alternative to the shrill disorder of industrial civilization had so seductive an appeal to Sherwood Anderson as a return to the primitive. Both as subject-matter—especially in his celebrated race-track stories, in *Tar, Dark Laughter* and *Many Marriages*—and as a touchstone of Anderson's own sense of himself as an artist, primitivism would seem to be an essential characteristic. "It may sound childish, but men will have to go back to nature more. They will have to go to the fields and the rivers. There will have to be a new religion, more pagan. . . ."[1] The reader and student of Anderson encounters such statements frequently. One recalls his description of how the theme of *Marching Men* appealed to "'my rather primitive nature,'"[2] and his letter to a friend claiming that "horses and Negroes seem to be the two things in America that give me the most ascetic [sic] pleasure. . . . We pay something . . . for our silly minds, don't we . . . ?"[3] Anderson as self-proclaimed primitive and primitivist has been echoed by some of his most influential critics. Oscar Cargill, for example, in his *Intellectual America*, includes Anderson under the heading of "The Primitivists," Maxwell Geismar calls him "an Ohio primitive," and Irving Howe concludes of Anderson's middle period that "the call to primitivism was tinged with a feckless irresponsibility."[4] While recent readings of Anderson have gone far in separating the author from the apparently guileless and groping, "primitive" voice behind much of his best work, Anderson's use of primitivistic materials in his writing deserves further examination.

What I would claim here is that much of what is called primitivism—and left at that—in Anderson is more meaningfully seen as pastoralism, and that the primitivist label as it has been so casually applied to Anderson fails to encompass the author's larger motives and methods, and distorts his most significant treatment of primitivistic materials. These materials—including the life of the senses, nature, childhood, the subconscious, and, for Anderson and his age, the Negro—are, of course, seen frequently in Anderson's work. But his use of these themes and

"Horses or Men: Primitive and Pastoral Elements in Sherwood Anderson," in *Sherwood Anderson: Centennial Studies*, ed. Hilbert H. Campbell and Charles E. Modlin (Troy, N.Y.: Whitson Co., 1976), 235–48. Reprinted by permission of the editors.

subjects is, for the most part, uncharacteristic of doctrinaire primitivism, in which the key element is a total rejection of or escape from civilization. Rather, Anderson's representative note is one of a struggle toward resolution between the character and a threatening society. If there is rejection or escape, it is typically undertaken so that the individual can somehow bring himself to cope with an inescapable and complex urban present. The essential tone in Anderson is reconciliatory, and in this sense his work may be seen as a contemporary version of pastoral.

The traditional literary genre of pastoral, as we all know, treats simple country people and manners. But it is concerned not so much with a celebration of rural life as it is with the contrast between rural simplicity and urban complexity, and with the need for those participants in this complexity, that is, the writer and his audience, to measure their world against the radical vision of country life. As John F. Lynen writes, "Though urban life is obviously superior in wealth and formalized knowledge, the country has its own special values. Pastoral plays the two against each other, exploiting the tension between their respective values, elaborating the ambiguity of feeling which results, and drawing attention to the resemblances beneath the obvious differences."[5] The essential element, then, in pastoral is this contrast which underlies its best examples whereby the relationship (as seen by the urban writer and his sophisticated audience) between complexity and simplicity, present and past, urban and rural, becomes the center of attention.

Pastoral has, through the ages since Theocritus and Virgil, undergone an expansion in its traditional subjects to a point where William Empson forty years ago in his influential study, *Some Versions of Pastoral*, extended the limits of pastoral even beyond the rural world. Nature, according to Empson, need not be an element in pastoral, but rather only nature's gift, simplicity of manners, the traditional quality of the shepherds of the old pastorals. Hence he classifies such diverse and apparently unlikely works as Gay's *Beggar's Opera* and *Alice in Wonderland* as pastoral because of the critical vision of simplicity which they embody. As Empson writes, "You can say everything about complex people by a complete consideration of simple people."[6] More recently, Leo Marx, in *The Machine in the Garden* (1964), has characterized nineteenth-century American literature and culture as another assertion of pastoral, with the dialectic formed around the contrarieties of America as nature and as machine civilization. Although Marx does not pursue his study beyond the end of the nineteenth century, it is clear that Sherwood Anderson, as perhaps no other writer of the twentieth century, embodies and reflects the main fact of American cultural history behind this pastoral tension: a comparatively simple agrarian life overtaken by an industrialized, urban civilization of bewildering magnitude and complexity. In Anderson may be seen both pastoral's thematic concerns for the countrified, the uncouth, the poor, and the naive, and its impulse for harmony and reconciliation between the opposing worlds out of which it draws its unique meanings.

The main body of Anderson's work, I would then claim, may be delineated in terms of pastoral. His first two novels, *Windy McPherson's Son* (1916) and *Marching Men* (1917), both define and explore what was always for Anderson the critical question: what are the possibilities for meaningful individual life in an urbanized industrialized America. Both concern young men from the hinterlands who come to the city and win success but find themselves still unfulfilled. Their search for meaning continues, along ever-widening lines of divergence. Sam McPherson denies the aspiration to money and power, forcing himself back into the "little" life of family and town. Beaut McGregor of *Marching Men* rejects such a solution and dissolves into a proletarian mist as the leader of a shadowy body of marchers, an example of "thinking big" which Anderson later repudiated, both in his own analysis of *Marching Men* and in the direction of his later work.[7] Along with his other pre-*Winesburg* book, *Mid-American Chants* (1918), these early novels express the pastoral tensions between country and city, quietude and shrillness, natural strength, simplicity and health, and the diseases of complexity and artificiality.

Winesburg, Ohio (1919) distills these tensions into a "moment" in which the small town and its inhabitants are poised in an uneasy equilibrium between an agrarian past and the threatening industrial age ahead. The keynote of *Winesburg* is the balancing of these two worlds in innumerable ways. The old world, the source of the book's evocation of a lost innocence and goodness, is the world of the setting, the fields and farms around Winesburg, as well as the simple round of daily life in the town itself. Set against this is the implicit presence of the city, which stands on the horizon of the book's scenes and events, an analogue of irresistible change. The "grotesques," the figures which move through the stories, are curiously isolated not only from one another and from the great world in the distance, but also from the natural self-sufficiency of the setting. George Willard, the artist as a young

131

man, seems finally both to express and to unify the attributes of village, grotesque, and great world. Standing Janus-like between the states of innocence and experience, youth and maturity, agrarian past and city future, he is a synecdoche for Winesburg itself. And the lesson of silence which he learns, the difficulty of meaningful human contact, leads, ironically, to the artist's understanding which may allow him one day to break down the walls of frustrated communication which surround the grotesques.[8]

If *Winesburg, Ohio* portrays the village and its attendant spirit, George Willard, in a state of arrested pre-experience, *Poor White* (1920) pushes them over the verge, "sweep[s] Winesburg into the modern industrial life. . . ."[9] Although Anderson's motive of reconciliation led him to treat his new hero, the industrialist-inventor Hugh McVey, as sympathetically as he could, nevertheless his ambivalent feelings toward "the machine" are reflected in the split between intention and feeling at the book's conclusion, and in the attitude of the other characters toward McVey. The creation of an uncomprehending mechanist-hero who destroyed the pastoral world which nourished him was the beginning point of a long search by Anderson for the means to reconcile the attributes of machine civilization with his characteristic association of the worthwhile life to natural and organic—rather than mechanistic and artificial—phenomena. Despite his heroic efforts to will himself toward its acceptance, the machine remains eternally hostile to the cornfield, and Anderson's sympathies remain firmly rooted in the natural world.

It is at this mid-point in Anderson's career that the primitivist themes become most insistent in his works. On such race-track stories as "I Want to Know Why" in *The Triumph of the Egg* (1921), "I'm a Fool" and "The Man Who Became a Woman" in *Horses and Men* (1923), and in his novels *Many Marriages* (1923), *Dark Laughter* (1925), and *Tar: A Midwest Childhood* (1926), Anderson's reputation as a primitivist rests. Yet despite his very real desire to present alternatives to the frustrations and pressures of machine-America and to re-enter what he saw as the restorative realms of sensation and simplicity—the world of the child, the race-track "swipe," and the Negro—Anderson's characteristic treatment of these themes exemplifies not the escapism of the primitivist, but the drive toward reconciliation of the pastoralist.

A close examination of one of these works, his well-known "I Want to Know Why," reveals how Anderson converts primitivistic material into pastoral expression. The story is narrated by a boy who loves racehorses and the track life, and who has discovered to his disgust and bewilderment that one of the horse-trainers whom he greatly admires can feel the same toward a hard-mouthed prostitute as toward a clean-limbed and magnificent thoroughbred race-horse. The boy, nearly sixteen now, looks back almost a year to the occurrence about which he has been puzzling ever since. "I'm getting to be a man and want to think straight and be O.K., and there's something I saw at the race meeting at the eastern track I can't figure out."[10] The boy's wish to "think straight and be O.K." contrasts sharply with his earlier behavior, which is an innocent celebration of the subrational life of his senses.[11] He is, at the time of the earlier incident, child enough to belong quite wholly to the primitive realm of the race-track, the horses and the swipes, the trainers, the sights and sounds, the feelings and smells of the racing world, his keen enjoyment of it recalling Huck's adoration of the Mississippi:

> Well, out of the stables they come and the boys are on their backs and it's lovely to be there. You hunch down on top of the fence and itch inside you. Over in the sheds the niggers giggle and sing. Bacon is being fried and coffee made. Everything smells lovely. Nothing smells better than coffee and manure and horses and niggers and bacon frying and pipes being smoked out of doors on a morning like that. It just gets you, that's what it does. (pp. 11–12)

In this primitive milieu of sensory impressions, of trainers and "niggers," of "aching" admiration for the hard and lovely thoroughbreds, the boy moves as naturally as a fish in a stream.[12]

In contrast to these primitive elements are the obligations of adult responsibility represented by the boy's parents, particularly his father. He seems a rather unsuccessful country lawyer who cannot afford to buy the boy things, as Henry Rieback's father, a gambler, does for his son. But the narrator's father does not disapprove of his associating with Rieback and Henry, as do the fathers of the other boys. The narrator's father emerges as a reserved but not uncompassionate figure, above all as a steadying influence upon his son. When the boy swallows a cigar to try to stunt his growth so that he may become a jockey, a course urged upon him by the town practical joker, and becomes ill, he says that most fathers would have whipped him for such behavior, but his didn't. The father understands the boy's love for horses and the track life and does not attempt to discourage it. "More than a thousand times I've got out of bed before daylight and walked two or three miles to the tracks. Mother wouldn't of let me go but father always says, 'Let him alone'" (p. 10). At the same time, the father will not allow his son to become a stable-boy.

Another father-figure is involved in the moral dilemma with which the boy has been struggling. He and three other young boys from the town had run away to see the big race meeting at Saratoga. Just before an important race, the narrator senses that Jerry Tillford, the white trainer of Sunstreak, shares his awareness of the "raging torrent" inside the horse. Sunstreak "wasn't bragging or letting on much or prancing or making a fuss, but just waiting. I knew it and Jerry Tillford his trainer knew. I looked up and then that man and I looked into each other's eyes. Something happened to me. I guess I loved the man as much as I did the horse because he knew what I knew" (p. 15). The boy feels himself, the horse, and the trainer drawn together into a bond of primal awareness. "Seemed to me there wasn't anything in the world but that man and the horse and me. I cried and Jerry Tillford had a shine in his eyes" (p. 15). "I liked him that afternoon even more than I ever liked my own father" (p. 16). Later, after Sunstreak has won the race with a record-breaking performance, the boy sets out to find Jerry Tillford, "like wanting to see your father at night when you are a young kid" (p. 17). He follows Tillford and some other men to an old farm-house, presented as a perversion of the clean and attractive sensory world of the track. The "lovely" race-track, the shiny, sweaty horses, the smooth, green lawns, and the riders in their colorful silks are here contrasted with the "rummy looking house" and the drunken men and women inside. "The place smelled rotten and there was rotten talk . . ." (p. 18). Unlike Sunstreak, who "wasn't bragging or letting on much, or prancing or making a fuss," Jerry Tillford "lied and bragged like a fool. I never heard such silly talk" (p. 18). Finally the boy sees Tillford looking at one of the prostitutes, his eyes shining as they had when he looked at Sunstreak. The boy becomes so angry that he wants to kill Tillford, but, instead, creeps away, gathers together the other boys, and starts for home, where, nearly a year later, he is still wondering why ". . . a man like Jerry Tillford, who knows what he does, could see a horse like Sunstreak run, and kiss a woman like that the same day" (p. 19).[13]

What the young narrator is struggling with is, above all else, his own incipient maturity, forced upon him after seeing the primitive confraternity of horse, child, and man shattered by the trainer's actions in the rummy farmhouse. Previous to the race, the boy has felt himself at one with the horses and the track Negroes in a ring of primitive understanding. Then, in the moment with Sunstreak before the race when he and Jerry Tillford "come alive" to each other, the realization suddenly comes to him that the trainer, a white adult who, unlike his own father, seems to share his devotion to the horses and the rarefied track life, also "belongs" within this primitive ring. The boy is ecstatic, having found an idealized, "spiritual" father. "I liked him that afternoon even more than I ever liked my own father. . . . It was the first time I ever felt for a man like that" (p. 16). But after seeing Tillford's actions in the farmhouse, the boy realizes that the trainer, who values a prostitute (who "was tall and looked a little like the gelding Middlestride, but not clean like him, but with a hard ugly mouth"), has betrayed the boy's vision (p. 18). Revealed as neither innocent nor noble, the trainer must be excluded from the boy's idealized world. "It was rotten. A nigger wouldn't go into such a place" (p. 18).

But anger at Jerry Tillford, alone, can hardly account for the boy's violent and protracted reaction to the incident. What is finally involved is his still-unacknowledged awareness that he himself must also follow Jerry Tillford out of the primitive circle. His first reaction to the scene in the rummy farmhouse, before the anger arises toward the trainer, is a wish that he had not seen what he did see: "I stood there by the window—gee!—but I wished I hadn't gone away from the tracks, but had stayed with the boys and the niggers and the horses" (p. 19). His anger at Tillford, which follows, only masks his primary realization of the beginning of his own loss of innocence. Similarly, as Arthur Sherbo points out, the act of following Jerry Tillford to the farmhouse (". . . I went along that road because I had seen Jerry and some other men go that way . . ." [p. 17]) suggests that the boy's life must henceforth lead him away from the clean, amoral world of the track.[14] Thus his continuing anger and bewilderment have less to do with Tillford than with his violent and painful initiation into a flawed world. That the boy's entry into maturity is neatly completed is suggested by the end of the story. No longer is he a creature of sensations. "At the tracks the air don't taste as good or smell as good. . . . I keep thinking about it and it spoils looking at horses and smelling things and hearing niggers laugh and everything" (pp. 19–20). But if the boy loses his sensory keenness, he has gained something in understanding and awareness of adult responsibility, the attributes of his father. Unlike Jerry Tillford, the father never crosses over into the boy's world. Although the father does not, therefore, share any blinding moment of awareness with his son,

135

neither does he betray him through disillusionment. The father remains blessedly predictable, someone the boy can count on.[15] And we sense that the father's presence and his settled values are helping the boy through his crisis. Certainly he has assimilated some of his father's calm stability: "I'm getting to be a man and want to think straight and be O.K." This attitude must be set against the boy's childish and impulsive actions at the beginning of the story which he is relating: running away from home, wanting to be a Negro so that he can be near horses ("It's a foolish thing to say, but that's the way I am about being around horses, just crazy"), and wanting to be a stable-boy (p. 6). His persistent questioning as he narrates the story—"I'm puzzled," "I can't figure it out," "I can't make it out," "What did he do it for?" "I want to know why"—suggest not merely bewilderment but also the beginning of a rational approach toward dealing with his dilemma and a responsible attitude toward himself. (The bewildered narrator is, of course, a concealment for the rhetorical stance of the author, who has carefully calculated his methods and effects. Anderson himself is not bewildered, as some of his critics seem to forget.) The emerging awareness of the narrator suggests that he will ultimately accept the fact that, because of his whiteness, his ties of family and responsibility, and time which reaps all innocence, he cannot return to the tracks "with the boys and the niggers and the horses" (p. 19).

Besides its internal integrity as a work of art, "I Want to Know Why" reveals important differences from doctrinaire primitivism. First of all, the primitive elements of the story, the innocence and purity of the horses, the boys, the swipes, and, for a moment, the trainer, are not simply celebrated, nor are we asked to reject society for their world. Rather, the story establishes clearly that this is a world closed to the audience, as it becomes closed to the narrator; "escape" is not even to be considered. The story's primitive elements are framed by the non-natural world through the comprehension of a narrator who is now beyond innocence. Although he is still close enough to the world of feeling to portray vividly the richness of its sensual life, he looks back upon it as the story closes from across a deep gulf. He speaks no longer for the primitive's world of sights and smells and tastes, but for the adult world of obligations and responsibilities, of complex moral problems. Thus, the primitive elements are viewed within the context of the real world—finally, the world of the reader. The juxtaposition of the two worlds suggests not primitivism so much as pastoralism, in its creation and exploration of a middle ground between the natural world and society. Primitivism leaps over this middle ground to a glorification of the natural world in terms which preclude any continuing alliance with the complex and the civilized state of man. Pastoral, in playing the natural world against the actual world, calls upon us to measure critically our own lives and surroundings by drawing attention to the simple and the innocent, as the young boy in the story is forced to measure his emerging awareness of himself against the innocent he had been before.

The central meaning of both "I Want to Know Why" and "The Man Who Became a Woman" is an awareness of a certain disillusionment, not with the natural life of the track, but with the narrator's *place* in such a life. The adult narrator of the latter story, especially, expresses clearly both regret at passing out of the primitive world and the understanding that one cannot call it back. And although he does not realize it, the actions of the narrator of "I'm a Fool" clearly reveal that he, too, has outgrown the track, even though he has, to his sorrow, not grown away from it. Hence, Anderson's three famous race-track stories resist the primitivist or escapist classification. They present the racing world as caught up in its own sensual music and finally lost to all but those from whom the narrator and his audience are inevitably separated. The direction of all of these stories is toward a letting-go of the dream of escape. As Anderson wrote to Alfred Stieglitz at the time of the publication of *Horses and Men*, "We have together the love of horses. In my own boyhood I went to them, lived with them, was groom to running and trotting horses . . . they were the most beautiful things about me. But it did not suffice. Will not suffice. The horse is the horse, and we are men."[16]

Anderson's autobiographical *Tar: A Midwest Childhood*, also concerned with the gulf between childhood innocence and maturity, similarly recreates the sensations and feelings of an earlier world while at the same time dramatizing the impossibility of remaining within it. But if the race-track stories and *Tar* correct the notion that one can hope to escape the demands of maturity and complexity by lingering forever in fields of clover, *Many Marriages* and *Dark Laughter* reject the opposite view that one must deny the sensual life entirely while upholding respectable appearances. Unfortunately, both novels lack the authorial control, the firm sense of presence, which one feels behind Anderson's best work. With *Dark Laughter* Anderson seems to have believed that the book's primitivist currency would carry it ("It is the kind of book that just now ought to arouse a lot of interest," he wrote to his publisher).[17] And the gestures of revolt in both works seem unexamined and sentimentalized, a sitting duck for the sharpshooting satire of Hemingway's *The Torrents of Spring*. Anderson's penetration into the primitive, as the failure of these two novels suggests, is, like Thoreau's, most successfully undertaken not as an end in itself, but as a way of coming to terms with society's nagging responsibilities.

In 1927, Anderson moved to Marion, Virginia, where he spent most of his later years. His return to the village is a remarkable metaphor of self-expression as well as an appropriate interpretation of his American experience. If the skeptical side of his nature warned him that he could not go home again, the artist-dreamer could envision the Marion venture as a return to the actual counterpart of the mythical town he never really left, to the lost boyhood villages in which his first four books of fiction are steeped, especially to the pastoral world of Winesburg where he knew by now that he had touched his highest mark as a writer. In those days of the late twenties when his reputation had begun to slide and he began hearing the whispers that "Anderson is finished," he sought in the town some new source of inspiration, a means of reestablishing himself. "I wanted to bury myself in the field and come up green," he wrote to Paul Rosenfeld after arriving in Virginia; "I'm done with cities."[18] While he was not, of course, done with cities, his statement affirms the spirit in which he moved to the South, the belief that the country offered possibilities for the renewal of communal life and hence for the rejuvenation of his own creative powers. In his later years it was the South which still provided, as both Anderson and the Southern Agrarians believed, the possibilities for the integration of the public and private self in modern America. Not nature, free and primitive, nor the machine-God of the city were to receive Anderson's final allegiance, but rather the emblem of their meeting, the town. Thus his last works center upon the small town and upon a renewed interest in individual lives during a period of social collectivism. His last two novels, *Beyond Desire* (1932) and *Kit Brandon* (1936), differ significantly from the proletarian modes of the time principally in their appeal for understanding and reconciliation. *Home Town* (1940) looks ahead with hope for the town as *Winesburg* had looked back with reverence. These last works are characteristic of Anderson's struggle to encompass the divisive oppositions of the old America and the new.

In his own personal involvement in both the simple life which he celebrates and the great world to which he finally belongs, Sherwood Anderson, it must be acknowledged, differs from the traditional pastoral artist. Distance was the hallmark of the old pastoral poet; he stood outside the mythical world and his call to return to it was not wholly serious. Both the artist and his audience knew too well that they could not take to the woods or the countryside. Yet Anderson's literary works as well as the record of his personal life suggest that he actually believed that there is the possibility, if not of reclaiming the idealized pastoral myth, of at least making a new start based upon some of its enduring values. He arrives at his pastoral stance, thus, not from a conscious awareness of the tradition, but from his adoption of the pastoral motive of reconciliation and new harmony: "I, myself a writer," he wrote, "have wanted more than anything else to make Americans in the civilization in which I am compelled to live, better known to each other."[19] His version of pastoral, like the traditional pastoral, was first of all a serious criticism of life. But more than that, the synthesis at which pastoral ultimately aims was the promise of a new life for himself, for that idealized artist-self whose importance we come increasingly to recognize, and for the America about which he cared so deeply.

Notes

1. Sherwood Anderson, *Perhaps Women* (New York: Liveright, Inc., 1931), p. 57.
2. *Letters of Sherwood Anderson*, ed. Howard Mumford Jones and Walter B. Rideout (Boston: Little, Brown and Company, 1953), p. xv. Hereinafter abbreviated as *Letters*.
3. *Letters*, p. 101. Anderson's attitude toward the Negro is discussed in n. 12, below.
4. Geismar's judgment is found in his edition of *Sherwood Anderson: Short Stories* (New York: Hill and Wang Company, 1962), p. xviii; Howe's remark is found in his *Sherwood Anderson* (New York: William Sloane Associates, 1951), p. 193. Paul Rosenfeld also describes Anderson's primitivistic impulses in his preface to the section entitled "Pastoral" in his *Sherwood Anderson Reader* (Boston: Houghton Mifflin Company, 1947), p. xx, but, I would argue, errs in calling these escapist tendencies pastoral.
5. *The Pastoral Art of Robert Frost* (New Haven: Yale University Press, 1960), p. 10. The subject of my essay here and throughout is treated at length in my unpublished doctoral dissertation, "Sherwood Anderson's American Pastoral" (University of Washington, 1964).
6. *Some Versions of Pastoral* (London: Chatto and Windus, 1935), p. 137.
7. Of *Marching Men*, Anderson recalled later that "it was not a success. I had been thinking too big. My imagination had betrayed me. When I later

returned, in my work, to life on a smaller scale, in the individuals about me, I was on solider ground" ("Man and His Imagination," in *The Intent of the Artist*, ed. Augusto Centeno [Princeton: Princeton University Press, 1941], p. 62).

8. This interpretation of *Winesburg, Ohio* is developed in my "*Winesburg, Ohio* and the Rhetoric of Silence," *American Literature*, 40 (March, 1968), 38–57.

9. *Letters*, p. 58.

10. *The Triumph of the Egg* (New York: B. W. Huebsch, Inc., 1921), pp. 8–9. Further page references will be incorporated into the text.

11. While I find myself in agreement with some of the individual points made by Donald A. Ringe in his "Point of View and Theme in 'I Want to Know Why'" (*Critique*, 3 [Spring–Fall, 1959], 24–29), I would place more emphasis upon the intimations of growing maturity in the narrator than does Ringe, who calls him "quite clearly a prisoner of his own five senses."

12. Anderson's portrayal of the Negro here is, of course, unacceptable to most of today's readers, nor can it be dismissed as merely attributable to the limited understanding of the boy-narrator, since it is quite consistent with Anderson's own conception of the Negro as "rather noble, but . . . physical, like the running horse or dog" (*Letters*, p. 101). Rather, Anderson's attitude in these race-track stories and in *Dark Laughter* reflects a popularly-held primitivistic stereotype of the Negro during the 1920's. (See, *e.g.*, Malcolm Cowley's *Exile's Return* [New York: The Viking Press, 1956], pp. 237–38). By the early 1930's Anderson's attitude had changed, as had the times. He satirized the writers of "nigger stories" in his "A Meeting South" in *Death in the Woods* (New York: Liveright, Inc., 1933), p. 225, and in a book review in *The Nation* of July 11, 1934, p. 49. In his own work, the picturesque "niggers" of the race-tracks and the New Orleans docks had become "Negroes," or "brown men," and Anderson was writing, "I can't see this sharp difference between the impulses of Negroes and myself. I think that decent Negro men and women have the same feelings I have" ("Look Out, Brown Man!" *The Nation*, Nov. 26, 1930, p. 579). The presence of the qualifiers "sharp" and "decent" suggest that Anderson may not have been wholly regenerate on the matter.

13. Arthur Sherbo, in his "Sherwood Anderson's 'I Want to Know Why' and Messrs. Brooks and Warren," *College English*, 15 (March, 1954), 350–51, corrects the misreading in Brooks and Warren's *Understanding Fiction* (New York: F. S. Crofts Company, 1948), pp. 348–49, of ". . . a man who knows what he *does*" to ". . . a man who knows what *he* does." Brooks and Warren's interpretation, it should be noted, is the first to treat the initiation theme in the story.

14. Sherbo, p. 351.

15. The most thorough and, in my opinion, judicious treatment of the father in the story is in John E. Parish's "The Silent Father in Anderson's 'I Want to Know Why,'" *Rice University Studies*, 51 (Winter, 1965), 49–57.

16. *Letters*, p. 106.
17. *Letters*, p. 143.
18. *Letters*, p. 171.
19. "The Sherwood Anderson Papers," *Newberry Library Bulletin*, ser. II (December, 1948), p. 65.

Mary Anne Ferguson

Though recent critics stress the importance of Sherwood Anderson's later works and most critics admire "Death in the Woods" as one of his best short stories, if not his masterpiece, the volume *Death in the Woods and Other Stories* (1933) has not been studied. Yet Anderson, always concerned with the "baffling question of form achieved or not achieved,"[1] took special pains with the book. When he was reading proof, he perceived unevenness in the quality of the stories and "threw out two or three"; he wrote a new story to complete the volume, "Brother Death," a story which in his opinion would "make the book"; "It is, I'm pretty sure, one of the finest stories I've ever done, and I even dare say one of the finest and most significant anyone has ever done." Anderson was especially pleased with these changes because, as he explained to Ferdinand Schevill, "I did want the book, dedicated to our friendship and my esteem for you and your mind, to have real integrity."[2] Anderson "sounds cocky," he admits; but as Schevill would have realized, such self-assurance with respect to a collection of short stories was a new note for Anderson. In his dedication to Dreiser of *The Triumph of the Egg* (1921) he wrote of his sense of inadequacy: "Many tales are dying in the street before the house of my mind"; and in the first selection in the volume "The Dumb Man," the persona reiterates this despair: "I have no words. . . . I cannot tell the story." In the Foreword to the collection *Horses and Men* (1923) Anderson says that he may be deaf, blind, and unable "with these nervous and uncertain hands . . . [to] feel for the form of things. . . ." In the Introduction to a collection of sketches, *Perhaps Women* (1931), he apologizes for his failure to have found a suitable form: "The whole thing is nothing but an impression, a sketch. I know that I have kept it by me for a year now. I have tried to give it better form but that now seems impossible

"Sherwood Anderson's *Death in the Woods:* Toward a New Realism," *MidAmerica* 7 (1980): 73–95. Reprinted with minor corrections by permission of the author, Professor Emerita, University of Massachusetts, Boston.

to me." Anderson's cockiness about having achieved his goal of "real
integrity" in *Death in the Woods* suggests that the volume may represent
a new departure for him. I find in the volume a movement away from
a persona seeking the meaning of life in "the preternatural or archetypal,"[3] a passive observer upon whom reality impinges itself, toward
a persona who shares the life he observes and locates the center of
reality outside himself. The change in the persona is associated in the
volume with a change in attitude toward women and toward death.

The story "Death in the Woods" is the first in the volume; "Brother
Death" is the last, and Anderson indicates that this arrangement was
his intention.[4] Obviously the volume is unified by the theme of death;
but it is not death alone. As he had elsewhere,[5] Anderson links the
topics death and woman. Of the sixteen stories in the volume, five
deal with the death of a woman and its effect upon a male character.
In "Death in the Woods" the male narrator is a stranger to the woman
whose death is an episode in his development. In three other stories—
"The Return," "Another Wife," and "The Flood"—the focus is on a
widower trying to find a substitute for his dead wife. The narrator of
"In a Strange Town" flees his wife and home in order to recover from
the depression he felt upon the death of a young woman student; he
consoles himself by meditating upon the meaning of life for a widow
he sees at a railroad station in a funeral party. These stories reflect the
conviction which led Anderson to publish *Perhaps Women* in spite of his
dissatisfaction with its form, his sense "that modern man is losing his
ability to retain his manhood in the face of the modern way of utilizing
the machine and that what hope there is for him lies in women."[6] Other
stories illustrate ways in which women may save men and make explicit
the faults from which men need to be saved. Their need for worldly
success is the primary life-denying fault, whether it be in a mountaineer moving to the city for work, a young man seeking sophistication
among expatriates, or a writer abandoning family and human values for
the sake of his craft. In one powerful story, "The Flight," Anderson
shows male rivalry as ruinous; in another, he shows jealous possessive-
ness as absurd. Through their interaction with other characters the
males in these stories either ironically reveal their illusions about themselves or gain self-knowledge. In a few stories Anderson focuses on the
positive qualities of the women characters—their wisdom and their
ability to deal with the realities of life—which enable them not only to
survive in a hostile world but to help men. Finally, in "Brother Death,"

he uses a female central consciousness to show that in the midst of death one can live fully.

The stories in *Death in the Woods* were written over a period of years—some were published as early as 1925—when Anderson was also writing the avowedly autobiographical works *A Story Teller's Story* (1924) and *Tar: A Midwest Childhood* (1926). But from these and many letters and passages in the *Memoirs* (1941) which tell about this period in Anderson's life, one cannot get a trustworthy chronology. The tantalizingly frequent parallels between his biography and his fiction cannot be made into a study of development.[7] But the changes I perceive in Anderson's male personae in the volume *Death in the Woods* are paralleled by changes in six versions of the title story which have survived.

Anderson considered "Death in the Woods" one of his best short stories, but, he added, it "was one of the stories I wrote, threw away, and rewrote many times." Recognizable versions of the story appear in three works unpublished during Anderson's lifetime: "Paris Notebook" (1921); "Father Abraham: A Lincoln Fragment"; and the recently discovered fragment "A Death in the Forest." Three published versions exist: as part of *Tar: A Midwest Childhood* (1926); as a separate short story in *American Mercury* (September 1926); and finally in 1933 in the volume *Death in the Woods*.[8] In a passage in which he compares the gestation of a story to pregnancy, "the telling of the tale . . . [to] the cutting of the natal cord," Anderson remarked that out of his private world of fancy, he would like to introduce and tell the story of, among others, "the old woman accompanied by the gigantic dogs who died alone in a wood on a winter day."[9] In "Death in the Woods" Anderson does tell the story of such a woman, using as narrator a grown man looking back to a memorable incident in his boyhood twenty years earlier. The narrator mentions that he did not understand the significance of the woman's story until later in life when he "had a half-uncanny mystical adventure with dogs in an Illinois forest on a clear moon-lit Winter night." In his *Memoirs*, Anderson describes such an experience when he was living in Chicago and spending weekends in the country nearby in order to write. The troop of dogs which accompanied him on a walk one snowy night "seemed excited"; they "ran in circles," and when Anderson stopped to doze, lying half-way up the slanting trunk of a fallen tree, they made a circular path in the snow beneath him, running head to tail; one by one they dropped out of the circle to run up the tree trunk and gaze into Anderson's face. Anderson felt "something of the mystery of the night," of the "strangeness" of the animals' reversion to a primitive state, but he thought that part of their ritual, their stopping to run to him, indicated their tie to civilization.[10]

Anderson ascribes a similar feeling of awe to Abraham Lincoln in "Father Abraham: A Lincoln Fragment." The narrator projects himself into the mind of Lincoln whom he imagines as the defense attorney for a woman accused of killing her employer. Like Anderson's mother a bound girl, the woman had no defense but violence when her master attacked her. Lincoln is able to imagine her feelings as well as those of the man who sees her as his rightful conquest; he knows that the man's wife tacitly condoned the rape as a way of keeping the girl bound to their service for life. With great insight Lincoln perceives the farmer as a misguided human being, not a brute; but his sympathy is for the victim. Earlier in "Father Abraham," Anderson wrote about Lincoln's passion for Ann Rutledge and his mourning for her at her grave in the snow on a winter night; Anderson presents Lincoln's love and loss as the experience which liberated him from the merely personal and allowed him to extend his sympathy and influence to strangers. In "Death in the Woods," Mrs. Grimes's early life as a bound girl parallels that of the woman on trial; the death scene bears many resemblances to that of Lincoln at Ann Rutledge's grave.[11]

The version of the old woman's story in "Father Abraham" is close to that of the sketch in the "Paris Notebook"; in both the emphasis is on the brutalized life of the old woman, told with compassion for all participants. In the "Notebook" the old woman, who has not attempted to murder the farmer, relives in dreams her youthful experience. The woman whom she served, habitually "silent & sullen," "did not mean to be unkind"; the farmer is not evil but amoral, perceiving the girl as his rightful prey. The man she married, "filled with wrath that was bottled up inside him" and which he did not understand, had in his youth expressed "a kind of love" in the only way he could, drinking and fighting. "Ma Winters" now dreams of herself as "frightened, a young girl in a torn dress," trying desperately to care for the animals which love her. In one of her dreams, trying to rescue herself and trapped animals from an airless barn, she cannot reach the bar which would open the door. "The bar she could not reach was cold as death. It was death. One raised death out of its sockets on the great door and then joy and light came in." Without raising death, she awakes. This version focuses on the meaning of death to the girl who is the central consciousness; her dream vision seems associated with Anderson's dreamlike experience in the Illinois forest.

But the bound girl's story, Lincoln-like compassion, and the dreamlike incident of the dogs were not always linked. In a recently published holograph version of the story entitled "A Death in the Forest" Anderson treats the old woman's death almost entirely as it concerns the narrator as a young boy. Anderson focuses on the boy's encounter with death and the nakedness of woman not as a rite of passage, made mysterious and "mystical" by the ritualistic circling of the dogs, but as the occasion for his finding a role model. At the death scene he meets Ben Lewis, a young man of the town who for five years has been a newspaper reporter in Chicago. His success and its importance to the narrator are symbolized by Ben's "grand overcoat . . . (all silk lined and everything)"; to the boy the most significant aspect of the death scene was Ben Lewis's giving his overcoat to him to hold:

> . . . the charge lay upon me with a delicious weight. Could men, actual flesh and blood men, who had been raised in our town, wear such gorgeous garments? Did such unbelievable things happen to young fellows who left our town and become reporters on city newspapers?
>
> The coat was of broad yellow and green plaid and to my fingers the touch of it was delicious. And it was lined with silk. How reverently I carried it home to our house and how good and kind I thought my mother when she laughingly permitted me to have the coat hanging in my own room overnight.
>
> I slept but little that night and often crept out of bed to touch the coat again. How deliciously soft the fabric. The death of Ma Marvin in the snow in the wood was forgotten. . . . Would I, could I, sometime, grow up, go away to a city, get a job on a newspaper and like Ben Lewis wear a coat like a king? The thought thrilled me beyond words. . . .
>
> As to the actual story of Ma Marvin's death, I found all about it in a rather queer way nearly twenty years later. Now I will tell you of that.

The manuscript ends here, but even if it had been continued, the story would not have been that of the old woman; the narrator has already dismissed that possibility in a few short paragraphs of narrative summary beginning "It was a poor little story after all." Obviously at this stage Anderson did not perceive a significant relationship between the woman's life and her death; the narrator dismisses the death as something beyond a boy's capacity to understand and immediately shifts his attention to the death as the cause for a gathering of the townsmen and the opportunity for him to hold Ben Lewis's coat. For the narrator, following in Ben Lewis's footsteps would lead to his heart's desire: success enough to buy luxury that would be visible to the townspeople.

Even for the adults in "A Death in the Forest," the old woman's death is not deeply significant. It occurs as an interruption to the town's happy preparation for Christmas and enjoyment of winter, "crowds of boys . . . shouting and laughing" as they jump on and are thrown from bobsleds on Main Street. The first sentence of the story announces the death bluntly: "It was December and snowing when Mrs. Ike Marvin—we knew her as Ma Marvin—died in the little hollow in the center of Grimes' woods, about two miles south of our Ohio town." The next two paragraphs personify the town: the return home of a few girls rich enough to have been away at boarding school and of Ben Lewis makes the narrator feel "one's town putting its nose up in the air like a fine pointer dog" on "a day to remember." The day is memorable because of the effect on the townsmen of the news of Mrs. Marvin's death: all activity in the town ceases, and the narrator recalls in detail what many of the townsmen were doing as "things went bang then, like putting a light out in a room." He recalls the bustle as the news is shouted by two young hunters who run down Main Street, figures remembered as "not quite human . . . more like Gods." The sudden cessation of activity is accompanied by a change in the weather as the townspeople, including "even women who had no babies to look after," went in a group to the scene. The old woman's life and the manner of her death, "just as plain as though there had been an eyewitness to her death there to tell the tale," are very briefly summarized. The narrator remembers the "white, half frozen little old figure, pitched a little forward," and the "pack of big ugly dogs"; he imagines "the stillness of death coming softly, night and the cold," but comments, "My boy's mind couldn't grasp it then," and goes on to give details of Ben Lewis's participation in moving the body and handing him the coat to hold. In this version it is the boy as part of the town, indeed, the town itself which is the center of the story.[12]

In the three published versions of the story the old woman's death and her life become the central memory of the adult narrator and the story becomes his attempt to perceive its true significance. The final version published in 1933 intensifies the mystical and mythical nature of the experience and its effect upon the narrator as a boy. All three of these versions omit any reference to Ben Lewis and his coat. The immediate impact of the death scene on the narrator and his brother is its function as sexual initiation for them: "She did not look old, lying there in that light, frozen and still. One of the men turned her over in the snow and I saw everything. My body trembled . . . and so did my brother's. It might have been the cold. Neither of us had ever seen a woman's body before" (20).

But before this scene the story of the old woman's life as a bound girl, as brutalized wife and mother, as a person totally isolated from human contact, has been amply told; the boy's previous impressions of her during a summer when he had observed her when he was idled by sickness, make his interest in her believable, his final view of her as a "feeder of animals" is made convincing when he presents it as arrived at "slowly, long afterward" (22).

Anderson gains credibility for the narrator in the published versions by carefully detailing his relationship to the old woman. An omniscient narrator first describes the old woman's trip to town on the fatal day as one of many such trips viewed "one summer and fall" by the boy. Her actions are presented as those habitual to "such old women" often seen by "all country and small-town people" but seldom understood by anyone. The use of the present tense to describe habitual action and of the conditional in verbs like "may own" and "might spend" is interrupted in the second paragraph by a specific statement about the boy's distaste for liver; now he becomes the central consciousness but the use of the habitual present continues. "The old farm woman got some liver . . ." is inconspicuous in the midst of the habitual present; it prepares the reader to believe the narrator's assertion that he had often observed the old woman. Continued shifts between the habitual present and the specific preterite are reinforced by apparently casual explanations of the narrator's knowledge both of the woman's past and of the day of her death. Such observations as "she got into my thoughts," "I remembered afterwards," "I later knew all about it. It must have stuck in my mind from small town tales, heard when I loitered about where men talked," augmented by conversational tags like

"You see," "Well," "Maybe," and rhetorical questions like "then what would she do?", subtly establish the tone of oral narration, of a tale being told. This tone not only achieves suspension of disbelief but imparts to the old woman's story the aura of myth. The detailed narrative of her death becomes part of a larger story; the sense of strangeness Anderson felt in the Illinois forest is communicated through dwelling on the dogs' return to their primordial origin as wolves, their memory of civilization and perhaps their fear of death expressed in their interrupting their circlings to come close to the old woman, who had stopped to rest against a tree trunk beside a clearing. Further details about the dogs' tearing into the old woman's bag of supplies and tearing off her dress "clear to the hips" prepare for the denouement when the narrator and his brother "saw everything" and perceived the body of the old woman as that of a slender young girl.

Even such a minor change from "A Death in the Forest" as omitting any women from the group of townspeople who went to the clearing, prepares for the climax as ritual: the old woman is completely alone among men who are reduced to silence by being in the presence of death and who treat her body with ritualistic reverence. Later the townspeople make her part of the community as she had never been in life, by banishing her husband and son, scapegoats for the townspeople's communal guilt for excluding her in life. The young brothers experience the scene as sexual initiation and as a story to be told; the inability of the older brother to tell the story properly increases the sense of its strange effect, which the narrator only later could understand as awe. He remembers the scene as if he had been a spectator of himself, seeing himself among "the men standing about, the naked girlish-looking figure, . . . the circle made by the running dogs, and the clear cold winter sky above," his angle of vision like that which Anderson had in the Illinois forest suspended on the tree trunk above the clearing. This distanced perspective of the adult narrator—like that of the tall Abraham Lincoln standing at Ann Rutledge's grave—along with new experience gained over time, enables him to see the woman's life and death as a cycle of feeding animal life, a cycle matching the dogs' ritualistic circle and representing a return to primordial origins. Mrs. Grimes becomes the archetype of female experience; the telling of her story brings her out of isolation into the reader's world. The substitution of the title "Death in the Woods" for "A Death in the Forest" underlines the mythical dimension.

That such a focus was deliberate is even more apparent when we examine other comparatively small but important changes among the three published versions. The version included in *Tar*, told in the third person, is quite different from the version published in the *American Mercury* in the same year as *Tar;* the shift to a first-person narrator, division into five parts, and many small changes in wording resulted in a story Anderson changed little for the 1933 volume. All the changes for the final version emphasize the mythical dimension. The words *lovely* and *charming* are added to the description of the body; the effect on the narrator is emphasized when "with some strange mystical feeling" is added to the sentence "his body trembled," and the words *the mind and* are inserted in the predicate of the sentence "something creepy steals over the body." Significant changes occur in the final paragraphs of the story summarizing what the narrator had gradually come to perceive as the meaning of the story, which become to him "like music heard from far off." In the sentence "The woman who died was one destined to feed animal life," the phrase "destined to feed" has replaced "who fed"; "animal life" has replaced "animals," preparing for the subsequent addition of the idea that "She was feeding animal life before she was born," a completion of the cycle which ends with her feeding animal life at her death. Such additional statements by the narrator as "I wonder how I know all this," "I remember now," "I have just suddenly now, after all these years, remembered her," and "It all comes back to me now" distance the adult narrator; dredging up the details from his memory, telling the story, is like perceiving the archetype. The narrator's "It is a story" near the beginning and "A thing so complete has its own beauty" near the end frame Mrs. Grimes's story, which has become also the story of the artisan's creation of the "thing so complete." This story is "a story teller's tory," an exemplum of the process by which the artist crystallizes experience into art.[13]

The other stories in *Death in the Woods* continue to reveal the creative process; the narrator-persona is confident and unapologetic, increasingly involved in the life described. One story, "The Flight," shows the necessity of putting aside childish views if one is to be taken seriously; another, "The Return," shows the futility of returning to childhood scenes and conditions—of going home again—in order to find a sense of adult identity. In twelve stories first-person narrators are adult males able to understand the meaning of events as they learn about or experience them in a specific environment, whether it be New York, Paris, the Virginia mountains, or the New Orleans of "A Meeting South." The locales are neither typical nor mythical; the narrators are at home in them. They are also more rational in putting two and two together in order to find a pattern than is the adult narrator of "Death in the Woods," and they rely on others than themselves for help in the process; they are very good at listening.

Many of the first-person narrators furnish an authoritative framework for their stories. Anderson had always taken ideas for stories from what he called "feeders," people who could tell him their stories but could not see their significance or write them.[14] In earlier collections "feeders" lack reinforcement as authoritative sources; they are casual acquaintances or unreliable characters: a "woman met on a train" ("War"), "a man" ("The Other Woman"), "my friend—his name is Leroy" ("Seeds"), a college professor unable to communicate with his own wife ("The Man in the Brown Coat"). "Feeders" in *Death in the Woods* are much more reliable. In the three stories about Virginia mountaineers, the narrators discourage disbelief by not demanding total belief. One has lived "for some time" among "These Mountaineers," but does not pretend to understand them when they reject his pity. Another has been told the story of "A Sentimental Journey" by a scholar who has become the friend of "a mountain man, named Joe, a man much older . . ."; the scholar tells the narrator Joe's story after first admitting to his earlier belief in "Romantic tales." In "A Jury Case" the narrator has most of his information from a mountaineer who participated in the crime and who is "something of a dramatist"; the narrator disarms disbelief by stating flatly, "His version is, to be sure, all a matter of fancy," and by not insisting on the truth of any version.[15] In "Like a Queen" a friend tells his story to the narrator after experience of thirty years has corroborated it; the story gains verisimilitude when Alice, who is the focus of the story, tells her own life history. In "A Meeting South" a young poet tells the narrator the "story of his ill fortune" as if he were "speaking of another"; his command of words wins the narrator's—and the reader's—belief. Being able to use language appropriate to the subject is a test for other narrators and "feeders." In "There She Is—She Is Taking Her Bath," the first-person narrator calls attention to his own use of clichés, a step which increases the verisimilitude of his self-revelation; and in "That Sophistication" the hostess's repetition of the word *corked* each time she pours out a new bottle of wine for her guests reveals her absurdity. The narrator of

"In a Strange Town" creates a story for us as an illustration of his techniques; because we know that the widow's life he has imagined is fiction, we tend to believe as fact the narrator's concluding story about his own experience. Unlike the persona of "The Dumb Man," this narrator has found a way to go beyond his first reaction of sitting "dumbly" upon learning of his student's death. Credibility for the narrator's perception of hidden truths about people is gained by repetition, at the beginning and end of the story, of examples of his amazing ability to hear sounds unheard by those familiar with them.

"In a Strange Town" more directly than "Death in the Woods" epitomizes the process behind this assured narrative voice. In his *Memoirs* Anderson recorded the centrality of this story to his concept of himself as a writer.[16] He tells us that his habit of wandering in strange towns, immersing himself in a "bath of new impressions, of people seen," often results in mystical self-loathing which brings him to the point of suicide—"and then something happens." This "something" makes "the person called Sherwood Anderson" disappear. But he does not commit suicide; he is able by writing to get "entirely rid of self," to project the "darkness," the "corrupt mass of self." Even as a child, he had felt the "selfishness and slickness in me," the tendency to "control and use men and women," had felt the need for salvation, to which others suggested religion as an answer. Anderson says that such an answer was not possible to him because he could not make the total commitment to art that imitating God as the supreme artist would entail; such a decision is impossible for him because he is not willing to let "everything else go." The creative process described in "In a Strange Town" allows the writer to make stories without controlling lives; the narrator need not feel self-loathing but through his art may achieve a catharsis of despair and self-centeredness.

The narrator of "In a Strange Town" is a professor of philosophy, "no longer young"; he has fled the familiar in order to renew his creativity by making up stories of the lives of strangers he encounters. He demonstrates this renewal by gradually imagining the story behind a group of people in the railroad station: he sees them as "people of no importance" who in becoming mourners have "suddenly become important [as] symbols of death. Death is an important, a majestic thing, eh?" (145), says the narrator, who has already shown the townspeople's sense of awe as they make a "litle path of silence" for the group. He "reconstructs" the life of the widow to illustrate his perception that all lives are similar but that "the little circumstances of no two lives any-

where in the world are just alike." From perceiving the "little odd frag-
mentary ends of things" he is able to perceive the mystery of life in
general which he represents in his reconstruction of the widow's life.
This process of relating the particular and the general is, of course,
appropriate for a professor of philosophy. Also appropriate to the mature professor is the fact that when he wanders in strange places he is
an observer, not a participant in life: he no longer picks up women but
tries to escape involvement. "It may be that I am a bit dirty with life
and have come here, to this strange place, to bathe myself in strange
life and get clean and fresh again" (150). Now, he tells us, he is re-
freshed. This could be the end of the story if it were meant like "Death
in the Woods" to exemplify the process by which the artist goes beyond
self or if the focus were on the imagined characters as symbols of death.
But the narrator goes on to reveal that the immediate cause of his wandering to a strange town was the sudden death of a young woman, his
student, whose attention had flattered him and whose experience had
often caused him to re-experience his youth. Her death has caused him
to take this trip in order to become "more aware," "more alive": as in
"Death in the Woods," a woman and her death have been the inspiration for a narrator; but his learning process here is the result of active
imagination, of purposefully weaving observed particulars into a pattern of meaning.

  The changes in the narrative voice in *Death in the Woods* are paralleled
by changes in the attitudes towards women revealed in the stories. All
of them go beyond the suggestion in "A Lincoln Fragment" and in "A
Death in the Forest" that a woman's death was more significant than
her life because it freed a man from provincial limitations, though
"Death in the Woods" itself comes close to this egocentric attitude.
Mrs. Grimes's nobility in suffering exalts her almost to the dimensions
of the mythical suffering servant who can redeem mankind, but this
exaltation is essentially demeaning to the character's humanity. However much the reader is inclined to sympathize with Mrs. Grimes's
stoicism, it is difficult to overlook its inadvertence. Her suffering is that
of a victim, not of an autonomous human being. In other stories about
women who are helpful to men because of their greater generosity and
nobility, Anderson creates more nearly autonomous characters. Alice in
"Like a Queen" arouses in the narrator a "great surge of love" when
she obtains a gift of a thousand dollars to support him in his work,
which she tries to convince him is a source of power. As a young beauty
she had given her lovers something; as an old woman she is still a

nurturer, acting as go-between for rich parents and their alienated children. Aunt Sally of "A Meeting South" is like a mother; she saves their nest-eggs for men who had patronized her gambling and drinking establishments, more than re-paying them for what they had paid her for her services. Significantly, Alice and Aunt Sally, though now old and ugly like Mrs. Grimes, are perceived as beautiful by the narrator, who dissociates them from any preconception of beauty.

Anderson's exaltation of women is distilled in *Perhaps Women*, a small volume he wrote after months of wandering to observe the impact of industrialization at the beginning of the Great Depression. The woodcut Anderson commissioned for the frontispiece of the volume shows a strong woman on an impressive steed leading a small man on a nag; Anderson felt this his friend Lankes caught exactly the meaning expressed in the volume.[17] But the repetition of "Perhaps Women" as the title of three separate sections within the book emphasizes the *perhaps;* Anderson sees women as potentially strong leaders of men but is not sure that they will actually become saviors. In fact, he feared that women, especially as consumers, might contribute to industrial man's castration; and he recognized that women too might stand in need of salvation. In the concluding section, "A Cry in the Night," he suggests that the factory women's calls to men may become only parts of a game, greeted by "an outburst of laughter from many women, ironic laughter." In spite of such doubts, the narrator persists in suggesting that women, because of their biologically-caused tenderness, may be able to bring back to life men deadened by their roles in industrial society.

Other stories in *Death in the Woods* show men's weakness and consequent need for the saving grace of women. Males who view women primarily as sex objects are shown to be foolish, if not vicious. The absurdly jealous narrator of "There She Is—She Is Taking Her Bath" ironically reveals his foolishness while defending his suspicions that his wife is committing adultery; the reader easily perceives the innocence of the wife who is merely taking a bath—symbolically renewing herself. The narrator in "The Lost Novel," shocked by the injustice of a novelist's perception of his wife as an object to be abused and used for literary purposes, perceives the novelist's self-deception. The narrator in "The Return" realizes that casual sex is no longer significant or even possible for him and that his marriage for the sake of professional advancement has been sterile. The difficulty men have in learning such lessons is wryly shown in "The Flood," in which a professor of philos-

Part 3

ophy intent upon finishing his lifework on values succumbs for the second time to marrying a frivolous woman. Although the woman in the story is not admirable, she is a tie to life more important than professional achievement. In these stories the women are more than objects; they have lives of their own and men must accept them as they are. In them Anderson moves away from exaltation of woman as a mythical creature to a realistic view of women sharing men's lives.

Two stories go further to show women as actively initiating involvements that will benefit men. "Why They Got Married" is a playful story in which a married couple tell the story of their courtship to an interested observer; both acknowledge the woman's skill in winning the man's love and his parents' approval, and credit her with their present happiness. As co-narrator as well as wife, the female character is on a par with the man; both relish the story of the wife's manipulation of her in-laws so that "marriage sure seemed like salvation to them" (268). In "Another Wife" a widowed doctor is happy to marry a woman who has, without regard to local mores, pursued him. The doctor realizes that his view of her as surrounded by admirers and therefore too good for him has been a stereotype, and he sees her as a person with her own specific life history, a unique identity. She is admirable, worthy of his love, and able to renew his self-confidence and vitality, but she is not above him on a pedestal. Through his new insight about her the doctor is able to end his own brooding introspection. In this last story the change in attitude toward women is accompanied by a significant change in the male character's view of himself.

In "Brother Death" Anderson went beyond perception of women as sharers of experience with males upon whom the stories focus; he uses a creative and wise female as the central consciousness.[18] No narrator intrudes between the reader and the characters. An assured but unidentified voice paints the scene and describes the characters before focusing on Mary Grey. Unlike the young boy in "Death in the Woods," Mary is already mature at fourteen. At the time the incidents of the story begin ". . . she was both a child and a grown woman. The woman side of her kept popping out at unexpected moments" (273), and she and her younger brother Ted understand life better than their elders. Like the narrator of "Death in the Woods," Mary does perceive the events of her childhood more completely when she grows up, but she never shares his naiveté. So sure is she of the validity of her own perceptions that she guards Ted, who has a heart ailment which they all know will soon kill him, from the overprotectiveness of the rest of

154

the family, and stands up to her mother, who spoils Ted's joy in life with her warnings. Mary and Ted both perceive that the very imminence of his death warrants his risking all for joy; embracing "Brother Death" is the only way for Ted to live. Later Mary realizes that living Ted's way, risking all for joy, is the only way to avoid "the more subtle and terrible death" in life that is the choice of their older brother, who sacrifices his independence to share in the materialism and success of his parents.

In making his mature voice a female, Anderson has blended his perceptions of the artist and of woman. It is not only the male free to roam—often freed by woman's sacrifice—who has "glimpses" that can become stories; woman living her life can have and fight for creative insights. Mary's wisdom coincides with the motto Anderson ascribes to Socrates as the ultimate wisdom, "Not life but the good life," and to Anderson's choice for the inscription on his grave: "Life not death is the great adventure."[19] *Death in the Woods* moves from a mythic view of woman and of the artist's quest to a definition of the good life, of the kind of success Americans need to substitute for the materialism that has blighted the fulfillment of their heroic quest for meaning.

In "Brother Death" Anderson goes beyond the kind of realism in which abstractions reveal meaning,[20] beyond myth which evokes "a connotative style approaching the idiom of poetry."[21] It is significant that Professor Tony Tanner, who found Anderson not only incapable of but opposed to rational analysis, focuses on *Winesburg, Ohio* for his examples.[22] Tanner epitomizes what he considers Anderson's childlike refusal to discriminate among random details in order to find the general behind the particular—his refusal to reason—by citing from *Tar* the child's concept of God as juxtaposed with his sensation of straw tickling his belly and the statement, "There's a lot to think about you can never really think about." "Brother Death" opens with a statement that two oak tree stumps were to two children "objects of wonder." But their wonder is no passive awe, no mystical feeling. Soon after seeing the trees cut, the two children start "wondering" about them, attempting to understand the event, to find reasons for it, to integrate it with their previous knowledge. They suggest that perhaps the stumps had bled, as they imagined the stump of an armless man they had seen must have; they argue over this idea, the girl insisting that a woman could have had an armless stump, so that the trees' experience could be compared with that of a woman just as well as with that of a war hero. Mary's "Why not? I'd like to know why not?" sets the keynote of the entire story in which the tree stumps become a rich symbol. She would like to have verified the hypothesis by touching the tree stumps to see if they were warm, but it is too late for that experiment, since she and her brother ran away "just as the trees fell." In the rest of the story they do not run away from experience; they escape into reality. Their escape is based upon the fact, the sure knowledge that Ted must soon die. The special bond between them because they accept the implication of their knowledge is verified by everyone who knows them; they are perceived as being "too serious" for childhood and they do not fit the romantic stereotype of the innocent, the ignorant child. It is the adults whose "recognition wasn't very definite"; Mary's sense of "something concerning her brother Ted" is not the result of an intuitive glimpse but stems from a reason, her knowledge of his condition and her rational facing up to its implications.

It is significant that Mary is not merely a passive observer of her brother's life and death; she participates in them, initiates action, though Ted too "was imaginative and could think of plenty of risky things to do." The children's actions are connected, purposive. Far from being passive, they create and re-create their own world daily; "being in their own created world, feeling a new security there, they could suddenly look out at the outside world and see, in a new way, what was going on out there in the world that belonged also to others" (282). They do not perceive the world as isolated details; they do not intuit some mythic world behind the perceived details. They create their own reality and use it to perceive the objective reality of others. The two children are reasoning; they are Man Thinking, inducing and deducing. The narration goes on to give the facts about the cutting down of the trees, about the irrationality and tyranny of the father who has ordered them cut, the ineffectiveness of the wife in trying to get him to change his mind, about the submission of the older son Dan after a brief rebellion against his father's will. The stumps can be taken to stand for the sterile lives of the father and son who make material success their goal, a living death far worse than the real death Ted experiences. They can be perceived just as physical facts without either the anthropomorphic meaning the two children suggest or the symbolic meanings of the struggle between father and sons or between the two sons, one literally dead and one metaphorically so. The stumps are a true symbol, open-ended in their meaning; Anderson has resisted the imposition of his own view of the world or that of characters in the story. Each reader must create his own reality. In going beyond the authoritative voice of other narrators in *Death in the Woods,* Anderson anticipates the modern critical view of the need for readers to participate in the creation of a text.

Even a partial analysis of the style of "Brother Death" shows Anderson's change from the paratactic style Professor Tanner considers his hallmark. Compared with the first two hundred words of "Death in the Woods," the opening of "Brother Death" is clearly in a hypostatic style. It contains almost twice as many subordinate clauses, one-third as many simple sentences; the average number of words per sentence is 15.4 compared with 11.8 for "Death in the Woods," a significant difference when linked by the preponderance in the latter of compound predicates joined by the paratactic *and* and in the former of participial embedding. One-line paragraphs found in "Death in the Woods"—there are nine—as portentous statements of simple narrative facts are used in "Brother Death" only for dialog; just a glance at the story establishes the paragraph length as much greater than that of any other story in *Death in the Woods,* the main reason being for continuous narrative. The style is also different in that it lacks the vagueness of "Death in the Woods" about the old woman as "one of those," "such a," one seen by all but unknown by any. "Brother Death" opens with the fact, "There were the two oak stumps" (Anderson added *oak* in revising an earlier version), and within four sentences begins direct discourse between the two children, who exchange ideas, even argue about the stumps.

The continuity of action in the story belies Anderson's fictional view of the writer's technique as the piecing together of isolated incidents, of understanding the general through erratic glimpses into the lives of others. The narrator of "Brother Death" knows the history of the land and the people in the story; he gives us details of the cutting down of the trees and the children's death-defying activities, but neither the trees nor the death of the younger brother becomes the focus of the story. Like "Death in the Woods," the story is beautiful because of its completeness. But it is not a completeness imagined by an observer of someone else's life; it is a completeness experienced by the characters. Their concept that death is the accompaniment, the fulfiller of life has the authority of direct truth, not of myth. The narrator of this story is no naive observer of life; he has gone beyond wonder to understanding.

"Death in the Woods" is probably Anderson's greatest story in the style of his early writing, his greatest achievement in mythopoesis. In

157

it he resolved the dichotomy between the observer and the observed by absorbing the external world into the mind of the observer. In the volume *Death in the Woods* he undercuts the authority of an observer as creator of the observed world by showing the absurdity of egocentricity, by increasing the credibility of other observers (his "feeders"), and finally, in "Brother Death," by allowing the meticulously reported details observed by the narrative voice to constitute the story, a story not about writing a story but about living a life. Perhaps this shift is the effect of Anderson's fully releasing the woman within himself. The old writer of "The Book of the Grotesque" felt that his creative force was a young woman within him, "wearing a coat of mail like a knight"— ready to go out and seek adventure. In "Brother Death" a young woman wise beyond her years creates the meaning of her brother's life; she leads him not because of superior strength and nobility, like the woman of Lankes's woodcut for *Perhaps Women*, but because of sympathetic sharing of his life. In Mary Grey the voice of Sherwood Anderson expresses the wisdom learned by living; "Brother Death" is a fitting climax to *Death in the Woods*.

Notes

1. Sherwood Anderson, *The Modern Writer* (San Francisco, 1925), p. 43. For a summary of critical attitudes toward Anderson, see Walter B. Rideout in *Sixteen American Authors: A Survey of Research and Criticism*, ed. Jackson R. Bryer, 2d ed. (New York, 1973). Michael Geismar was one of the first critics to see the importance of *Death in the Woods;* he saw as the unifying theme of the volume a deepening of Anderson's commitment to "the realm of ordinary human relationships . . . the mysteries of the commonplace" (pp. xix, xx, Introduction to Geismar's edition *Sherwood Anderson: Short Stories* [New York, 1962]). A more recent assessment is that of David D. Anderson, who considers *Death in the Woods* Anderson's "most consistently high-level collection . . . an integrated and mature examination of Anderson's belief that reality must be separated from appearance. . . ." See his "Sherwood Anderson after Twenty Years," pp. 246–56 in *The Achievement of Sherwood Anderson: Essays in Criticism*, ed. Ray Lewis White (Chapel Hill, 1966). See also his "Anderson and Myth," pp. 118–44 in *Sherwood Anderson: Dimensions of His Literary Art, A Collection of Critical Essays*, ed. David D. Anderson (East Lansing, Michigan, 1976). Interestingly, the imputation of form to *Winesburg, Ohio* and its designation as a "novel" instead of a collection of stories is a post-facto critical phenomenon; as John H. Ferres points out, early critics saw no form in it at all (see his Introduction to *Winesburg, Ohio: Text and Critical Edition* [New York, 1966]). William L. Phillips has shown, however, that Anderson conceived the stories

of "The Book of the Grotesque" as complementary parts of a whole, unified by setting and the character George Willard; see his "How Sherwood Anderson Wrote *Winesburg, Ohio*," in *The Achievement of Sherwood Anderson*, pp. 62–85.

2. Letter to Schevill, March 2, 1933, in *Letters of Sherwood Anderson*, ed. Howard Mumford Jones and Walter B. Rideout (Boston, 1953), pp. 277–78. In July, 1933, Anderson reiterated his high opinion of "Brother Death" to Paul Rosenfeld, saying that the story was "written last winter after the rest of the book was in press" (p. 292). That this was only partially true is apparent from a study of a collection of notes and six versions of the story; see Earl Hilton, "The Evolution of Sherwood Anderson's 'Brother Death,'" *Northwest Ohio Quarterly*, XXIV (Summer, 1952), 125–30.

3. Benjamin T. Spencer, "Sherwood Anderson: American Mythopoeist," *American Literature*, XLI (March, 1969), p. 3 (rpt. in *Sherwood Anderson: A Collection of Critical Essays*, ed. Walter B. Rideout [Englewood Cliffs, N.J., 1974], pp. 150–65). Professor Spencer has brilliantly shown that Anderson's prevailing style up to and including "Death in the Woods" involved the process of turning into myth his observations about American life; and that his attempts, like those of Whitman, "to project the democratic beyond concept into myth," contrast with the techniques of "such contemporary naturalists or realists as Dreiser or Lewis."

4. See the letter to Paul Rosenfeld referred to above, *Letters*, p. 292.

5. One of the main foci in *Winesburg, Ohio* is the death of George Willard's mother; in fact, David Stouck considers death "a persistent preoccupation" in Anderson's work, though he does not discuss *Death in the Woods* per se; see his "*Winesburg, Ohio* as a Dance of Death," *American Literature*, XLVIII (January, 1977), 525–42. In the first selection in *The Triumph of the Egg*, the tale the "dumb man" could not tell was that of the relationship of a woman to four men, one of whom "may have been Death; / The waiting eager woman may have been Life." The long story "Unused" from *Horses and Men* is about a young boy's first view of death; he sees the bloated distorted body of a woman who had committed suicide because she could find no man who could accept her proffered love.

6. Introduction, *Perhaps Women* (New York, 1931; rpt. Mamaroneck, N.Y., 1970). For Anderson male impotence was not just a sexual but a total failure, essentially a failure to be an individual. To him women represented not just sex but the sense of life. For more detailed considerations of Anderson's view of women as a civilizing force, his debt to Henry Adams and rejection of Freudian formulas, see Rex Burbank, "The Artist as Prophet," pp. 107–23 of his *Sherwood Anderson* (New York, 1964), and Frederick J. Hoffman, "Anderson and Freud," reprinted in the Ferres edition of *Winesburg, Ohio*, pp. 309–20. In a study limited to Anderson's short stories, William V. Miller links Anderson's life experiences with women to his artistic view of them as idealized but limited to their biological roles. Miller points out as a "new note . . . the objectivity, the irony, and the narrator's [comparative objectivity]" in a

story of 1936 but fails to find the evidence for this new note that I believe exists in *Death in the Woods*. See Miller's "Earth-Mothers, Succubi, and Other Ectoplasmic Spirits: The Women in Sherwood Anderson's Short Stories," *Mid-America I* (Fall, 1973), 64–81.

7. For dates of publication of the stories, see *Sherwood Anderson: A Bibliography*, ed. Eugene P. Sheehy and Kenneth A. Lohf (Los Gatos, Cal., 1960). Of the sixteen stories in the volume, four were published for the first time in *Death in the Woods:* "Like a Queen," "That Sophistication," "The Flood," and "Brother Death," Anderson seems to have used the writing habits described by Phillips for *Winesburg:* he frequently changed single words but seldom whole paragraphs or the original narrative order. The stories with previous magazine publication, except for "Death in the Woods," were almost unaltered for the volume. Anderson's shaping of the volume depended largely on the arrangement of the stories and the final writing of "Brother Death." None of the stories can be specifically linked to incidents which must have deeply influenced his ideas about women and about death, such as the death by suicide of his second wife, Tennessee Mitchell, in 1929, her body discovered in her apartment several days afterwards; and the lonely life and death (1927) of his youngest brother Earl who never found a woman to rescue him. But Anderson does explicitly credit his fourth wife, Eleanor Copenhaver, whom he married shortly after *Death in the Woods* was published and with whom he was traveling when he put the volume together, with "awakening in me again the desire to participate in life at any cost." See his letter to Paul Rosenfeld, *Letters*, p. 292.

8. See Michael Faning, *France and Sherwood Anderson: Paris Notebook, 1921* (Baton Rouge, La., 1976), pp. 62–65, for what Fanning thinks may be Anderson's first attempt at "Death in the Woods." "Father Abraham: A Lincoln Fragment" appeared in *The Sherwood Anderson Reader*, ed. Paul Rosenfeld (Boston, 1947), pp. 530–602; Rosenfeld thinks the piece may have been alluded to in a letter of 1925, and there is a reference to "working on Lincoln" in a letter of April [1924] to Jerome and Lucille Blum (see *Sherwood Anderson: Centennial Studies*, ed. Hilbert H. Campbell and Charles E. Modlin [Troy, N.Y., 1976], p. 9). "A Death in the Forest" was edited by William V. Miller as an appendix to *Tar: A Midwest Childhood*, ed. Ray Lewis White (Cleveland, 1969). The first and only edition of *Death in the Woods* was published by Horace Liveright in New York; the volume appeared on April 8, 1933, in the depth of the depression, and Liveright went out of business a month later. This fact may account for the scarcity of reviews elicited by the volume—there were only seven—and the scarcity of subsequent attention, though preoccupation with *Winesburg, Ohio* as Anderson's most important if not only significant work was also a cause of neglect of the volume. All quotations from the story are from the 1933 final version in *Death in the Woods* except when specific reference is made to one of the earlier versions.

9. *A Story Teller's Story* (New York, 1924), pp. 122, 121.

10. *Memoirs*, ed. Ray Lewis White (Chapel Hill, N.C., 1969), pp. 425–26. In the first edition of the *Memoirs* (New York, 1942), the incident appears as part of Book IV, The Literary Life, entitled "Old Mary, the Dogs, and Theda Bara," pp. 306–12. The specificity of the title makes the incident seem biographically credible; if it occurred, it would have had to be between 1920–22, according to Professor Walter Rideout, who kindly gave me this information in a letter dated February 3, 1978.

11. Anderson had long been fascinated by Lincoln and identified himself with him. See David D. Anderson, "Sherwood Anderson's Use of the Lincoln Theme," *Lincoln Herald*, LXIV (Spring 1961), 28–32. Lincoln's mysticism Sherwood Anderson associates with his "being alone in the forest on still summer afternoons" ("A Lincoln Fragment," p. 567). The fact that Anderson added a comment about the cruelty encountered by bound children to the 1933 version of "Death in the Woods" indicates that the Lincoln story may have been in his thoughts at the time, though his own fictionalization of his mother's life as a bound girl may have been uppermost in his mind; see *A Story Teller's Story*, p. 7.

12. The town as Anderson's mythopoetic creation is discussed by Professor Spencer in part three of the article cited in n. 3 above.

13. Many critics have seen the focus on the artist as the center of the story; see Jon S. Lawry, "'Death in the Woods' and the Artist's Self in Sherwood Anderson," *PMLA*, LXXIV (1959), 306–11; and Sister Mary Joslyn, "Some Artistic Dimensions of Sherwood Anderson's 'Death in the Woods,'" *Studies in Short Fiction*, IV (Spring 1967), 252–59. Professor Mary Rohrberger has explored the story as the narrator's retrieval of myth from the subconscious suggesting that underlying the image of Mrs. Grimes are those of the goddesses worshiped in the Eleusinian mysteries, Demeter, Proserpine, and Hecate; see her "The Man, the Boy, and the Myth: Sherwood Anderson's 'Death in the Woods,'" *Midcontinent American Studies Journal*, III (Fall 1962), 48–54.

14. See *Memoirs*, ed. White, pp. 376–81, for Anderson's account of his friend George Daugherty as a "feeder."

15. Anderson's objectivity in these stories was apparently deliberate; in a letter dated October 29, 1929, he wrote to friends that "These Mountaineers" was "just a description of some people, all my own feeling left out. I think it was good" (*Letters*, p. 196). In the Introduction to *No Swank* (c. 1934; rpt. Mamaroneck, N.Y., 1970), Anderson comments that his "glimpses" are not "a complete or even a just picture" of his friends.

16. Pp. 435–37.

17. See Welford D. Taylor, "Two Dismounted Men: Sherwood Anderson and J. J. Lankes," in *Sherwood Anderson: Centennial Studies*, pp. 224–34. See also Sherwood Anderson, "Mr. J. J. Lankes and His Woodcuts," *No Swank*, pp. 25–29.

18. In his article on "Brother Death" cited in n. 2 above, Earl Hilton

points out that the use of Mary as central consciousness occurs in Anderson's notes as well as in all six versions of the story; and that one of the main effects of Anderson's changes is to give more of the story through Mary. Hilton's view that the evolving central theme is "success" as a living death is borne out by Anderson's comment in a letter written in the spring of 1933 (to Roger Sergel; quoted by William V. Miller, "In Defense of Mountaineers: Sherwood Anderson's Hill Stories," *Ball State University Forum*, XV [Spring 1974], p. 57). In the context of *Death in the Woods*, the major theme seems to be a definition of life lived fully, the life lived *with* "Brother Death."

19. *Memoirs*, pp. 558–60.

20. Walter B. Rideout ("The Simplicity of *Winesburg, Ohio*," reprinted in Ferres's edition, pp. 287–300) considers Anderson's realism in the early work as "a means to something else, not an end in itself" as it was for more traditional writers such as Sinclair Lewis; the result was that Anderson produced a "highly abstract kind of reality," one effect of which was to "depreciate the values of surfaces."

21. Spencer, p. 3.

22. Professor Tanner's view of Anderson as expressing in appropriately static paratactical style his passively glimpsed fragments of life is found in "Sherwood Anderson's Little Things," pp. 205–27 in *The Reign of Wonder: Naivety and Reality in American Literature* (New York, 1965).

Appendix

Excerpts from "*Winesburg* and Clyde, Fictional/Real Places" *by* Thaddeus B. Hurd

Thaddeus Hurd's father was Herman Hurd (1877–1963), a lifelong resident of Clyde, Ohio. He ran a grocery store on Main Street, as had his father and grandfather before him. Sherwood Anderson and Herman Hurd were neighbors and of the same age. They became close friends in boyhood, a friendship that lasted through life. Sherwood Anderson died in 1941; Herman Hurd in 1963. In Herman Hurd's later years, he often talked with Thaddeus about his boyhood in Clyde and his association with Sherwood.

Thaddeus was born in Clyde in 1903 and graduated from Clyde High School in 1920. He knew the same social environment, the same buildings, the same streets and places his father and Sherwood Anderson had known. From his own recollections, and from conversations with his father, he has been able to identify many fictional places in Winesburg, Ohio *which are based on real Clyde places. Thaddeus died in 1989.*

Sherwood Anderson was born in Camden, Ohio, west of Dayton, in 1876. He moved to Clyde, Ohio, in 1884, at the age of 7, and lived there until age 22.

There is a close relation between the fictional Winesburg, Ohio, and the real town of Clyde, Ohio, where Anderson grew up. Many of the fictional places in the book bear a close resemblance to real places in Clyde. This study identifies many of them.

Winesburg, Ohio is a collection of 25 interrelated short stories. They concern lives of people in a large rural village in northern Ohio in the

"*Winesburg* and Clyde, Fictional/Real Places," by Thaddeus B. Hurd appears by permission of the Clyde Heritage League, Inc. This is its first publication. These excerpts were edited and revised by Robert Allen Papinchak.

late 1800s. In the twenty-first story, "The Untold Lie," Anderson writes: "People from the part of Northern Ohio in which Winesburg lies will remember Windpeter by his unusual and tragic death" (*CW*, 3:245). He thus fixes the location of the fictional village. In the fourteenth story, "The Teacher," Anderson writes: "By ten o'clock all but four of the eighteen hundred citizens of the town were in bed" (*CW*, 3:186). He thus fixes the town's size, similar to the real Clyde. Clyde, like Winesburg, is in north central Ohio. It stands in eastern Sandusky County, nine miles south of Sandusky Bay on Lake Erie. Although now a small city (5,489 in the 1980 census) its population in 1890 was 2,327. In both location and size, the fictional Winesburg closely matches the real Clyde.

The list which follows shows real places in Clyde, Ohio, which Anderson had in mind when he created their fictional counterparts.

Groups 1–3 and 7 of the list tabulate the following information: place identification (real street and number or real name) followed by its present real name (now); its former real name, 1880 or after (was); and its fictional name as used in *Winesburg, Ohio* (book), followed by the title of the short story in which it appears, and corresponding page number. For some entries, a passage from the book is quoted if it involves a character or place name.

In Groups 4–5, real place names are listed as *now;* in group 6, well-known real American place names, by *book*. Group 8 lists only the fictional name following *book*.

This is a listing of major landmarks, not a complete index. Less significant places at some distance from Clyde are listed in Group 6. Fictional places which I cannot tie firmly to real Clyde places are listed in Group 8. Though I can approximate many of them, the correlation has been omitted from this study because of imprecision.

The reference, "See MAP," is to the map of Clyde, Ohio, which appears at the end of this appendix.

In this study, identification of fictional *Winesburg* places with real Clyde places are grouped as follows:

	numbers	total	sum
Group 1: Clyde Buildings Extant 1988	B1–B23	23	
Group 2: Clyde Outdoor Places Extant 1988	O11–O7	7	30

Group 3: Clyde Streets & Alleys Extant 1988	S1–S9	9	39
Group 4: Clyde Nearby Places Extant 1988	N1–N9	9	48
Group 5: Major Distant Places	D1–D8	8	56
Group 6: Other Distant Places	X1–X13	13	69
Group 7: Clyde Places Non-Extant 1988	G1–G17	17	86
Group 8: Clyde Places Uncertain	U1–U24	24	110

The stories in *Winesburg, Ohio*, all take place in the fictional village of Winesburg and surrounding rural areas in Ohio in the mid-Victorian years of the 1880s. The 25 stories and key characters in each are:

1. "The Book of the Grotesque"
2. "Hands" [Wing Biddlebaum]
3. "Paper Pills" [Dr. Reefy]
4. "Mother" [Elizabeth Willard]
5. "The Philosopher" [Dr. Parsifal]
6. "Nobody Knows" [Louise Trunnion]
7. "Godliness I" [Jesse Bentley]
8. "Godliness II" [Jesse Bentley]
9. "Godliness III" [Louise Bentley]
10. "Godliness IV" [David Hardy]
11. "A Man of Ideas" [Joe Welling]
12. "Adventure" [Alice Hindman]
13. "Respectability" [Wash Williams]
14. "The Thinker" [Seth Richmond]
15. "Tandy" [Tandy Hard]
16. "The Strength of God" [Rev. Hartman]
17. "The Teacher" [Kate Swift]
18. "Loneliness" [Enoch Robinson]
19. "An Awakening" [Belle Turner]
20. "Queer" [Elmer Cowley]
21. "The Untold Lie" [Ray Pearson]
22. "Drink" [Tom Foster]
23. "Death" [Elizabeth Willard]
24. "Sophistication" [Helen White]
25. "Departure" [George Willard]

The *Winesburg* stories take place in the 1880s when the railroads were a major element in American life. The action of the stories centers on the railroad passenger depot and the New Willard House hotel which faces it across the tracks. The hotel, actually the Empire House, was demolished in 1940, the depot in 1960. The railroad tracks came up in 1980. Of the story action center, only the brick depot platform remains.

Group 1: Clyde Buildings Extant 1988

B1. 100 North Main Street
  now: Wilson's men's clothing store, side door on Buckeye Street
  was: post office
  book: post office. "The Teacher" (157); "Queer" (197); "Departure" (246, 247)
  247. "He [George Willard] thought of little things—Turk Smollets wheeling boards through the main street of his town in the morning, a tall woman, beautifully gowned, who had once stayed overnight at his father's hotel, Butch Wheeler, the lamplighter of Winesburg, hurrying through the streets on a summer evening and holding a torch in his hand, Helen White standing by a window in the Winesburg post office and putting a stamp on an envelope."

B2. 101 North Main Street
  now: DTE Photographic. Second floor vacant.
  was: Jackson Hardware Store. Clyde Enterprise newspaper office of second floor.
  book: Winesburg Eagle newspaper office. "Hands" (27); "Mother" (44); "The Philosopher" (49, 50); "Nobody Knows" (58, 59, 60); "A Man of Ideas" (106, 107); "Adventure" (112); "The Strength of God" (153, 155); "The Teacher" (163, 164); "Queer" (190); "Drink" (218)
  58. "Looking cautiously about, George Willard arose from his desk in the office of the Winesburg Eagle and went hurriedly out at the back door."

B3. 103 North Main Street
  now: Vacant, recently a video parlor, previously a pet shop.
  was: Louis Hock's saloon
  book: Tom Willy's saloon. "The Philosopher" (49); "Drink" (217)
  49. "In the late afternoon Will Henderson, owner and editor of the Eagle, went over to Tom Willy's saloon. Along the alleyway he went

and slipping in at the back door of the saloon began drinking a drink made of a combination of sloe gin and soda water."

B4. 105 North Main Street
  now: Town Tavern bar
  was: Miller's tailor shop
  book: Sinning's Hardware Store. "Mother" (41); "A Man of Ideas" (105). The real Sinning's Hardware Store was at 122 S. Main Street, now Clyde Hardware.

B5. 107 North Main Street
  now: Dewey Law Office
  was: H. H. Rabe's Drug Store
  book: Sylvester West's drug store. "Mother" (41); "Nobody Knows" (61); "A Man of Ideas" (104)
  41. "For a long time there was a feud between the banker and a grey cat that belonged to Sylvester West, the druggist."

B6. 109 North Main Street
  now: Danish Pastry Shop
  was: C. D. Arnold's Bakery
  book: Abner Groff's Bakery. "Mother" (41); "The Thinker" (133)
  41. "By turning their [Elizabeth Willard and son George] heads they could see through another window, along an alleyway that ran behind the Main Street stores and into the back door of Abner Groff's bakery."

B7. 101 South Main Street
  now: Part of Corner Pharmacy, had been Stanley Widner's Corner Store
  was: S. R. Hartzel's cigar store
  book: Wacker's Cigar Store. "The Thinker" (136); "Drink" (216)

B8. 103 South Main Street
  now: Corner Pharmacy
  was: John Surbeck's saloon
  book: Ed Griffith's saloon. "Nobody Knows" (58); "Respectability" (122, 123); "The Teacher" (157); "An Awakening" (180)

B9. 106 South Main Street—first floor
  now: Board of Education Office, north half
  was: People's Banking Company, then Clyde Savings Bank
  book: Winesburg Savings Bank. "Godliness II" (78)

B10. 108 South Main Street
  now: Board of Education Office, south half
  was: First National Bank, then Clyde Savings Bank
  book: Winesburg National Bank. "The Strength of God" (149); "An
Awakening" (179)

B11. 110 South Main Street—third floor over present Cindy's dress
shop
  now: vacant; stage and proscenium remain
  was: Terry's Hall, Terry's Opera House
  book: Opera House. "Sophistication" (241)
  241. "In Winesburg the crowded day had run itself out into the long
night of late fall . . . In the Opera House a crowd had gathered to see
a show and further down Main Street the fiddlers, their instruments
tuned, sweated and worked to keep the feet of youth flying over a
dance floor."

B12. 112–112 South Main Street—second and third floors
  now: vacant
  was: Richards Block
  book: Heffner Block. "Paper Pills" (35); "Loneliness" (174, 175);
"Death" (220). The real Heffner Block was 217–225 North Main
Street, demolished 1966, its namestone now in Clyde Museum.

B13. 112 South Main Street—first floor
  now: Gift Box, north half
  was: George S. Richards & Co. Dry Goods Store, then Herrick &
Heiteshu Men's Clothing Store, then Winfield Adare's Men's Clothing
Store
  book: Paris Dry Goods Store. "Paper Pills" (35); "Death" (220);
Herrick's Clothing Store. "Death" (220)

B14. 112 South Main Street—second floor
  now: vacant
  was: office of Dr. Stephen T. Finch, then Dr. A. R. Lord
  book: Dr. Reefy's Office. "Paper Pills" (35); "Death" (221); "Sophistication" (233)
  220. "The stairway leading up to Dr. Reefy's office, in the Heffner
Block above the Paris Dry Goods Store, was but dimly lighted."

B15. 114 South Main Street—first floor
  now: Gift Box, south half

was: Alfred Pawsey's shoe store
book: Win Pawsey's shoe store. "A Man of Ideas" (108)

B16. 124 South Main Street
now: LaMar Wott Real Estate
was: Hurd's Grocery
book: Hern's Grocery. "A Man of Ideas" (105); "Queer" (198);
"Drink" (214); "Sophistication" (237)
214. "In Hern's Grocery they would be roasting coffee on Friday
afternoon, preparatory to the Saturday rush of trade, and the rich odor
invaded lower Main Street."

B17. 131 South Main Street
now: Heritage Hall, community and senior center
was: Clyde Village Hall, built 1882
book: Town Hall. "The Thinker" (136)

B18. 137 South Main Street
now: Pine Rose Inn (John and Bonnie Pickett)
was: Dr. E.D. Soper residence and office
book: Kate Swift house. "The Strength of God" (148, 149); "The
Teacher" (158, 160)

B19. 552 South Main Street
now: Robert Dugger residence
was: Michael Kiefer house (brick)
book: Richmond House (stone). "The Thinker" (128, 139); "The
Strength of God" (150)

B20. 136 West Buckeye Street
now: Harkness Davenport residence
was: Emmons D. Harkness house
book: Banker White's new stone house, "Hands" (29); Banker
White's brick house, "The Thinker" (128, 137); Banker White's new
brick barn, "Drink" (212)

B21. 160 West Buckeye Street
now: Clyde Masonic Temple
was: First United Methodist Church
book: Methodist Church. "Adventure" (117)

B22. 117 East Forest Street
now: apartments, owned by Lois S. Hall

was: Rader House (brick)
book: Tom Hardy's brick house. "Godliness II" (74, 78); "Godliness III" (87)

B23. 113 West Forest Street
  now: First United Presbyterian Church
  was: Presbyterian Church
  book: Presbyterian Church. "The Strength of God" (147, 148);
"The Teacher" (160)

Group 2: Clyde Outdoor Places Extant 1988

O1. Depot Platform
  now: Abandoned brick walkway, runs west from North Main Street just north of Railroad Street, and a section which runs southwest along West Maple Street
  was: Depot platform
  book: Station Platform. "Mother" (42); "A Man of Ideas" (109); "Respectability" (122); "The Thinker" (136); "Death" (229); "Departure" (245)
    109. "It was seven-thirty and fast growing dark when Joe Welling came along the station platform toward the New Willard House. In his arms he held a bunch of weeds and grasses."

O2. Fairgrounds (See MAP)
  now: East half is grounds of South Main Street Elementary School; west half is Marlene Drive housing development
  was: Clyde fairgrounds with ½ mile track
  book: Fairgrounds. "A Man of Ideas" (108); "The Thinker" (128, 140); "The Teacher" (163); "Loneliness" (174); "An Awakening" (187); "Sophistication" (233, 239, 240, 242)
    239. "The Fair Grounds stands on top of a low hill rising out of the valley of Wine Creek and from the grand-stand one can see at night, over a cornfield, the lights of the town reflected against the sky."

O3. Waterworks Pond (See MAP)
  now: Waterworks Pond
  was: Waterworks Pond
  book: Waterworks Pond. "A Man of Ideas" (108); "The Strength of God" (151); "The Teacher" (157, 161); "An Awakening" (187); "Sophistication" (240)
    187. "When George [Willard and Belle Carpenter] had finished talk-

ing they turned down a side street and went across a bridge into a path that ran up the side of a hill. The hill began at Waterworks Pond and climbed upwards to the Winesburg Fair Grounds."

O4. Waterworks Hill (See O3)
   now: East Hill of Waterworks Pond and Raccoon Creek Valley
   was: same
   book: Waterworks Hill. "Sophistication" (240, 242)

O5. Raccoon Creek (See MAP)
   now: Raccoon Creek, locally "Coon Crick," large creek flowing north through west part of Clyde. Feeds Waterworks Pond.
   was: Raccoon Creek
   book: Wine Creek. "Godliness I" (73); "Godliness II" (79, 84); "A Man of Ideas" (104, 105); "Adventure" (113, 114); "The Teacher" (157); "Sophistication" (239–40)
   157. "Past the pond and along a path that followed Wine Creek he [George Willard] went until he came to a grove of beech trees." See also O2.

O6. Piety Hill (See MAP)
   now: Race Street area
   was: Piety Hill area, level land west of Waterworks Pond and Raccoon Creek Valley, not a hill
   book: Gospel Hill. "The Strength of God" (151); "The Teacher" (161)
   151. "One evening when they [Rev. and Mrs. Curtis Hartman] drove out together he turned the horse out of Buckeye Street and in the darkness of Gospel Hill, above Waterworks Pond, he put his arm around Sarah's waist."

O7. Cemetery (See MAP)
   now: McPherson Cemetery, the Clyde city cemetery
   was: McPherson Cemetery
   book: Winesburg Cemetery. "A Man of Ideas" (108)

Group 3: Clyde Streets & Alleys Extant 1988

S1. Main Street (See MAP)
   now: Main Street, North and South, divides at Buckeye Street
   was: Main Street
   book: Main Street. "Hands" (28); "Mother" (41, 42, 45, 47); "The

Philosopher" (55, 56); "Nobody Knows" (61); "Godliness III" (90); "A Man of Ideas" (103); "Respectability" (123); "The Thinker" (132, 136, 137); "The Strength of God" (147, 150, 153); "The Teacher" (157, 159, 163, 164); "An Awakening" (182); "Drink" (213, 216); "Death" (222, 228, 230); "Sophistication" (233, 237, 241); "Departure" (245)

61. "When George Willard got back to Main Street it was past ten o'clock and had begun to rain. Three times he walked up and down the length of Main Street."

S2. Buckeye Street, East (See MAP)
   now: East Buckeye Street
   was: East Buckeye Street
   book: Maumee Street. "Loneliness" (174); "Queer" (190, 191)

174. "Enoch Robinson and George Willard met beneath a wooden awning that extended out over the sidewalk before Voight's wagon shop on Maumee Street, just off the main street of Winesburg." (See also S8)

S3. Buckeye Street, West (See MAP)
   now: West Buckeye Street
   was: West Buckeye Street
   book: Buckeye Street. "The Thinker" (136); "The Strength of God" (147, 151); "An Awakening" (179)

S4. Duane Street (See MAP)
   now: Duane Street
   was: Duane Street
   book: Duane Street. "Drink" (213, 216)

S5. Forest Street, East (See MAP)
   now: East Forest Street
   was: East Forest Street
   book: Elm Street. "Godliness II" (74, 78); "Godliness III" (87)

S6. Alley #1 (See MAP, L-shaped, off Railroad Street)
   now: No name
   was: No name
   book: alleyway (behind Abner Groff's Bakery, Sylvester West's Drug Store, Sinning's Hardware Store, Willy's saloon, Eagle office). "Mother" (41); "The Philosopher" (49); "Nobody Knows" (58, 59); "The Thinker" (133); "The Teacher" (159); "Drink" (218).

S7. Alley #2 (See MAP; "Alley" west of 4, Main Street)
  now: Harkness Drive
  was: No name
  book: alleyway. "Nobody Knows" (58); "The Teacher" (159)

S8. Alley #3 (See MAP; "Alley" east of 4, Main Street)
  now: Terry Drive
  was: No name
  book: alleyway. "The Teacher" (159); "Queer" (190)
  190. "Beside the [Cowley & Son's] store (Maumee St.) an alleyway ran behind the Main Street stores and all day drays and delivery wagons, intent on bringing in and taking out goods, passed up and down. The store itself was indescribable." See also G15.

S9. McPherson Highway (See MAP)
  now: McPherson Highway, U.S. 20
  was: The Maumee & Western Reserve Turnpike, "The Pike"
  book: Trunion Pike. "A Man of Ideas" (104, 108); "Tandy" (143); "The Teacher" (161); "Loneliness" (167); "Drink" (210); "Death" (227); "Sophistication" (233); "Departure" (244)
  210. "His [Tom Foster] grandmother had been raised on a farm near the town and as a young girl had gone to school there when Winesburg was a village of twelve or fifteen houses clustered about a general store on the Trunion Pike."

Group 4: Clyde Nearby Places Extant 1988

N1.
  now: The Frank Farver Farm, 3 miles south of Clyde on Route 101, on right as it turns west at Kuny's Corners
  was: The William E. Lay farm
  book: The Bentley Farm. "Godliness I" (63, 64); "Godliness II" (74, 76, 78, 79)

N2.
  now: Green Springs, Ohio, small village 6 miles southwest of Clyde
  was: Green Springs, Ohio
  book: Unionville. "The Untold Lie" (202)

N3.
  now: Fremont, Ohio, 8 miles east of Clyde on McPherson Highway, U.S. 20; county seat of Sandusky County which includes Clyde

was: Fremont, Ohio
book: the county seat. "Godliness III" (96); "The Thinker" (130); "An Awakening" (182)

N4.
now: Sandusky, Ohio, 18 miles northeast of Clyde on Sandusky Bay of Lake Erie
was: Sandusky, Ohio
book: Sandusky on Lake Erie. "An Awakening" (180, 181)

N5.
now: Cedar Point, a recreational theme park on Cedar Point peninsula which encloses the east part of Sandusky Bay, separating it from Lake Erie
was: Cedar Point, a summer resort amusement park
book: Cedar Point. "An Awakening" (181)

N6.
now: Sandusky Bay, 8 miles due north of Clyde, at mouth of the Sandusky River
was: Sandusky Bay
book: Sandusky Bay. "Departure" (246)

N7.
now: Lake Erie, 15 miles due north of Clyde, north of the Marblehead Peninsula which encloses the north side of Sandusky Bay
was: Lake Erie
book: Lake Erie. "The Thinker" (129); "An Awakening" (180, 182); "Drink" (217); "Departure" (245)
182.   "For days the weather had been bitter cold with a high wind blowing down on the town from Lake Erie, eighteen miles to the north, but on that night the wind had died away and a new moon made the night unusually lovely."

N8.
now: Seneca County, 3 miles due south of Clyde. Raccoon Creek rises here.
was: Seneca County
book: Medina County. "A Man of Ideas" (105, 107). The real Medina County is two counties southeast of Clyde.

N9.

now: Tiffin, Ohio, a county seat of Seneca County, 17 miles south-west of Clyde

was: Tiffin, Ohio

book: Tiffin, Ohio. "A Man of Ideas" (104)

Group 5: Major Distant Places

A number of major distant places (real cities) are mentioned in the collection of stories. In Ohio, these cities are Toledo ("The Thinker," 129); Cleveland ("Godliness I," 68; "Godliness IV," 98; "Adventure," 113, 114; "The Thinker," 132, 134; "Tandy," 143, 146; "The Strength of God," 147; "The Teacher," 158; "Queer," 199; "Sophistication," 235; "Departure," 245); Columbus ("Respectability," 125; "The Thinker," 138); Dayton ("The Philosopher," 52, 54; "Respectability," 123, 125, 126); and Cincinnati ("Drink," 210, 211, 212, 215, 217). Other cities named are Chicago, Illinois ("The Philosopher," 51; "Adventure," 114; "Departure," 245) and New York, New York ("The Strength of God," 149; "Loneliness," 167, 168, 170, 171, 172; "Drink," 210). The state of Pennsylvania is noted in "Hands," 31, 32, 33.

Group 6: Other Distant Places

Other distant places names are Illinois ("The Philosopher," 51); Iowa ("The Philosopher," 51); The State University ("The Thinker," 138); Muncie, Indiana ("The Strength of God," 149); Paris ("Loneliness," 167); Washington Square ("Loneliness," 167); Philadelphia ("Loneliness," 172); Brooklyn ("Loneliness," 172); Connecticut ("Loneliness," 172); Portland, Oregon ("The Untold Lie," 207); Kansas ("Drink," 210); Canada ("Drink," 210); and Covington, Kentucky ("Drink," 210).

Group 7: Clyde Places Non-Extant 1988

G1. Empire House Hotel (See MAP-3)

Demolished 1940. Stood north of Lake Shore tracks, west of North Main Street and opposite depot

now: West part of Industrial Savings & Loan office parking lot

book: New Willard House. "Hands" (27); "Mother" (42, 44, 47);

"Nobody Knows" (61); "A Man of Ideas" (107, 109); "Respectability"
(122); "The Thinker" (132); "Tandy" (143, 144); "The Teacher"
(158); "Queer" (200); "Death" (228); "Departure" (245)
    27. "With George Willard, son of Tom Willard, proprietor of the
New Willard House, he [Wing Biddlebaum] had formed something
like a friendship."

G2. board sidewalk
    obsolete now in Clyde
    now: replaced by brick, flagstone, or concrete
    was: of thick boards crosswise on wood stringers
    book: board sidewalk. "Mother" (42); "Tandy" (144); "An Awak-
ening" (183)
    144. "Tom Hard sat in a chair before the New Willard House with
his daughter, then a child of five, on his knees. Beside him on the
board sidewalk sat young George Willard."

G3. railroad (See MAP)
    Two of the three railroads in Clyde are now defunct, their rails hav-
ing been removed 1979–1980
    now: right-of-way grass covered, encroached on by adjacent
landowners
    was: Lake Shore & Michigan Southern Railroad and the Big Four
Railroad (Cleveland, Cincinnati, Chicago, & St. Louis). A third railroad, the Wheeling & Lake Erie, built 1882, still operating, does not
appear in the *Winesburg* stories.
    book: railroad. "Tandy" (144); "Departure" (245)
    144. "It was late evening and darkness lay over the town and over
the railroad that ran along the foot of a little incline before the hotel."

G4. Big Four (See MAP)
    A railroad from Sandusky city on Lake Erie to Dayton and Cincin-
nati on the Ohio River
    now: defunct; see G3
    was: The Cleveland, Cincinnati, Chicago & St. Louis Railroad,
nicknamed the Big Four
    book: Big Four. "The Philosopher" (52)

G5. Railroad Passenger Depot (See MAP-2)
    Demolished 1960. Along Railroad Street, west of North Main Street
    now: Eagles Lodge parking lot along Railroad Street
    was: Passenger depot of two railroads, the Lake Shore & Michigan

Southern and the Big Four
  book: railroad station, depot. "The Thinker" (134); "Queer" (197, 200)

G6. depot area
  Became parking lot in 1960
  now: Eagles Lodge parking lot, on railroad property leased by city
  was: depot grounds
  book: station yard. "Mother" (42); "Respectability" (121); "The Thinker" (135)
      Station lawn. "Respectability" (123); "The Thinker" (136)

G7. telegraph office
  In depot, destroyed 1960
  now: See G5
  was: In depot's northwest corner, at angle of building's L
  book: telegraph office. "Respectability" (122)

G8. express office
  In depot, destroyed 1960
  now: See G5
  was: At east end of depot's Lake Shore wing
  book: express office. "Mother" (42)
  42. "In the station yard, after the evening train had gone, there was a heavy silence. Perhaps Skinner Leason, the express agent, moved a truck the length of the station platform. On Main Street sounded a man's voice, laughing. The door of the express office banged."

G9. small frame building
  Demolished 1965–1966
  now: Parking lot, south part, Industrial Savings & Loan office
  was: Small wood building just east of brick part of Empire House. Sat north side of railroad tracks. Used as a barber shop.
  book: small frame building. "Mother" (41)
  41. "They [George Willard and his mother, Elizabeth] sat by a window that looked over the roof of a small frame building into Main Street."

G10. 106 Railroad Street
  Demolished ca. 1958
  now: Eagles Lodge, east addition
  was: Mrs. Henry Baker's bakery and restaurant, later William M.

Smila's bakery
    book: Biff Carter's lunch room. "The Philosopher" (51); "The Thinker" (134).
    51. "He [Dr. Parcival] slept in the office that was unspeakably dirty and dines at Biff Carter's lunch room in a small frame building opposite the railroad station."

G11. 114 Railroad Street
    Demolished about 1940
    now: City parking lot, west of Eagles Lodge
    was: Harvey & Whitaker livery stable
    book: Wesley Moyer's livery barn. "Adventure" (113); "Loneliness" (173); "An Awakening" (181); "Death" (226); "Sophistication" (238)
    238. "He [George Willard] came to Wesley Moyer's livery barn and stopped in the shadows to listen to a group of men who talked of a race Wesley's stallion, Tony Tip, had won at the Fair during the afternoon."

G12. 111 North Main Street
    Wood building moved from here to 514 Duane Street in 1908
    now: Arrow Cafe bar (brick)
    was: Henry ("Penny") Weissert's notions store (wood)
    book: Winney's Dry Goods Store. "Nobody Knows" (61); "Adventure" (112, 114, 115)
    61. "On the sidewalk at the side of Winney's Dry Goods Store where there was a high board fence covered with circus pictures, he [George Willard] stopped . . ."

G13. 210 North Main Street
    Demolished 1977 to build Clyde Municipal Building
    now: North part of Clyde Municipal Building site
    was: C.J. Miller's Billiard & Pool Room, later Town Tavern Bar
    book: Ranson Surbeck's pool room. "An Awakening" (182)

G14. 106 East Buckeye Street
    Demolished 1981
    now: Terry Drive parking lot
    was: B. F. Rogers cobbler shop, later Mann & Shaw Coal & Feed Store
    book: Cowley & Son's store. "Queer" (190, 199); see S8 and G15.

G15. 119 East Buckeye Street
Demolished 1975
now: Union Bank & Savings Company drive-in office
was: George Adams' carriage shop
book: Voight's Wagon Shop. "Loneliness" (174); "Queer" (190)
The real Vogt Bros. wagon shop was at 111 Duane Street
190. "Cowley & Son's store did not face the main street of Winesburg. The front was on Maumee Street and beyond it was Voight's wagon shop and a shed for the sheltering of farmers' horses."

G16. 133 West Buckeye Street
Demolished 1938 to build post office
now: West half of post office site
was: Dr. J. F. Whittemore office and residence, then later Dr. James E. Ott office and residence
book: Dr. Welling's house. "The Thinker" (136)

G17. 521 Vine Street
Demolished 1937 to build new high school, now Junior High School
now: Clyde Junior High School site
was: Clyde public schoolhouse (Union School) built 1870
book: Winesburg High School, high school building. "Godliness IV" (87); "Death" (229)

Group 8: Clyde Places Uncertain

These are Winesburg fictional places which are not firmly identified with real Clyde places. I can approximately tie some of these to a real Clyde place or otherwise make a Clyde connection but not as firmly as in the preceding groups.
U1. Myerbaum's Notion Store; "Nobody Knows" (58)
U2. Williams' barn; "Nobody Knows" (59)
U3. Jake Trunion house; "Nobody Knows" (59)
U4. bridge over a tiny stream; "Nobody Knows" (61)
U5. store for sale of buggies and wagons; "Godliness III" (87)
U6. Daughtery's feed store; "A Man of Ideas" (106)
U7. brick house opposite the cemetery; "A Man of Ideas" (108)
U8. cider mill on Trunion Pike; "A Man of Ideas" (108)
U9. Alice Hindman's mother's house; "Adventure" (118)

Appendix

U10. Kate McHugh's millinery shop; "Respectability" (123); "An Awakening" (179)

U11. barrel stave factory; "The Thinker" (139)

U12. Ned Winters' barn; "The Teacher" (161)

U13. Sucker Road; "The Teacher" (161)

U14. Ike Smead's chicken farm; "The Teacher" (161)

U15. Comstock's mill; "Loneliness" (169)

U16. house of prostitution; "An Awakening" (182)

U17. Cal Prouse's barber shop; "An Awakening" (183)

U18. picket fence near a street lamp; "An Awakening" (183)

U19. day laborer's section of town; "An Awakening" (184)

U20. Belle Carpenter's house; "An Awakening" (179, 186)

U21. The Wills Farm; "The Untold Lie" (202)

U22. sawmill; "The Untold Lie" (202)

U23. lane along the creek; "The Untold Lie" (206)

U24. tumbled down house by the creek; "The Untold Lie" (209)

A Map of Clyde, Ohio

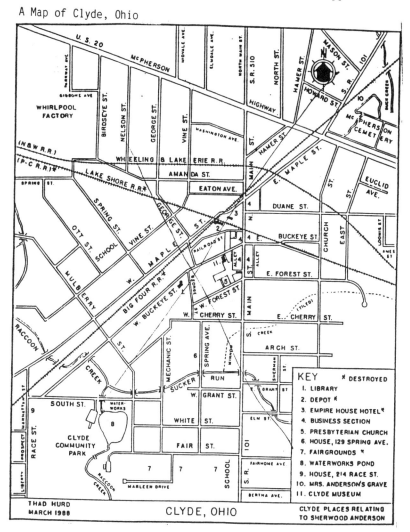

KEY   ⚔ DESTROYED

1. LIBRARY
2. DEPOT ⚔
3. EMPIRE HOUSE HOTEL⚔
4. BUSINESS SECTION
5. PRESBYTERIAN CHURCH
6. HOUSE, 129 SPRING AVE.
7. FAIRGROUNDS ⚔
8. WATERWORKS POND
9. HOUSE, 214 RACE ST.
10. MRS. ANDERSON'S GRAVE
11. CLYDE MUSEUM

THAD HURD
MARCH 1988

CLYDE, OHIO

CLYDE PLACES RELATING
TO SHERWOOD ANDERSON

181

Chronology

1873 Parents, Emma Smith and Irwin Anderson marry.

1874 Brother, Karl, born.

1875 Sister, Stella, born.

1876 Sherwood Anderson is born 13 September in Camden, Ohio.

1877 Brother, Irwin, born, Mansfield, Ohio.

1879 Brother, Ray, born, Caledonia, Ohio.

1883 Anderson family moves to Clyde, Ohio. Brother, Earl, born.

1888 Sister, Fern, born, dies in 1890.

1894 Mother dies.

1896 Arrives in Chicago.

1900 Graduates Wittenburg Academy. Accepts advertising job with Crowell Publishing Company in Chicago. Becomes copywriter for Frank B. White Advertising Agency.

1904 Marries Cornelia Platt Lane.

1906 Moves to Cleveland. Works for United Factories Company.

1907 Son, Robert Lane, is born 16 August in Elyria, Ohio.

1908 Son, John, is born, 31 December.

1911 Daughter, Marion, is born, 29 October.

1912 In November walks out of Elyria; is found dazed and is hospitalized in Cleveland, Ohio, on 1 December.

1914 Separates from Cornelia in March. First short story, "The Rabbit Pen," is published in *Harper's*. Meets Marietta (Bab) Finley.

1915 "The Book of the Grotesque" and "Hands" are published in *Masses;* "Sister" is published in *The Little Review.*

1916 In January "The Story Writers" is published in *The Smart Set;* in March "Vibrant Life" is published in the *The Little Review;* in June "Blackfoot's Masterpiece." Divorces Cornelia 27 July; marries Tennessee Mitchell 31 July. *Seven Arts* magazine begins publication. First novel, *Windy McPherson's Son*, published in October.

1917 *Marching Men* published.

1918 "Seeds" is published in the *The Little Review*. Moves to New York; meets Anita Loos; by December returns to Chicago.

1919 *Winesburg, Ohio* is published in May. Father dies.

1921 In Chicago visits the Domicile; meets Ernest Hemingway. In Paris meets Gertrude Stein. *The Triumph of the Egg* published. Receives first *Dial* award.

1922 Leaves Chicago; in New York meets Elizabeth Prall.

1923 *Many Marriages* published; *Horses and Men* published.

1924 Divorces Tennessee Mitchell; marries Elizabeth Prall. *A Story Teller's Story* published. Moves to New Orleans.

1925 *The Modern Writer* published; *Dark Laughter* published. Purchases Ripshin Farm, Virginia.

1926 *Sherwood Anderson's Notebook* published; *Tar: A Midwest Childhood* published.

1927 Buys, edits, and publishes two Marion, Virginia, newspapers.

1929 *Alice and the Lost Novel* published. Separates from Elizabeth Prall.

1930 Meets Eleanor Copenhaver.

1932 Divorces Elizabeth Prall. *Beyond Desire* published.

1933 Marries Eleanor Copenhaver. *Death in the Woods* published.

1936 *Kit Brandon* published.

1941 During one of several farewell parties in New York, swallows a toothpick, which perforates his intestine, causing peritonitis. Sailing on the Grace Line's *Santa Lucia*, is taken on 4 March from the ship at Cristobal to Gorges Hospital at Colon, Panama Canal Zone, where he dies four days later.

1942 *Sherwood Anderson's Memoirs* published.

Selected Bibliography

Primary Works

Short Story Collections

Alice and the Lost Novel. London: Elkin Mathews and Marrot, 1929. Contains "Alice" and "The Lost Novel."

The Complete Works of Sherwood Anderson. 21 vols. Edited by Kichinosuke Ohashi. Kyoto, Japan: 1982 (*CW*). Vol. 3, *Winesburg, Ohio;* vol. 9, *The Triumph of the Egg;* vol. 10, *Horses and Men;* vol. 11, *Alice and The Lost Novel* and *Death in the Woods and Other Stories;* vol. 20, *The Sherwood Anderson Reader;* vol. 21, *Appendix: Twenty Uncollected Stories* ("The Rabbit Pen," "Sister," "The Story Writers," "Vibrant Life," "The White Streak," "A Ghost Story," "Pop," "Off Balance," "I Get So I Can't Go On," "Samovar," "Mr. Joe's Doctor," "Feud," "Nice Girl," "Harry Breaks Through," "Hard-Boiled," "Two Lovers," "Pastoral," "A Landed Proprietor," "Italian Poet in America," and "The Persistent Liar").

Death in the Woods. New York: Liveright, 1933. Contains "Death in the Woods," "The Return," "There She Is—She Is Taking Her Bath," "The Lost Novel," "The Fight," "Like a Queen," "That Sophistication," "In a Strange Town," "These Mountaineers," "A Sentimental Journey," "A Jury Case," "Another Wife," "A Meeting South," "The Flood," "Why They Got Married," and "Brother Death."

Horses and Men. New York: B. W. Huebsch, 1923. Contains "I'm a Fool," "The Triumph of a Modern," "Unused," "A Chicago Hamlet," "The Man Who Became a Woman," "Milk Bottles," "The Sad Horn Blowers," "The Man's Story," and "An Ohio Pagan."

The Sherwood Anderson Reader, ed. Paul Rosenfeld. Boston: Houghton Mifflin, 1947. In addition to stories from the other collections, also contains "Nobody Laughed," "Blackfoot's Masterpiece," "The Contract," "When We Care," "A Part of Earth," "The Yellow Gown," "Morning Roll-Call," "Justice," "A Dead Dog," "Daughters," "The Corn-Planting," "A Walk in the Moonlight," "His Chest of Drawers," "Not Sixteen," and "Tim and General Grant."

The Triumph of the Egg. New York: B. W. Huebsch, 1921. Contains "I Want to Know Why," "Seeds," "The Other Woman," "The Egg," "Unlighted Lamps," "Senility," "The Man in the Brown Coat," "Brothers," "The

Door of the Trap," "The New Englander," "War," "Motherhood," "Out of Nowhere into Nothing," and "The Man with the Trumpet."

Winesburg, Ohio. New York: B. W. Huebsch, 1919. Contains "The Book of the Grotesque," "Hands," "Paper Pills," "Mother," "The Philosopher," "Nobody Knows," "Godliness (Parts 1 and 2)," "Surrender (Part 3)," "Terror (Part 4)," "A Man of Ideas," "Adventure," "Respectability," "The Thinker," "Tandy," "The Strength of God," "The Teacher," "Loneliness," "An Awakening," "'Queer,'" "The Untold Lie," "Drink," "Death," "Sophistication," and "Departure."

Uncollected Story

"Moonshine." *Missouri Review* 12, no. 1 (1989): 135–45.

Novels

Beyond Desire. New York: Liveright, 1932.
Dark Laughter. New York: Boni and Liveright, 1925.
Kit Brandon. New York: Charles Scribner's Sons, 1936.
Many Marriages. New York: B. W. Huebsch, 1923.
Marching Men. New York: John Lane, 1917.
Poor White. New York: B. W. Huebsch, 1920.
Windy McPherson's Son. New York: John Lane, 1916.

Correspondence

Letters of Sherwood Anderson. Edited by Howard Mumford Jones and Walter B. Rideout. Boston: Little, Brown, 1953.
Letters to Bab: Sherwood Anderson to Marietta D. Finley, 1916–1933. Edited by William A. Sutton. Urbana: University of Illinois Press, 1985.
Sherwood Anderson's Love Letters to Eleanor Copenhaver Anderson. Edited by Charles E. Modlin. Athens: University of Georgia Press, 1990.
Sherwood Anderson: Selected Letters. Edited by Charles E. Modlin. Knoxville: University of Tennessee Press, 1984.

Memoirs

France and Sherwood Anderson: Paris Notebook, 1921. Edited by Michael Fanning. Baton Rouge: Louisiana State University Press, 1976.
The Sherwood Anderson Diaries, 1936–1941. Edited by Hilbert H. Campbell. Athens: University of Georgia Press, 1987.
Sherwood Anderson's Memoirs. Edited by Paul Rosenfeld. New York: Harcourt, Brace, 1942; vol. 19 of *CW.*

Sherwood Anderson's Memoirs: A Critical Edition. Edited by Ray Lewis White. Chapel Hill: University of North Carolina Press, 1969.
Sherwood Anderson's Notebook. New York: Boni and Liveright, 1926; vol. 14 of *CW*.
A Story Teller's Story. New York: B. W. Huebsch, 1924; vol. 12 of *CW*.
Tar: A Midwest Childhood. New York: Boni and Liveright, 1926; vol. 13 of *CW*.

Nonfiction

The Buck Fever Papers. Edited by Welford Dunaway Taylor. Charlottesville: University Press of Virginia, 1971.
Hello Towns! New York: Liveright, 1929; vol. 15 of *CW*.
Home Town. New York: Alliance Book, 1940; vol. 17 of *CW*.
The Modern Writer. San Francisco: Lantern Press, 1925; reprint, Arden Library, 1979; vol. 14 of *CW*.
No Swank. Philadelphia: Centaur Press, 1934; vol. 16 of *CW*.
Perhaps Women. New York: Liveright, 1931; vol. 16 of *CW*.
Puzzled America. New York: Charles Scribner's Sons, 1935; vol. 17 of *CW*.
Return to Winesburg: Selections from Four Years of Writing for a Country Newspaper. Edited by Ray Lewis White. Chapel Hill: University of North Carolina Press, 1967.
Sherwood Anderson: Early Writings. Edited by Ray Lewis White. Kent, Ohio: Kent State University Press, 1989.
The "Writer's Book" by Sherwood Anderson: A Critical Edition. Edited by Martha Mulroy Curry. Metuchen, N.J.: Scarecrow Press, 1975.

Poetry

Mid-American Chants. New York: John Lane, 1918; vol. 18 of *CW*.
A New Testament. New York: Boni and Liveright, 1927; vol. 18 of *CW*.

Plays

Plays: Winesburg and Others. New York: Charles Scribner's Sons, 1937; vol. 18 of *CW*.

Secondary Works

Anderson, David D., ed. *Sherwood Anderson: Dimensions of His Literary Art: A Collection of Critical Essays*. East Lansing: Michigan State University Press, 1976.

————, ed. *Critical Essays on Sherwood Anderson*. Boston: G. K. Hall, 1981.

Atlas, Marilyn Judith. "Sherwood Anderson and the Women of Winesburg." In Anderson, *Critical Essays*, 250–66.

Bunge, Nancy. "Women in Sherwood Anderson's Fiction." In Anderson, *Critical Essays*, 242–49.

Burbank, Rex. *Sherwood Anderson*. New Haven: College & University Press, 1964.

Campbell, Hilbert H., and Charles E. Modlin, eds. *Sherwood Anderson: Centennial Studies*. Troy, N.Y.: Whitson, 1976.

————. *The Winesburg Eagle*, vols. 13–15 (1987–90). Sherwood Anderson Society, Virginia Polytechnic Institute, Blacksburg, Va. This is a continuing series.

Curry, Martha Mulroy. "Sherwood Anderson and James Joyce." *American Literature* 52, no. 2 (May 1980):236–49.

————. "Anderson's Theories on Writing Fiction." In Anderson, *Anderson: Dimensions*, 90–109.

Ferguson, Mary Anne. "Sherwood Anderson's *Death in the Woods:* Toward a New Realism." *MidAmerica* 7 (1980):73–95.

Fetterly, Judith. "Growing up Male in America: 'I Want to Know Why.'" In Judith Fetterly, ed., *The Resisting Reader: A Feminist Approach to American Fiction*, 12–22. Bloomington: Indiana University Press, 1978.

Gado, Frank. "Introduction." In Frank Gado, ed., *Sherwood Anderson: The Teller's Tales*, 1–20. Schenectady, N.Y.: Union College Press, 1983.

Geismar, Maxwell. "Maxwell Geismar Writes of Anderson's *Winesburg*." *New York Times Book Review*, 18 July 1943, 4.

Howe, Irving. *Sherwood Anderson*. Stanford, Calif.: Stanford University Press, 1951.

Ingram, Forrest L. "Sherwood Anderson: Winesburg, Ohio." In Forrest L. Ingram, *Representative Short Story Cycles of the Twentieth Century: Studies in a Literary Genre*, 143–99. The Hague: Mouton, 1971.

Love, Glen A. "Horses or Men: Primitive and Pastoral Elements in Sherwood Anderson." In Campbell and Modlin, *Anderson: Centennial Studies*, 235–48.

Lovett, Robert Morss. "Sherwood Anderson." *New Republic*, 25 November 1936, 103–5.

Malmsheimer, Lonna M. "Sexual Metaphor and Social Criticism in Anderson's 'The Man Who Became a Woman.'" *Studies in American Fiction* 7 (Spring 1979):17–26.

Miller, William V. "Earth-Mothers, Succubi, and Other Ectoplasmic Spirits: The Women in Sherwood Anderson's Short Stories." *MidAmerica* 1 (1973):64–81.

————. "Portraits of the Artist: Anderson's Fictional Storytellers." In Anderson, *Anderson: Dimensions*, 1–23.

Papinchak, Robert Allen. "'Something in the Elders': The Recurrent Imagery in *Winesburg, Ohio.*" *Winesburg Eagle* 9, no. 1 (November 1983):1–7.

Phillips, William C. "How Sherwood Anderson Wrote *Winesburg, Ohio.*" *American Literature* 23 (March 1951):7–30.

Rideout, Walter B. "'I Want to Know Why' as Biography and Fiction." *Midwestern Miscellany* 12 (1984):7–14.

———. "The Simplicity of Winesburg, Ohio." *Shenandoah* 13 (Spring 1962):20–31.

Rosenfeld, Paul. "Sherwood Anderson." *Dial* 72 (1922):29–42.

Somers, Paul P., Jr. "Sherwood Anderson's Mastery of Narrative Distance." *Twentieth Century Literature* 23 (1977):84–93.

Taylor, Welford, ed. *Winesburg Eagle*, vols. 1–12 (1975–86). University of Richmond, Richmond, Va.

White, Ray Lewis, ed. *Sherwood Anderson: A Reference Guide.* Boston: G. K. Hall, 1977.

Williams, Kenny J. *A Storyteller and a City.* Dekalb: Northern Illinois University Press, 1988.

Index

Index

The Author

Robert Allen Papinchak received his Ph.D. in American literature from the University of Wisconsin-Madison. He has taught creative writing, literature, and composition at the University of Wisconsin-Madison, the University of Pittsburgh, and Boise State University.

He has been the program director of a writers and artists series co-sponsored by the National Endowment for the Arts, as well as an adviser and editor for a national award-winning literary magazine.

His fiction, nonfiction, poetry, criticism, and essays have been published in *Kansas Quarterly, Studies in Short Fiction, Alaska Quarterly Review, Journal of Advanced Composition, South Jersey Monthly, Winesburg Eagle, Byline, Family Weekly, The Oregonian, Journal of Canadian Literature, American Review of Canadian Studies,* and elsewhere. The Canadian Studies Center at Duke University published his monograph on modern Canadian literature in its Outreach Series. He maintains an interest in creative writing, the short story, the contemporary British and American mystery novel, and English-Canadian literature.

The Editor

Gordon Weaver earned his Ph.D. in English and creative writing at the University of Denver in 1970. He is professor of English at Oklahoma State University. He is the author of several novels, including *Count a Lonely Cadence, Give Him a Stone, Circling Byzantium*, and most recently *The Eight Corners of the World* (1988). His short stories are collected in *The Entombed Man of Thule, Such Waltzing Was Not Easy, Getting Serious, Morality Play, A World Quite Round*, and *Men Who Would Be Good* (1991). Recognition of his fiction includes the St. Lawrence Award for Fiction (1973), two National Endowment for the Arts fellowships (1974 and 1989), and the O. Henry First Prize (1979). He edited *The American Short Story, 1945–1980: A Critical History* and is currently editor of *Cimarron Review*. Married and the father of three daughters, he lives in Stillwater, Oklahoma.